Dell Boy

Russell Budden

Dell Boy

Russell Budden

Published by Archers Milton Ltd

Published by Archers Milton Ltd

First published in 2017.

ISBN 978-0-473-39753-1 soft cover version
ISBN 978-0-473-39754-8 Kindle edition

Typeset in Garamond 11pt

Cover photographs: foreground Kellie Budden;
background: Russell Budden
(The Dell, Southampton versus Brighton and Hove Albion, 26th May, 2001);
Design and finish: Shauna Budden and Sarah Budden;
Back cover photograph: Russell Budden;
Design and finish: Shauna Budden.

On the first day in May, at the start of the long hot summer of 1976, a father closes his brown and orange curtains to block out the bright sunshine. He settles down nervously to watch his team play in the FA Cup final – the biggest match in British football – on his colour television. His four year-old son is alongside him, about to be invited into the world of a football fan that will captivate father and son alike, for the rest of their lives.

This book is dedicated to my Dad

"Football's just a bunch of ugly blokes running around kicking nothing more than a pig's bladder and kissing each other like girls."

Mrs. Portsmouth *
My next door neighbour when I was eight years old,
remonstrating with me with a particularly nuanced
argument, after I'd knocked on her door and politely
asked for my ball back from her garden (again).

* that was actually her real name

.

Contents

Foreword 11

Introduction 15

Red and White 22

1976 32

1979 42

Going for it 53

1982 62

No Ticket 72

1984 81

1986 92

The Long Haul 99

Playing the Game 108

2001 115

2003 133

Leaving for Home 146

Black and Blue 162

Saints in NZ 174

Saturday 196

Dignity 211

2017 234

Monday 249

Going Home 256

Afterword 268

Acknowledgements 274

References 278

YouTube videos 283

Pictures 291

Foreword

Foreword

By Kellie Budden, the football widow.

Having a baby is perhaps the most wonderful experience you can have in this world. However, I know more than most, that there are some times that are better to have a baby than others. For instance, having strong contractions during rush hour traffic can be stressful for mum and for baby. Parents-to-be may be concerned about having a baby overnight when it is perhaps thought that there are less qualified staff on, such as midwives or doctors. However, I know the most stressful time to have a baby is at around three o'clock on a Saturday afternoon when the football is on.

On Saturday, the 24th of August 1996, I was contracting rather well. We had a little room to deliver in at Winchester hospital. My midwife was busying herself, carrying out her checks, making sure mum and baby were nice and comfortable. I remember there was a student midwife there too, sat by the bed, trying to absorb everything my midwife was doing, and helping out where she could. Then there was my husband, Russell, who was pacing up and down the room concerned. Not because his wife was having a baby though, but because his football team – Southampton, or the Saints – were playing a match.

Thankfully the match was away from The Dell, Southampton's home ground, because then I would wonder if he would have been at the birth at all. There was a radio in the room and at just before three o'clock, he had turned off my Bon Jovi cassette and had put on Radio Solent to listen to the match.

I remember at some point during the match the midwife thought I needed some support, and believed that my husband should be taking more interest in his wife rather than the radio.

"You do realise your wife is having a baby, don't you?" she said to him sarcastically.

Just then, Russ suddenly let out a cry of pain and started to mutter to himself. He hadn't hurt himself – something had happened in the football match that he wasn't happy about. I wasn't listening to the match you understand, I was otherwise pre-occupied.

The midwife was already cross at Russell, but this was the last straw as far as she was concerned. She marched over to the radio and confiscated it from him.

"You're not having this back!" she said crossly to him.

"But West Ham have got a penalty!" Russ argued. He pleaded for the radio to be put back and tuned back in but the midwife wasn't having any of it, and he was forced to look after me instead.

This gives you a taster as to what it is like for me being a football widow. No doubt there are hundreds of thousands of other wives in the same situation as me.

Please don't get me wrong, he is not at all a bad husband – quite the opposite. He's actually a wonderful husband – he's caring, a great father and he makes me laugh. We've been married now for nearly twenty-two years, and have been together now for nearly thirty. Time flies, and we have had great fun together and are very happy.

However, I have to tolerate the behavioural swings of a man with a football team. Often this is harmless, like when he drifts off in to his own little world, daydreaming football thoughts. When Saints lose, I know just to step back a little bit, give Russ some space to let him stew. He can get grumpy, feel hard done by, and when Saints got relegated one year, he was grief stricken for days. It really was as if he had lost a loved one. Eventually though, he always comes back into the real world. When Saints win, it's a bit of relief really, and I am glad I don't have to tread on egg shells that day.

I enjoy the football too. My dad was a football referee and my brother liked football too, but until I met Russell I had no idea how much devotion a person could have to a team.

Family events have always had to be organised around the demands of football, and particularly The Saints. When we got married in 1995, we made sure the registry office was booked on a weekend when Saints were playing away from home. Visits to family and friends at weekends had to be on the Sunday, unless Saints were playing that day. Holidays were planned around home matches or if possible, at the end of the season, but never near cup final day, just in case Saints ever got there.

Nowadays we live in New Zealand, about as far away from The Dell as it is possible to get. When we plan holidays back to England to see family, we have to consider the fixture list to see what matches we can fit in.

You'll be pleased to learn that Sarah was successfully born that day in 1996 although I never did get my Bon Jovi cassette back. For the arrival of our next daughter, Shauna, I was once again planned to be induced. This time I didn't make the same mistake again, and organised a date with my doctor during the week to have the baby, not on a weekend. Thinking about it now, we even engineered the birth date of our daughter around the bloody football!

Shauna is now nineteen and Sarah is now twenty. Nothing has changed with Russell from then to now. Obviously in New Zealand, he can't go to the games so instead watches the matches live on telly, in the early hours of Sunday morning, because of the time difference. Although he tries hard to be quiet, bless him, he has woken me up many, many times with his cheering, groaning and arguing at the referee who can't hear him through the telly. He was woken the girls up many times too – he even used to wake Shauna up deliberately so he had some company to watch the match with. And it won't surprise you to learn that on occasion neighbours have been awoken because of the noise.

When Saints got to the League Cup Final this year, I was genuinely thrilled. When we moved here we made a promise that should this ever happen (and I never thought it actually would) that he should go back for the match. It was really nice that he could go. In truth though, I was absolutely delighted to get rid of him. He was unbearable in the lead up to the game and it was a blessed relief that he got on the plane.

Russell inhabits a completely separate world where me and the girls are rarely invited. It's not fair to suggest that he puts The Saints first ahead of me and the girls. After all, emigrating across the other side of the world is a big decision, and it was a decision that he wanted to make. But if you put a gun to his head and told him that he had to decide between either his wife and kids or The Saints, it would be a decision he would think about very carefully before choosing us.

At least I think he'd choose us.

PS, please enjoy the book, he'll be ever so grumpy if you think it's rubbish! Kellie xxx

Foreword

Introduction

Have you read Nick Hornby's book 'Fever Pitch'? It's certainly a better book than this one so I would recommend getting that book instead. It's about Nick's love affair with his football team, Arsenal, and how it forms part of his life. It's an amazing book. He captures the thoughts, behaviours and dreams of thousands of football fans perfectly. It is almost a text book of anybody wanting to understand about football fanaticism, about what makes people travel hundreds of miles to an away game at the other end of the country, on a cold Tuesday night, for a match which will have no meaningful bearing on their team's season. He exposes how illogical and ridiculous football fans can be and how this ridiculousness invades his life.

My book, albeit wholly inferior and apologetic in comparison, is about me, me, me, and my support of my team, Southampton, or The Saints. Southampton, unlike Arsenal, do not win trophies. The last major trophy that Southampton won was forty-one years ago.

I am very roughly still in my late thirties. I have an amazing wife, two incredible daughters, two dogs and a football team. But not necessarily in that order. There are many types of football fans out there, from the casual observer to the football nutter. I sit somewhere closer to the nutter than the observer I expect, and I'll leave you to judge exactly how close I am to the nutter end of the scale. It means though that my team jostles for prominence in my life in competition with my wife, Kellie, and my kids, Sarah and Shauna – sometimes successfully. Don't get me wrong, my family mean everything to me, like any normal father, it's just so do my team. And I know it's wrong, but I have never been able to stop it, control it, lessen it even. It would be rather nice to one day get it all into rather better perspective.

Some evidence: in my lounge, I have a football shirt signed by Matt Le Tissier (greatest player ever) wishing me a happy birthday. I have three large pictures in my study that used to be in my lounge – one's a picture from the last ever game at The Dell, one's a picture of one of the first games at our new stadium, St Mary's, and one's a picture of the FA Cup Final in 2003 between Saints and Arsenal. The common link between the three is that me and my Dad are in them all, albeit a spec in the cup final one.

I had a cat called Matty (after Mr. Le Tissier). I refused to get married on a day of a home game (we got married when Saints were beaten by Chelsea at Stamford Bridge 3-0, in 1996 – I remember the great Ruud Gullit scored for Chelsea that day, not sure of the date though). When my first child, Sarah, was due, I still went to matches. On the day she was born, we were playing West Ham United away. I was listening to the radio in the hospital whilst Kellie was huffing away, until my unruly response to Saints conceding a penalty resulted in the midwife confiscating the radio (we lost 2-1). I refused to allow my other daughter Shauna to wear a Liverpool shirt in the house, or out with me with it on (it had been a gift from The Boyfriend). I would not allow other kids into my house with a football shirt on other than a Southampton one, even though they were only six or seven and probably had no idea who Thierry Henry or Arsenal was. My own company name is called Archers Milton Ltd, after the names of the stands at each end of The Dell, the Archers Road end and Milton Road end.

I have The Saints 2017 calendar, I have an actual seat, number '24' from The Dell, before the ground was knocked down. I have a football signed by the 1982 team including Alan Ball, Mick Channon and Kevin Keegan. For crying out loud, I even have a flip top Saints bin in the bathroom. Being a football fan must look to others like being a moron.

It's true. If you think about it, we generally all happily co-exist together. Football fans are like normal people, as a breed we are courteous to people, polite and respectful, just like anybody else, and we go about our business each day with a general sense of decorum. When we watch football, and particularly when our team is playing, we degenerate into some form of human sub-species incapable of rational thought or intelligence. Our minds learn to dislike and hate opposition players, our rational thinking warps into extreme bias towards our own. Our thoughts leading up to a game dwell on what might happen, who will play, what do we need to do to win. We convince ourselves that our team can win even when the odds are firmly stacked against us. We get nervous before a match starts, as we might at an interview for a job or our wedding day. We shout at the match knowing no one can hear us, either at the game or at home watching the TV. The shouting includes abuse at the players we dislike or the referee. Our ability to know what is happening around us fades as we focus only on the match, what is happening on the pitch, what is going to happen in the game. We erupt with noise when our team scores, or regress into depression if our team concedes a goal.

It's like a form of road rage I suppose; we get into the car and become this aggressive, irrational being, beeping our horns, screaming at other drivers or cyclists, until we arrive and get out of the car, and we are instantly restored to our normal mild manner. Except with football fans, losing a match leaves a lasting fog with us that can last for days, whereas winning a match illuminates the world in a much brighter perspective.

That's how I am. A reasonable, approachable, law abiding, normal human being, until my team plays football and then, I'm afraid, all bets are off. I blame my Dad for all this.

My life's earliest memory is the FA Cup in 1976, when Southampton played Manchester United in the final. I was four. Southampton was my local team, so it is no surprise that they were whom I should support, with my Dad being a supporter for years and a youth team player for Southampton before that. So I grew up with the team all around me, soaking up football during those times, picking up ephemera, mostly from Dad that solidified my support. Then I went to watch Saints play with my Dad. Even though these were times blighted by unbelievably bad hooliganism, Dad ensured we stayed safe week after week, and the matches were a wonder to me.

As I grew up, I was playing too. By the time I was sixteen I was playing senior football on Saturdays so stopped watching the Saints for a while. Dad came to watch me instead, although your team never goes away. You still follow them seriously, and when there is a free weekend or a midweek game, you still go along. Once I stopped playing, I went back to watching, and eventually sat back with Dad as we moved home grounds, from The Dell to our new St Mary's Stadium.

Suddenly, I moved my family to New Zealand to live for, we hoped, a better life. Of course, it was a momentous decision and the biggest adventure of our lives, and whilst we were all leaving our families behind, I was also leaving my team behind, which seemed to have a galvanising effect to me. It is natural to become more patriotic when you move to live or stay in another country, but I do not believe I have met many, or any, ex-pats with the same levels of devotion to my team than me. And whereas most football supporters can switch off from their team to enjoy another match in another league or another country, I'm just too partisan to be that interested. This invariably means that teams who have beaten Saints, at crucial times in history, who have burst my own bubble of hope and expectation, are thereafter consigned to the pits of my loathing and disdain. It seems to me that some people have 'love' and 'hate' tattooed on their knuckles, whereas in a football world I seem to have the words burned on my cranium.

Football invades the life of a football fan. Life moves around the requirements of football. Saturdays are for football. You may be watching a home game, or listening to the away game on the radio. Occasionally you'll go to an away game. If the game is on Sunday, then Sunday is off limits to anything other than football too. Midweek games are not missed either and are prioritised over parent meetings at the school, swimming lessons or the possibility of work overtime. Conversation with people are tested with football – if they have no interest in football, it is unlikely you'll have any interest in them. Friendships are formed around football, and you may know little or care less about anything else in their lives.

I'm not envious of fans of Liverpool, Chelsea, Arsenal, Manchester United, or any other team who win lots of trophies. I suspect for the fans of these teams, the joy of winning must be considerably diluted. I would imagine that forever lifting trophies, going to Wembley so many times, winning things so often must become a quite a chore. I am envious of the Swansea City's, the Leicester City's, even the Portsmouth's of this world who have won trophies in recent times. For Swansea and Portsmouth, they had the added luck of playing teams in lower leagues to maximise their chances of winning, which they duly did. And what of Leicester City who unfathomably won the Premier League in 2016 after nearly being relegated in 2015? How did that happen, and why could that not have been my team? Leicester also won two League Cups in the Nineties – why should football's version of Lady Luck shine on them and not us?

I just want my team to win a trophy, one of the big ones, just once. I'm not greedy, but I want to experience that exultation and joy, I want to sing 'we won the cup!'. But time is ticking. There are no guarantees as to when your next cup final opportunity will be. Saints nearly went out of existence altogether in 2009, so I don't take it for granted that since we are back in the Premier League, that we will be regular visitors to a final or occasional challengers for the Premier League title.

I am not getting any younger. I am twenty years from retirement. The opportunity to go to a cup final in ten or twenty years' time just won't be there as our lives start to slow down, both financially and socially. And, quite frankly, I don't want my team to be so prominent in my life then. Sure, I will always follow them, watch them on telly and look up their scores on the Internet (maybe in 20 years I could be watching as a virtual spectator anyway – my nephew has shown me the future and it is amazing). But I don't want to get up at 2:00 a.m. or 4:00

a.m. on a Sunday morning any more to watch them play, depending on daylight savings, when I'm old and saggy. I don't want almost my entire wardrobe to be decked out in red and white colours, emblazoned with the club emblem.

I am sure that if we could win something; if I could celebrate something really big, I could start to let go.

In February 2017, the Saints once again become my primary focus in life. They've reached the final of the League Cup, to play Manchester United, and I want to be there to see it. Living in almost certainly the furthest city to London anywhere in the world, is just a detail. Even though we've not long been back to England, ten months prior to in fact, and the fact that this match comes at a busy time for us, is inconsequential.

But this is it. An opportunity to win a cup. An opportunity to exorcise my demons. It doesn't matter that this season, the team have been poor, and started to regress after years of excellent progress. It doesn't matter that since Christmas we seemed to be getting beaten by everybody. It doesn't matter that we have loads of long term injuries, and only one fit central defender in the club. It doesn't matter that we are playing a Manchester United team who have purchased Paul Pogba for a world record fee of 90 million pounds, and have world class players in each position of the team. In my biased and warped football mind, we still have a decent chance.

It was planned as an epic trip. I would leave New Zealand in Summer, arrive in England in Winter, staying there into Spring, and arrive back in New Zealand in Autumn, all within nine days, just to see my team play in a big match.

I'm no professional writer. Actually, that's not true, I was – my first job was as a technical author / technical writer, creating manuals (step 1; insert the CD-ROM into the CD-ROM drive – that kind of thing – not very exciting, I know), but that's not the point. What I mean is, I am an amateur as far as writing something *interesting*. I don't know if this is any good, coherent, or relevant. It might even be totally self-centred and egotistical. If it is, then it wasn't my intention. But I wanted to have a good old college try and, for better or worse, this is the result.

Incidentally, I make no apologies for my writing style. I tend to start sentences with the word 'and' which I remember my English teachers frowned on. And I also start sentences with the word 'but' when I should be using a 'but' only after a comma. But worst of all is my use of 'me and Dad' or 'me and Dan' or 'me and Kellie' when I should of course be using 'Dad and I', or 'Daniel and I' or 'Kellie and I'. That sounds a little bit posher/poncier than I would actually say, so you'll all have to make do with my misuse of personal pronouns. I do have a bit of a vocabulary when I put my mind to it, and am especially pleased that I got the word 'discombobulate' (to feel disconcerted or confused) into the book, albeit only in this particular paragraph.

I did take the time out to do some decent research on non-fiction writing. Publisher and historian Juliet Gardiner wrote an article in The Guardian about writing non-fiction. She stated: "And if you ever start a sentence with 'meanwhile' you have literally lost the plot". This confused me greatly because I have started many sentences with 'meanwhile' and don't think I have lost the plot any more than I had already, and she started her sentence with the word 'and'! What am I supposed to do?

Meanwhile, it is important to understand that I started to write this muddle of a book (if you can call it a book, I am sure Mr. Hornby would feel pretty peeved that this kind of tat can find its way on to Amazon), only once I decided to go to the final, whilst I was in England and then completing it on my return to New Zealand. So, whilst not structured like a diary, there is a kind of diarised approach to the narrative, even if it is not evident from the chapter structure.

I also have a habitual problem of using brackets to re-enforce a particular statement (like this one in order to illustrate the use of the closed brackets). I apologise if you find this a bit irritating (I'm not sure why, I even edited a few out), but I am sure you will be able to persevere (I'd be mortified if you had a copy of the book and then wouldn't read it owing to the volume of parenthesises). I did explore the use of footnotes too[1].

I realise that some folk reading this will also be Saints fans and will be completely up to date with events and our history. I am equally aware that some readers may not be totally aware of the structure of football in England or even how intrinsically woven football is into English culture. My daughter Sarah, for example, thought we were playing in the 'Wembley Football Cup thing' (oh the shame!) so it is important that I explain stuff in the fullest context possible not to lose some of the readership that don't follow football fully, but who are part of my target audience. I thought it also important to dwell on who the key players are, for instance who was Mick Channon and why was he a Southampton legend? As surprising as it may seem to some, not everyone would be aware of him. I have tried to hang about on such matters when prudent to do so; apologies if I am preaching the obvious to some.

---

[1] But I found footnotes to be too formal, and distracted the reader from their current reading position.

I've tried to apply some rigid rules to the narrative. Everything described is true to the best of my knowledge. I'm sure there are a few misunderstandings and misconstrued elements kicking around somewhere. I have provided some football wisdom and 'frank' opinion (Frank Opinion, former French international in the Fifties) but only when relevant to underpin the narrative – there are no soap boxes in this book. Also, in chapters looking back into my memory, I've sought to use my memory first and foremost, but allowed myself to use resources such as YouTube and Wikipedia as a basis for fact checking. Wikipedia often is criticised for the quality of its information, but there is seldom an error, I find, when it comes to football matches. I do acknowledge on occasions where the facts don't match my memory, although I won't concede that the facts are actually right!

Why am I like this? Why is life continually compromised by the balancing the needs of my family with the needs of my team. When I moved to New Zealand, why couldn't I leave my team behind? What is my excuse for some of my baffling behaviours? For example, if someone were to walk by my house, I would almost certainly ignore it. But, if this person walked by my house in a Portsmouth shirt (our deadly rivals), I would most likely race out and demand he walk on the other side of the street. Why is it that some people can take a defeat with an 'ah well' and a smile on their face, whereas for me I have to brood with a dark cloud almost visible above my head – sometimes for days if the defeat was a particularly bad one. I want to make sense of it all. I hope this book helps, and acts as catharsis. If it doesn't it'll be a waste of a number of weeks and a few reams of paper.

I hope you find this book interesting and worthwhile, and I hope you enjoy the read. For some of you, and you know who you are, I hope you treasure it.

Red and White

November 1885, meeting of the St Mary's Young Men's Association at Grove Street schoolrooms near St Mary's church, Southampton.

To begin to unravel this, we first need to understand a bit about my family, both people and football club.

Surprising as it may seem, I am happily married to my wife Kellie, who is happily married to me, apparently. She is definitely not one of these stereotypical wives whose eyes roll and tuts every time the football is on. She has never, ever, demanded that I turn the telly over from the football to Eastenders or Coronation Street. She is fully conversant with the laws of the game – none of this "Can he do that?" nonsense whenever there is a throw in, unlike the stereotype. Her knowledge of the intricacies of the offside law as it applies to Active Play stirs my loins in a most agreeable way.

She has limits though. Decorating my house full of flags, scarves and balloons for instance. during a World Cup, drives her mental. For the 2014 World Cup I also dragged out my huge Subbuteo collection (table football game) including advertising boards, dugouts, terraces, spectators, managers, substitutes, referees, linesmen, ball boys, cameramen, photographers, television gantry, perimeter fencing, standby St Johns Ambulance service, police presence, mascot and female streaker. I certainly try her patience.

My eldest daughter is now twenty (twenty! It sure goes quick!). She somehow missed my ongoing lectures on how important football is, or how brilliant the Saints are. She has grown up to have no sporting genes in her body whatsoever. At school, she excelled at Netball and Swimming. I was an embarrassment to her when cheering her on watching Netball, I'd shout "Handball!" at every pass, which was funny for about the first minute of the new season but the joke would lose its lustre with other parents twelve weeks later whilst watching her team play stood in the driving rain. I would want to de-construct each match afterwards with her in miniscule detail, but she was just happy to play the game win or lose. When she clocked a new personal best at swimming she would be oblivious to it. She doesn't seem to have a competitive bone in her body. That is not to say that she is timid, there is a certain steel and focus about her and she does a very cool Angry Sarah. It's just that sport isn't her thing. I envy her, I really do. Supporting the Saints can be such a curse at times and an obsession – she is free of all that. She doesn't spend her free hours thinking about who Saints might sell to Liverpool during the English summer transfer window. She doesn't calculate how many points Saints need to avoid relegation and who those points might be against. She doesn't have to think about whether we will play one striker in our next game or whether we will push two up front. She doesn't need to count down the days before you can order the new home football shirt from the team's club shop web site, and spend over the odds getting almost exactly the same shirt as was purchased last year.

She has come to matches with me, but her interest is in the good-looking number 20 playing, or the suave Italian right back on the other team. She has no interest in the team, the score or the match itself, other than knowing the score to predict my mood.

Shauna however, has got into the football and am happy to report she does support the Saints, despite the aberration regarding the Liverpool shirt. Perhaps she thinks she might be tossed out on the street if she were to admit an affiliation to Liverpool? She might be right. At nineteen she has had six different home or away Saints shirts with 'Shauna' emblazoned on the back. This is not proof that she is a fan but she does wear the shirt, although fortunately not the offensive 2017 home shirt that look like pyjamas.

At school, she nagged me to get into a football team. "No, no, no," I told her, "you're a girl – you have to play Netball". She did that for a year, and although more sporty and athletic than Sarah, she wanted to play football. My sexist attitude toward female football disappeared when New Zealand hosted the Under 17's Woman's World Cup. It was fantastic full of exciting, honest, breathless football. We even saw England win a penalty shootout (no, really, we actually did). So, with that I relented apologetically, and Shauna played football with the boys for a few years. Eventually she stopped, but she still follows the game either with me or The Boyfriend (although that could be a deception when I think about it. "Dad? Can I go with Ryan [The Boyfriend] to see the Champions' League Group Stage clash between Fenerbahçe and Shakhtar Donetsk?") Anyway, whenever we or she gets to go back to England, she gets to go to games. When back in England in 2013 we went to St Mary's to see Saints play Tottenham Hotspur at the

Northam Stand end which holds the most vocal of supporters. When Saints scored the opening goal, she got the same thrill of noise thundering through her as I did when I first went, and it was addictive to her. I was very disappointed with her however in one of the next home games against West Bromwich Albion, where we sat close to the pitch. Luke Shaw, our former full back, raced down the left in front of us causing Shauna to swoon and almost fall out of her seat full of the besotted crush young teens tend to get over superstars. It made me reflect whether having boys would have been better.

One worry is the fact that The Boyfriend supports Liverpool. Once those red-shirted spermatozoa fuse with Shauna's candy-striped eggs sometime in the distant future (separate rooms and separate beds are the order of the day until she turns 30 – them's the rules), my concern will be which way will the grandchild go, Scouse or Saint? It's a dilemma I have right now and have no idea how this will turn out or what I will be able to do about it.

Back in England is my family. There is lots of them and they are like the mafia. The boss, the *capofamiglia*, is my Mum. Oddly, she has never been to a game of football and will certainly never get to one. She has never even seen me play when I was a kid, which was a shame because I was quite good. That's not to say she doesn't follow Saints. She has to, with Dad's moods and temperament almost exclusively governed by the fortunes of Saints in the same way that the tides are controlled by the Moon. And with most of her family being Saints fans it just won't do to be behind with recent events. She even joins in with my Fantasy Football Premier League game on the Internet and takes it super-seriously, studying player form and informing me on a weekly basis who's in and who's out for the next week's matches. Much to the consternation of the other fifteen participants in my league, Mum has been winning.

Another big part in this story is Big Sister Debbie. Debbie is much, much older than me. In the year-of-our-Lord-2017 she will be 60. Properly old. She is the *consigliere*, the 'underboss' who reports into the boss, but is the one who makes things happen. She is the heartbeat of my family back in England. She looks after Mum, drives her where she needs to go, and has her own family to look after. Debbie never stops.

And she supports Saints, along with husband Chris. Debbie doesn't normally go to games, but will watch on telly or listen on radio, always ironing. It's a superstition; all footballers and football fans are superstitious. In my twenties, mine was always having a Kentucky Fried Chicken before matches, or wearing the same pair of socks. The problem always was that sometimes (often, in some seasons) Saints lost even though you followed through completely with your superstition.

That meant you still needed to follow through with the same routine next week because 'sometimes you might win' rather than because 'you will win'. The worst text you can get from Debbie is the panicky one I sometimes get before a match starts: "I've got no ironing to do!"

"Just iron something in the airing cupboard then!" I'd reply.

I'd always know if she did do this based on the result. For the cup final, I expect the volume of ironing would be mountainous.

Chris has a superstition of sorts too. Often, during a match, Saints would score when he went for a wee. Dad would always cajole Chris to push off for a wee when Saints needed a goal.

Debbie has three kids. Daniel is the eldest. Dan is my only nephew and he has a lot of Dad's personality in him. He has a successful animation business in Bristol, and is a properly talented fella. I am very proud of him. He's a big Saints fan, and we've been to games many times together. He lives with his girlfriend Sama (pronounced 'Summer'), who thinks, sadly, that football is just a game.

Then there's Kate, another Saints fan, who goes to games with hubby Ian, and their kids Luke (10) and Ryan (8). Kate is hilarious because she has this complete inability to keep a secret. So when I drop back in to England every few years it is always best to tell Kate first, tell her it is a secret, just to ensure everyone knows by the end of that day. Coming over for the cup final I decided to keep the trip secret from my Mum. In order that Kate or the boys did not blurt out the news to her on their weekly visits to Mum, they had to feign a rare strain of flu and kept away.

Hayley is the youngest at 27... Yup, another Saints fan. She lives with a Portsmouth fan would you believe? How that works out, Lord only knows! (At this point you are thinking that this book is entirely made up, first he reckons England won a penalty shootout and then he has the temerity to suggest that a Southampton fan would live harmoniously with a Portsmouth fan – what a load of hogwash! All I can say is, whilst extremely far-fetched, it is all true.) If I had met a girl who suggested she was a Portsmouth supporter I would be so disappointed, but I would do the right thing by her, and agree never to see her again. Of course, the youngsters of today are very different and live by a different ethical code, but I still find it hard to fathom. Has she thought about the child issue at all? I endlessly wrestle with the Liverpool/Southampton problem that could exist with Shauna's kiddo, so goodness knows what on earth is Hayley putting her poor father through? Chris could be sitting at home in five or six years' time, his grandson happily bouncing on his knee, at his absolute happiest in his life, when all of a sudden the grandson looks up longingly at Chris and says, "Grandpapa? Dada took me to a Portsmouth match on Saturday! I loved it so much!" Oh, the shame, the shame!

I've another sister, Tracey – who is also really old, but like Sarah football and sport washes over her, and thus so does this book. When I have a desire to write a book about hairdressing or BBC Radio Four, she will be the centre of attention. Hannah and Laura, Tracey's girls, two more nieces of mine, have quite happily missed out on the Southampton DNA and have no compunction about visiting Ikea on a Saturday afternoon instead. Tracey's bloke, Colin, is a Dirty Leeds supporter, so nobody in that part of the family follows football at all.

But this book is as much about my Dad as it is about me. I've always wanted to write about him. I was brought up to love the club through 'thick and thin' by my Dad. My memories of growing up are dominated by both my team and my father. It seemed that where there was Dad, there was the Saints. Where there was the Saints, there was Dad. In my memory they are intrinsically linked somehow. He was like my football fan's mentor, guiding me through the rocky terrain of good seasons and bad seasons, achievements and disappointments.

Weekends were all about football, Saturday with the Saints, Sunday about me and my team. Sometimes football would bleed into a weeknight with midweek games either at The Dell or on the radio. Some nights in summer Dad would say to me, "Hey, Russ, let's go up the pub!" seemingly on a whim. He would drive us for what seemed like hours through the back of Winchester through the countryside. He would find a pub in the middle of nowhere and park up. If there was a beer garden with a trampoline I was allowed out of the car; if there was no beer garden I would be left in the back of the car with the window wound down a bit for some air circulation. He'd come out of the pub after a few minutes and hand be a bottle of coke with a bendy straw, and a bag of salt 'n vinegar Golden Wonder crisps.

With a grin on his face, he'd wink at me and say, "Hey Russ, guess who's in the pub?" One time it was David Peach, another time Mick Channon (I'd hang out with his son on the climbing frame), another time Graham Baker, another time Ted MacDougall. All former Saints players. He'd find out through the grapevine at his work at Ford's Transit plant in Eastleigh, about which players would hang out in which pubs in the area. Like a professional stalker, off he would go with me in tow to meet the latest football club legends, with the hope they were in the pub that night, having a pint.

I'm not complaining, I loved those nights. I always had toy cars and football stickers and Subbuteo ready in the back of the car if needed, but mostly played in the beer garden with the other kids, some of whom whose Dads had also gravitated to the same pub for the same reason. Of course, I never got into the pub to say 'hello' – these were days when kids under fourteen never got into pubs. For me, it was all part of the world of football reverence I was in.

That is not to say that all my memories of my childhood with Dad are football related. There are loads of crazy non-football memories kicking around inside my head. But it is true to say that many of my memories are certainly related to football.

When we talked about the Saints, we spoke of them in terms of it being our team or my team. People would ask Dad in the pub how did 'you' get on at the week end – meaning how did Saints get on, and Dad would respond – as every fan does – by saying 'we' won/drew/lost. You'll find me writing in this book that 'we' beat whoever, or that a team beat 'us'. You use the terms 'we' and 'us' because as a fan you are part of it, you are part of the journey, and for the majority of us, it is a journey you can't just decide to get off.

Saints' journey began in 1885. They were formed in the November as St Mary's Young Men's Association Football Club, following a meeting chaired by Arthur Baron Sole at the local Grove Street schoolrooms near St Mary's church, in the St Mary's parish of Southampton, one of the poorest and neglected areas of the city.

Southampton as a city took off around 1838 when Southampton Docks were opened to support the industrial revolution and the ambition of the British Empire. The population boomed but oddly St Mary didn't, and became known as a den of iniquity, a place to go to find drink and women. At the turn of the twentieth century Southampton became a major shipbuilding centre and built, fitted, repaired and restored ships in both World Wars. It is well known that RMS Titanic sailed on its maiden voyage from Southampton Docks in 1912. More than 540 people from Southampton alone went down amongst 1,083 other lost souls – almost as many that died during the Blitz in Southampton in World War II. Many on the Titanic came from St Mary's and the surrounding parishes of Northam, Shirley and Freemantle.

To support the war effort, the Spitfire aircraft was designed, constructed and delivered from Southampton. It's conceiver, R.J. Mitchell lived in the city. The Spitfire, of course, became a trump card in the war and is widely regarded as the machine above all others responsible for protecting English shores. Southampton was one of several industrial targets that received heavy bombing during the Second World War, and Dad was evacuated from his home to families in the countryside, whom he had never met, on a number of occasions.

St Mary's first match was against the Freemantle Association, and was played under the rules of 'association football', or 'soccer', known as the 'dribbling game', to be distinguished from the more prominent sport of the time, rugby, or 'rugger', which was known as the 'running game'. The 'Saints' as they were nicknamed even in their early years prevailed 5-1.

For the first few years, St Mary's played mainly friendly matches. But the club was becoming more competitive and entered the FA Cup for the first time in 1891. In the 1895 season they joined the Southern League. Also that season, Saints changed their name to Southampton St Mary's, having proven themselves to be the dominant team in the city. Three years later they changed their name again to simply 'Southampton Football Club'.

In the north of England, the popularity of football was exploding. In 1888, the Football League was formed with twelve inaugural teams. The working class would spill out of the factories with their weekly pay cheque on a Saturday lunch time and go straight to a football match in the afternoon. However, the most southern of teams in this league were Aston Villa, in Birmingham. Despite great progress in their initial years, the southerly geographic location meant that there was no way that Saints could join this elite group. However, the Southern League was an adequate competition, and by the turn of the century was drawing comparison to the Football League proper.

Saints won the Southern League three years in succession, in 1897, 1898 and 1899. They missed out on the title the following year, but I think Saints had a decent excuse: that season, in 1900, Saints reached the FA Cup final – the first time any non-league team had reached the final. The match was played at the Crystal Palace in front of a massive 69,000 people. Their opponents, Bury, scored three times in the first twenty-five minutes and eventually ran out easy winners in the end 4-0. The following year, one of Saints' rivals in the Southern League, Tottenham Hotspur went one better and became the first non-league club to actually win the FA Cup. It was consolation to Saints that they pipped Tottenham to the Southern League title that same year. The following year, in 1902, Saints managed to get to the FA Cup final again, losing out again – this time to Sheffield United in a replay. The initial game had ended 1-1, with Saints equalising with two minutes to go, but in the replay Saints lost 2-1. It would be another seventy-four years before Saints reached a final again.

Even in those days, Saints had star quality in their team. None more so than C.B. Fry. Fry was a dual international and was nicknamed 'The Almighty'. He was England's cricket captain, and whilst a Southampton player, had earnt his first England cap for football, against Ireland in 1901. He was well known throughout the country, not only for his exploits in cricket and football, but in other sports, writing, politics and poetry. He was also, believe it or not, the long jump world record holder at the time. It's also understood that Albania had even asked him to become king there (presumably some representatives thereof, not the entire country). It didn't seem possible but Fry also had time for football by the association rules, and played for Saints as an amateur between 1900 and 1903.

Charles Miller is a little-known name but no less notable than Fry. The fantastically moustachioed Miller was part of the Saints team a little earlier, from 1892 to 1894. He left Saints in 1894 and travelled to Brazil, with 'two footballs and the laws of the game from the Hampshire Football Association'. A year later he fashioned the first ever football match in Brazil between The Gas Works and São Paulo Railway. Things went rather well for Brazilian football after that, I'm led to believe. Brazil have been widely regarded as the world's best team and football nation since the Fifties. They have won the World Cup more than any other nation, five times, and been runners-up twice. They've won the Copa América (South American Championship) eight times and been runners-up twelve times. They have produced some of the best players the world has ever seen, with the most exotic of names, Pelé, Garrincha, Jairzinho, Tostão, Rivellino, Zico, Sócrates, Ronaldo, Romário, Kaká, Neymar – the list is endless. Brazilian football is also synonymous with exciting, attacking, flamboyant football – the football equivalent of the Harlem Globetrotters or the All Blacks. Former Saint Charles Miller is considered in Brazil as the 'father' of Brazilian football after setting up the Liga Paulista – the first football league in Brazil.

Saints had been moving from ground to ground, but in 1898, the club moved from Hampshire Cricket's County Ground to The Dell, which would become their home for more than 100 years. It cost the princely sum of 10,000 pounds. The opening match in 1898 was against Brighton United. By the end of the 1920's, both main stands had been rebuilt by the famous architect Archibald Leitch and had a grand capacity of 30,000. The Dell was where almost all of my young football memories were made. It was my church. It was Dad's church too. Saints eventually moved to a modern stadium in 2001, named after their roots – St Mary's Stadium.

Saints persevered in the Southern League until 1915 when the Great War suspended all football. It wasn't long after football resumed that the entire Southern League was swallowed up by the Football League in 1921 and rebadged as Football League Division Three. Just a year later Saints won promotion to Division Two, where they stayed until the break out of World War II that suspended football again in September 1939.

Three years after the end of the second World War and the resumption on hostilities on the football field, Saints looked set to break into Division One at last. With seven matches to play, Saints led Division Two by seven clear points from Fulham and West Bromwich Albion. With only two points awarded for a win in those days, it seemed a matter of 'when' not 'if' Saints would get promoted. They had one of the best strikers in the country, Charlie Wayman, banging the goals in (he scored an incredible seventy-three goals in 100 games for the Saints). Saints had just beaten Tottenham Hotspur away 1-0, but Wayman got injured. There were no substitutes in those days, so Wayman had to soldier on hurt. And soldier on he did, bashing in the heroic winning goal that day. But his injury cost Saints, who limped through the rest of the season much like Wayman had to in the Tottenham match, and somehow missed out on promotion in third place, behind both Fulham and West Brom. It was a disaster for the Saints which they never recovered from. Wayman soon left for Preston North End, and Saints soon left Division Two, although in a downward not upward direction, back into Division Three.

In 1955, Saints appointed former player Ted Bates as their manager, and slowly but surely Saints halted their decline and became upwardly mobile again. Saints gained promotion back to Division Two at the end of the 1960 season.

In 1963, Saints got to the semi-final of the FA Cup to play Manchester United. My Dad was there to see Saints unfortunately beaten by a fortunate Dennis Law goal. This was the Saints' fourth semi-final appearance in sixty-one years, since the final loss to Sheffield United and had lost them all. But, in 1966 – a couple of months before England won the World Cup – Saints managed to finally get promoted to Football League Division One for the first time. That year, they even had representation in the England squad – Terry Paine, Saints' tricky winger. Paine only played once in the tournament, in the win against France in the group stages, but played for Saints with distinction a staggering 815 times.

Now Saints had the opportunity to mix it with the 'big boys', which they did quite comfortably for a few years, giving some of the bigger sides a bloody nose in the process. Early in the 1970 season Saints beat Manchester United at Old Trafford 4-1. After Liverpool were beaten 1-0 also in 1970, their legendary manager Bill Shankly labelled the Saints team 'ale-house brawlers'. It wouldn't be the last time that a fine Liverpool team left The Dell with their tail between their legs and demonstrating a distinct lack of class.

It didn't last though. For the 1974 season, Ted Bates – who had served the club magnificently – had stepped aside for a new manager to come in, the tall Geordie Lawrie McMenemy. The team looked comfortable at Christmas near mid-table, but a disastrous run in the second half of the season plummeted Saints to third from bottom. That year 1974 was the first season that three teams would be relegated rather than two, and it was just Saints' luck that they fell through the trap door back into Division Two as the team third from bottom.

Saints had a long history, but not a particularly great one. The sum total of their achievements were just a couple of cup finals and promotions, as well as having a player who gave football to a country that would become the best at it. There were not too many heroic stories, and their history was littered with mediocrity not trophies. In fact, there was not a single major trophy in their trophy cabinet. But it was at this point, things took an interesting turn.

1976

FA Cup Final 1976, Manchester United versus Southampton. Wembley Stadium, London, Saturday, 1st of May.

In the beginning, there was darkness. Then there was light. My first memory as a little person is the 1976 FA Cup Final. Before this day there was nothing. I think. It may be possible that some earlier memories have been inadvertently re-organised to a later time in my mind, probably as a result of such a momentous occasion at such a young age, but for all intents and purposes, this was my earliest recollection. I was four.

In England, there are two major domestic cup competitions, the Football Association Challenge Cup (the FA Cup) and the Football League Cup. The FA Cup was first played in 1872 and is the oldest football competition in the world. It is a knockout competition where teams are drawn together without seeding or weighting. The winning team progresses to the next round until only two teams remain. Any team can conceivably enter the competition, from league champions to village green teams. In the 2017 competition, 736 teams entered the competition that started in August, 2016.

Saints had unexpectedly reached the 1976 FA Cup Final to play Manchester United. In those days, we were still stuck in the Second Division, after being relegated in 1974 with Norwich City and – would you believe – Manchester United. The United team would be rebuilt in 1975 and gained promotion straight back up to Division One, and finished an excellent third place in their first season back in Division One in 1976. Saints, on the other hand, wallowed in sixth place in Division Two that year. This meant that Manchester United would be favourites for the match, with Saints at such far out odds as 5-1 to win. United had beaten Derby County in the semi-final and the Manchester United manager Tommy Docherty implied that that match was the real final. Saints beat Crystal Palace, who were in the Third Division, in their semi-final, winning 2-0 in a very tense encounter.

The Saints manager, Lawrie McMenemy had a number of good players in his Southampton team, even though some of them were past their best. He'd not enjoyed a great time in the job since he took over in the 1974 season. In the first season he oversaw Saints' relegation, and in the two years since, found getting back into the top division beyond his team. Indeed, the exciting cup run in 1976 put paid to Southampton's promotion hopes that year.

The team still had Mick Channon, a fully-fledged England international who would go on to become Saints' highest ever goal scorer with 185 goals from 510 matches played. He menaced defences with a distinctive scruffy look and I remember his shirt was always outside his shorts – something I liked to emulate much to Dad's frustration.

The 1976 side also had the very experienced Scottish international Jim McCalliog, who had signed from Manchester United. McMenemy had also purchased more experience in Peter Osgood from Chelsea, who in 1970 became one of the few players to score in every round of the FA Cup, including the final, which they won beating Dirty Leeds after a replay. There was more experience in defence in the form of the thirty-two year old captain and Welsh international Peter Rodrigues, and the central defensive partnership of Mel Blyth and Jim Steele who between them had over 500 career matches behind them.

On this day, I would watch the game with Dad at home. We lived in a small bungalow on the main road through Colden Common, near Winchester. It was a sunny day (this would be the first summer day that would turn into the famous drought of 1976), so our brown and orange Seventies curtains needed to be firmly drawn shut to maximise the viewing experience.

I was already being primed as a Saints fan. I remember I knew it was the cup final and that I knew it was important. I knew we were playing Manchester United and that the game would be very hard. I would soon have my first Saints shirt, a plain red and white striped number. You could buy number transfers that you could iron on to the back of your shirt (well, Mum could, I was much too young to do ironing then. In fact, Kellie won't let me do ironing now). I had the number three, as David Peach, who was our reliable left-back and penalty taker. I recall that I chose this number but I don't remember why; I really ought to have chosen Channon's number, number eight. My shirt had a big red patch on my back as Mum burnt a massive hole through the back of the shirt as she tried to iron the number transfer on it. I also had a poster of the team that was presumably given away at Esso petrol stations as it had the red and blue Esso logo on it, which I didn't understand at the time.

I had my own plastic 50p ball from the newsagent next door and I had the perfect playmate in our Old English Sheepdog Dougal. I would call him the Dulux dog as Dougal looked like the dogs on the advert. Dougal would always be Newcastle United, owing to his black and white coat. We had a long back garden where I could run and play, and further up the garden, near some spooky woods Dad had even made me what seemed like a huge goal post. Cows once found their way into the garden which Mum found really scary, and made me disappointed as it ruined my intended football match against Newcastle that day.

The matches with Dougal never lasted long. The imaginary referee would blow his imaginary whistle, and the game would start with Newcastle making an uncompromising challenge on the slender blonde Southampton player, pick up the ball in his mouth, run off with it and burst it. After treatment from the physiotherapist (Mum) to the Southampton player, the game would be abandoned owing to a lack of essential playing equipment. Soon after I would be marched next door to the newsagents for another ball and off we would go again.

For the cup final, a snazzy new lemon yellow and blue kit would be the order of the day for the Saints. Manchester United would be in red shirts and white shorts. This confused me completely. Dad explained that this was because of a colour clash and two teams can't wear the same kit otherwise the players would get mightily confused. I thought that was wrong, after all Saints were red with white stripes on the shirt, not just red – surely the players would notice the difference? Then I realised I had forgot, if you looked at the Saints shirt from the back, you'd see it was predominantly red, owing to this giant patch. Therefore, I submitted and agreed to Dad's logic.

Cup final day in our house was always a special day. Because of 1976, the FA Cup was always a special competition to us and we always dreamt that watching the final next year we might be there instead of watching it on the telly. Each year, we would watch the entire day's television, always BBC, never ITV, and the extensive build up to the day. The original BBC synopsis from the Radio Times for the event was as follows.

'BBC Cup Final Grandstand, direct from the Empire Stadium, Wembley with David Coleman, Frank Bough and Jimmy Hill. The 1976 FA Cup Final between Manchester United versus Southampton. BBC outside broadcast cameras bring you the whole of this Royal occasion, with slow-motion replays of the game's outstanding moments, and interviews with the players.'

'11:15 a.m. Cup Final Morning. Frank Bough introduces Grandstand from Wembley. Barry Davies and John Motson talk to the players of both teams at their Cup Final hotels. Tony Gubba meets the supporters on their way to Wembley.'

'12:00 The Women's FA Cup Final between Southampton and Queens Park Rangers. Highlights of the Women's Football Association match of the year, for the Mitre Trophy, played at Bedford Town FC. Southampton, the holders, have won the Cup four times out of the five previous competitions.' Saints Ladies would win this one 1-0 – I remember it clearly. It was like a normal football match, but with girls – yuck!

'12:20 p.m. Cup Final Knockout. The excitement of It's a Knockout as teams from the supporters' clubs of Manchester United and Southampton compete in this special contest for Cup Final Day. Among the personalities joining in are present and past players, and celebrity supporters. Introduced by Eddie Waring and Stuart Hall. Referee: Arthur Ellis.' It's a Knockout was a Seventies incarnation of Total Wipeout. I thought it was very funny but it was taken very seriously – the UK winners would qualify for the European It's A Knockout, called 'Jeux Sans Frontières'. Looking back on YouTube I am shocked at just how crap it is: I can't believe I was duped into watching this on a Friday night in Summer. There was always a cup final version, a staple element of cup final day.

'1:10 p.m. Racing from Ascot.' Racing was boring!

'1:20 p.m. Boxing. The World Heavyweight Championship between Muhammad Ali and Jimmy Young (Champion) (USA). This morning's title fight in Baltimore, USA – Ali's sixth defence since he regained the title in 1974. Young, who stopped Richard Dunn two years ago, is unbeaten for three years. Commentator: Harry Carpenter.' Ali would win on points after 15 Rounds. I remember the fight, being twitchy and anxious about how long the boxing would continue and would we miss the football. Dad told me it was alright and he told me all about how amazing Muhammad Ali was. (I didn't remember the result of the fight– I had to look it up.)

'1:45 p.m. Inside Wembley. The Cup Final atmosphere mounts as the teams arrive to inspect the Wembley turf. Followed by Goal of the Season: see the winning goals, and find out who has won the 200 pounds worth of Premium Bonds in this popular annual competition.' I had no idea what a Premium Bond was.

'Followed by Action Highlights of the road to Wembley. Meet the Teams. Action profiles of the players. The Final Word from Jimmy Hill, Bobby Charlton and Frank McLintock.' I remember at this point Dad went potty. Absolutely mental. Bobby Charlton, the distinguished former Manchester United and England legend, had predicted Manchester United would win 6-0. This wasn't Sir Bobby's finest moment – he was clearly speaking as a biased supporter rather than an impartial football observer. Dad jumped around our small lounge and called him a prick. Mum told Dad off.

'2:45 p.m. Abide with Me, the return of the Cup Final hymn.' I'm not a hymn person, and not at all religious, although when we are one goal down with five minutes to go, I will most certainly pray to the footballing gods. Abide with Me is tradition on cup final day and actually an amazing experience at a football match.

'2:50 p.m. Presentation of the Teams to HRH The Duke of Edinburgh.' The teams had come out to a rapturous reception from the fans, and lined up in the middle of the pitch ready to be met by royalty. The captain of each team walked the VIP through each of the players in turn and introduced them, followed by the manager. That day, the Queen was in attendance watching from the royal box.

'3:00 p.m. The FA Cup Final: Manchester United versus Southampton'. It was time for the match! The Manchester United team had a big reputation from the season just completed. They had two troublesome attacking wingers in Gordon Hill and Steve Coppell who were a menace to defenders. They were also strong at the back with Martin Buchan, a Scottish international in the centre of defence, and Alex Stepney in goal. Stepney was a survivor of the 1968 European Cup final when Manchester United had beaten Benfica to become the first English team to win that trophy.

The match had barely begun when Coppell shot at our goalkeeper, Ian Turner. Instead of gathering the ball, Turner parried the ball into a crowd of Manchester United players. Then it was Hill's turn to cause panic in the Saints defence with Turner having to save from close range. Hill was then sent clean through but his attempted lob was able to be parried again by Turner. Dad was edgy, his booming voice sending shivers right through me.

But with each minute in the game passing, Saints were growing stronger, belief mounting with the players. Turner, in the Southampton goal had got over his nerves in the early moments and now looked much more comfortable. Close to half-time, Saints had their best chance, with McCalliog sending Channon through on goal with a beautiful long pass. Channon tried to poke the ball past the onrushing Stepney but Stepney was sharp enough to meet and save with his right foot.

At half-time, it was 0-0 and it was time for the traditional half-time marching display by the 'Massed Bands of The Guards Division'. At about four o'clock every day, Mum would start to scoot around the house getting ready for work. She worked at Britain's first and largest hypermarket, Carrefour. Normally Dad would take her at five o'clock, and I can't imagine what would happen if the match went into extra time to make Mum late!

In the second half both teams toiled in attacking the goals in which most of their fans were behind. From a corner, Manchester United hit the crossbar, the in-swinging corner nodded on at the near post and headed on to the bar from close range. Saints had survived another near miss but in truth, were handling Manchester United very well.

I remember Dad being on the edge of his seat on the sofa, living every minute, with me sunk on the sofa next to him, and Mum buzzing around in her dressing gown getting ready.

Channon received the ball on the edge of the penalty box and skipped inside two Manchester United defenders, before flashing a shot just wide. Shortly after, United removed one of their most dangerous players and substituted Gordon Hill; a sure sign that the United coaching team were not happy about Saints gaining some ascendency in the match. With twenty minutes to go the match could not have been more finely poised. Peter Osgood was played in by Channon but could only stretch as he shot and Stepney saved comfortably. Bobby Stokes, Channon's young strike partner, received the ball twenty-five yards out and also flashed a shot just wide.

Then, the moment that all Saints fans remember had arrived. The time was about 4:38 p.m. on Saturday the 1st of May, 1976. There was seven minutes left in the FA Cup Final. Ian Turner had the ball in his hands, caressing it before placing the ball down to take a goal kick. He sent his goal kick up to half way out to the right. Channon flicked the ball inside to McCalliog, who played a fantastic instant through ball to Stokes, over the top of the Manchester United defence. Stokes was lightning quick to get beyond the defence, and hit the ball first time which fired along the deck and past Alex Stepney right into the corner of the goal.

When this happened at home, Dad leapt out of his chair arms aloft and screamed so loud, I just burst into tears. Not only did he celebrate the goal but he and Mum needed to reassure me everything was okay. I had never heard my Dad shout so loud, even at me, and it frightened me so much I was inconsolable! I'm not sure Dad ever shouted like that again since! Once things had settled down a little bit, Saints just needed to see out the last couple of minutes. When the whistle went at the end of the match, up went Dad again, this time Mum putting her hands over my ears.

Peter Rodrigues led the Saints players up the famous thirty-nine steps to collect the trophy from the Royal Box (it was actually thirty-five steps, I know, I counted them when Dad took me to a Wembley open day. We got to walk out of the tunnel, sit in the dressing room, and even go to the royal box and lift a facsimile cup). Waiting for the players was the glorious FA Cup, decorated in yellow and blue ribbons, and also Her Majesty The Queen who would present the medals in a blue outfit. Interestingly, the Queen has not returned to a cup final since 1976. Legend has it she's a Saints fan and won't return until Saints get to Wembley again. Rodrigues lifted the trophy towards the Saints fans, the crowd cheered, and Southampton had won the FA Cup.

Of course, what I do remember from the day is very little, just short segments of detail and flashes of colour. Over the years, the game has gone into Saints folk lore and often repeated. The FA Cup Final 1976 DVD is a staple title in any Saints' fan DVD collection, so over the years you become more familiar with the details of the match.

Re-watching the match today, it was interesting that the Manchester United team, with nothing to show for their efforts after twenty minutes were mentally unable to compete thereafter, their confidence waning. Southampton, although a division below had all the experience necessary to steer the ship on the day, with the younger United players freezing on the big occasion. In some respects, by the end of the match it was absolutely no surprise that Saints had taken the lead and won the match.

When you watch the winning goal again it's easy to forget what a super goal it was. Manchester United ex-players have argued over the years that Stokes was offside when he scored, but looking at it I very much doubt that he was, even though in those days, a striker only needed to be level with the defender to be deemed to be in an offside position.

Stokes was a small, quick player with good technique who drifted in and out of the Saints side in the years he was there. Ironically, he was from Portsmouth, and joined Southampton when he was young simply because Portsmouth didn't have a good enough infrastructure to bring players through. Even during the 1976 season Stokes nearly transferred over to Portsmouth. Every time I see that cup final winning goal, I am not ashamed to admit that the hairs on the back of my neck stand up and I get a bit wet around the eyes (I said the eyes!) – although not nearly as bad as the day itself. There are only two pieces of film that make me a bit emotional, Dobby the house elf dying in Harry Potter and that Bobby Stokes winning goal.

I've been reading the book 'Tie a Yellow Ribbon' which is the definitive account of Saints achievement that year. I wanted to find out some information about the aftermath of the match until the following Monday, when Mick Channon had his testimonial friendly match against Queens Park Rangers. The funny thing is, nobody seems to have any information about it – it's as if the next forty-eight hours were a complete blur to the people of Southampton. I bet there were some fantastic parties that night!

On the Sunday, the cup was paraded through the streets of Southampton to the Guildhall in the centre of town. An open top bus was hired so the players could show off the cup from on high as they slowly travelled through the city. I have pictures that show just a sea of people hanging out of every window, from every rooftop, with thousands upon thousands of fans there to welcome the team home with the cup, whilst the bus tries to carefully navigate on its route behind a brass band. When in England in 2016 we went to the Premier League match against Manchester City that coincided with the fortieth anniversary of the cup win. They managed to locate the original bus and the remaining players still going got to parade the trophy once again from the open upper deck. It was a nice touch and great to see the bus and players at the match.

Missing from this fortieth anniversary celebration was Peter Osgood who sadly died of a heart attack in 2006. Also missing was the little legend Bobby Stokes, who tragically died at just forty-four, in 1995, from bronchial pneumonia. Author Mark Sanderson has done a wonderful service to Bobby by charting his career in his 'Bobby Stokes' biography. In it, the author describes how scoring the winning goal in the cup final and acquiring that legendary status was something that Bobby was not prepared for and never really came to terms with.

Each year, Dad and I would watch the FA Cup Final together. It was always an important day in the Budden calendar irrespective as to who was playing and I would never miss it. It's in part because of what happened in 1976 and how it happened. It was as if each year we would try to recreate the atmosphere of 1976 even though Saints weren't there. Like 1976 Dad would formally draw the curtains as we would sit and watch all the pre-match guff, through to the winning captain lifting the trophy. Dougal, who sometimes spent his afternoons sleeping on the window ledge would pick a spot on the floor, waking up each time Dad or me cried out at the incident in front of us. We would adopt a team, usually the underdog and cheer them on. Sometimes we backed the winner, such as Ipswich Town in 1978 or Coventry City in 1987, but more often we were left slightly miffed, such as Tottenham Hotspur beating Queens Park Rangers in 1982 or Manchester United beating Brighton and Hove Albion in 1983. One year we even got tickets for the final, in 1988, when Wimbledon caused an upset to beat Liverpool 1-0 (hugely enjoyable).

Although Saints would invariably be missing in this final match each year post-1976, the matches would not necessary be without tension. This was normally caused by Dad's neighbours rather than the football though, who, realising it was only stupid football on the telly, would decide to mow their lawns. Each year, cue the teams coming out of the tunnel on to the pitch to the bellows and cheers of the crowd, there would suddenly be this buzzing sound of a small motor roaring into action, followed by Dad going off on one…

"Can you hear that, Russ? Is that a bloody mower? I don't bloody believe it! Don't they know its sodding Cup Final day?"

It would appear the grass would be longest and needing the most attention closest to Dad's garden boundary and closest to the lounge window, and thus the noise would increase as would Dad's anger until eventually (normally as the referee was tossing the coin to see who would kick off) Dad would stick his head out of the window.

"What the bloody hell do you think you are doing?" he'd bark. At first the neighbour would not hear Dad's call for reason. However eventually he would clock Dad's head hanging out the window, turn off the mower's engine, and ask Dad if everything was all right.

"The bloody Cup Final's on!" Dad would say. This always seemed to explain everything, and the neighbour would always relent and retire back into his house and wait until five o'clock when the match would be over.

In 1983 however, there was extra time, and the neighbour trotted back out assuming the match to be over. On went the mower, up jumped Dad and off he went again. It became almost tradition for the neighbour to receive a bollicking from Dad.

By 2002, Dad had invested in satellite television. But instead of getting the vastly superior and popular BSkyB service, Dad opted to get the vastly inferior and cheaper OnDigital. I don't know if you remember OnDigital; this was a service launched by ITV in 1998. By 2001 it had pretty much had it. Problems with picture quality caused by weaker than expected broadcast power plagued their service causing their subscribers to switch to BskyB in their droves. But Dad knew better, so that year we would watch Arsenal versus Chelsea in 'high' quality digital.

Except the picture quality was dreadful. The build up to the match was marred by pixelated formations on the screen and jarring pops and squeaks as the sound would pause then collide with itself as it tried to keep up with the pictures. The marching band, so often a staple of cup final day would be scattered across the screen as if the individual guardsmen were making a run for it, their music sounding like a scratched and mutilated record. By the time the final kicked off, we could only see the legs of the players in the bottom quarter of the screen. With the neighbour already banished back into his home with his mower, Dad set about first trying to fix the problem on the satellite decoder, then argue with it, before hitting it. After about five minutes, I made a run for it and legged it to Debbie's and Chris's house in the next street. By half-time Dad had arrived too, looking as though he had been in a fight rather than calibrating the television.

The next month, in June of 2002, OnDigital folded and Dad would have to invest in BskyB in time for the next year's final. Little did he know, he wouldn't need it the following year.

1979

English Football League Cup Final 1979, Nottingham Forest versus
Southampton. Wembley Stadium, London, Saturday, 17th of March.

Saints got to the League Cup Final in 1979 to play the mighty
Nottingham Forest, managed by the legendary Brian Clough. The
League Cup is the other major knockout trophy in England. It is a
similar format as the FA Cup, except it is only open to the ninety-two
Football League teams. Unlike the FA Cup Final which is the
showpiece match at the very end of the football season in May, the
League Cup final is in February or March.

At this time Forest were the reigning league champions and were
the current holders of the League Cup so would be defending their
crown. A couple of months after the final they would also become
European Champions, and had just purchased Trevor Francis, the first
ever one million pound footballer who, thankfully, wasn't able to play
that day. They were top calibre opposition and were certainly more
formidable than the Manchester United team Saints beat three years
earlier.

That year, Saints were back in Division One for the first time in five
years. They were promoted the previous May after finishing Second in
Division Two. The team had adjusted to the higher standard admirably
and, whilst they were one or two players short of a good team, they
were never in danger of relegation, and as well as getting to the League
Cup final, had a great chance in the FA Cup, where they were due to
play Arsenal for a place in the quarter final only forty-eight hours after
this match.

The Saints team were unrecognisable from the cup winning team of
1976. Nick Holmes and David Peach were the only survivors of that
day. The team had been rebuilt almost as soon as Peter Rodrigues lifted
the trophy. Indeed, the hero Bobby Stokes, was gone before the end of
the 1977 season. Major new arrivals included Phil Boyer, an underrated

forward player who was brought into the club to replace Mick Channon who had finally got his wish to move into Division One with Manchester City.

The team now had a smattering of internationals, such as Chris Nicholl, Northern Ireland's centre back, and Ivan Golac from Yugoslavia, who had arrived at The Dell in an era when there were only a few 'foreign' players in the English game.

Lawrie McMenemy had also purchased Alan Ball from Arsenal, who famously won the World Cup with England in 1966. He would prove to be another inspired signing by Southampton, even though he was beginning to enter his 'senior' years as a footballer. Dad was put out by Mr. Ball when I asked both him and Steve Williams (latest youth player to ascend to the first team with great credit) for an autograph, whereupon Mr. Ball snatched my pen, grunted ("sure can"), scribbled some lines on my autograph book and handed it back. In retrospect, I am not quite sure what he was supposed to say. I did discuss this incident in depth with Alan when he visited New Zealand – a genuine legend.

The team additionally included an ex-boyfriend: Malcolm Waldron, Saints other central defender, dated my sister Debbie. She brought him home when I was about five whereupon by shyness to 'real' footballers was mistaken for abusive behaviour. I had told him not to kick my football (yellow ball with black spots, 50p, from Hayles Newsagents next door) because he might burst it (particularly astute for a young boy of five, I thought). I am sure I got a wallop at some stage after from Debbie; I don't remember the exact slap because I had so many (usually deserved – I was a horrible child), but I am sure I would have.

Saints had beaten Dirty Leeds in the semi-final. They were 2-0 down into the second half of the first leg at Elland Road, but Steve Williams and Phil Boyer responded to give us the edge in the two-legged semi-final. In the second leg at The Dell, Tony Curran, a mercurial winger who endured a single poor season for Saints that year, scored his only goal for Saints that night, and the only one he would get playing for us.

But back in March I was seven and three-quarters. To this point, Dad had taken me to The Dell to watch the reserves play in front of a smattering of supporters (I remember Peter Osgood playing against Bristol Rovers), but never for a 'first team' match – a real match.

I asked Dad one time as to why he had not gone to the 1976 Final. He told me that he had seen Saints play Blackpool back in 1953 in an FA Cup fifth round match, when Stanley Matthews single-handedly beat them at The Dell. Having lost that game, he went to Villa Park in the 1963 FA Cup semi-final, when Saints had given a good account of themselves but were undone by a single Dennis Law goal to miss out on the final. So he had decided to avoid FA Cup matches as he was clearly the cause of the ongoing heartache.

But in 1979 that changed. He acquired two tickets for the Final. Dad's reasoning that I couldn't see a real match up to that point was because of the hooligan problem that blighted the sport. But, he said, Wembley was different – you never see any fighting at Wembley. To perhaps test that theory he acquired two bench seats close to the edge of the greyhound track, in amongst all the Nottingham Forest fans.

To me, not only did being in another cup final feel fantastic but to get a ticket to go to the game was unbelievable. I would be allowed to look at the small blue and white ticket with thin stub as it is were some rare gem, proclaiming the match to be played at 'The Empire Stadium, Wembley' no less. Ironically Dad thought it best for him to look after the tickets himself, and then I would imagine promptly walking off wondering what he had done with his car keys.

It didn't matter, I'd find the tickets in the study room downstairs in the writing drawer whilst I was looking for my felt tip pens that he kept stealing from me (he would use the pen, then leave the lid off, drying the pen!). I'd stare at the tickets as if they were the most precious thing in the world.

As a kid time moves so much slower. I can't remember the time between getting the tickets and going to the game, but it felt like the longest time ever. Debbie had given me a badge with a thumbs-up logo on it saying, '17th March All Saints Day'. I also had a yellow and blue rosette, that was still the thing in those days.

Dad had acquired a yellow and blue scarf that I wore on the day, which Dad commandeered afterwards and wore to all matches thereafter. He also brought home from work an enormous top hat made out of cardboard covered with yellow and blue electrical tape. Across the front was the word 'SAINTS' which was made out of the letters that made up the word 'TRANSIT' on the back of the Ford vans. I thought it was amazing but wondered if there would be a Transit Van sold as FORD TR's because there were letters missing. The hat fitted but was very heavy. Dad would have enormous fun by banging on the top of the hat and wedging it across my forehead until my head ached and scratched and no doubt reshaped my head to look like an egg for a while. It had pretty much collapsed by the day of the game so would have to stay home.

I got no sleep the night before. I was beside myself with excitement. I had previewed the match extensively with Subbuteo. I didn't have a red team (for Forest) nor a yellow team for Saints, so out came by Southampton home team (red and white stripes circa 1973, reference number 9) – two or three players still manfully clinging to their bases, whilst all other players had been severed or crushed in some way and would take to the field with blu tac around the ankles. Forest would wear something akin to their change strip, and would use my Holland team for them (reference number 13). For some reason those players kept well, I still have six of those players in good order now. Full commentary and crowd noise would be required, no doubt reaching down the street. I felt comfortable that, although Saints were underdogs, and Forest were current League champions, Saints would surely win 3-2. I even remember how the goals would go in: Saints score first, Forest hit back with two goals, then Saints storm back to win 3-2 with a magnificent goal from outside the box in the last minute.

The 17th of March was in a spring that followed the harshest, coldest, snowiest winter in my memory. There was snow on the ground that day, still thawing from some days before. But the day was bright, and we travelled to the match with one of Dad's friends. I have no idea who this man was, or his son. I had never met them before, and never saw them again after. Dad had a circle of friends that would crop up periodically in my childhood, but this guy is a blank to me today, and I remember I didn't think much of his son either whom I recall was about the same age. I didn't have time to play – this was serious – this was a cup final. I wonder if the lure of the tickets and the ride up were a contributory factor in this particular friendship? It certainly would be something that would cross my mind searching for a ticket in 2017.

We drove up in a small, strange, car for what seemed like an eternity, and included the obligatory stop at Fleet services. We arrived near the ground in good time, and true to form, Dad decided he knew where to go (although this was his first time at Wembley too). In no time, his job was done and got us completely lost. I had seen some funny orange signs up with a diamond shape on it and an arrow. I asked Dad if we followed these arrows we might get to the ground? He told me to shut up. Eventually his friend suggested we try this and sure enough, we ended up circling the Wembley complex.

I can't remember where we parked but I do remember the walk to the ground. Dad had told me to try and look around and take things in otherwise I would forget. I was desperate to remember everything. At first all I could see was an incredible myriad of people, singing Saints songs, milling about the streets. It would have been still about ninety minutes to kick off but I had never seen so many people in my life. Soon we were walking up Wembley way, a huge straight of concrete angling up from the road level to the stadium's enormous twin towers. I had my Cup Final programme (20p) and my yellow flag 'Southampton, The Saints'. Our entry gate was on the opposite side of the towers, and then we were inside Wembley stadium for the first time. We took our seats along a bench close to the front and looked up to take in as much as I could.

Whereupon I realised I couldn't see a thing!

I could see a fence and a greyhound track, but I had to look really hard to see the pitch and the goals through the fence grille. No matter, Dad promised to lift me up when Saints went forward so I could see better.

But this was the most incredible place I had ever been to. There were hundreds of flags hanging from inside the roof all the way around its oval perimeter. I could see two giant scoreboards at either end, a manual one with the letters of the teams neatly spaced at one end, and an electronic scoreboard at the other with a "Sport For All" logo either side of it. I could see portions of the greyhound track running around the perimeter of the pitch with a large semi-circular space between the turns of the track and the back of the goal, with advertising hoardings spaced out at angles. There were still mounds of snow thawing across the greyhound track and large black tarpaulin that had presumably been covering the pitch during the snow. Soon there would be 100,000 people in the ground.

As the ground started to fill up, the realisation dawned on Dad that we were in a Nottingham Forest part of the ground. We were along the side but behind the goal that Southampton defended in the first half. There was a mass of Saints fans near us to my right in the main standing enclosures behind the goal, but from the enclosure I was in all the way round to the other goal in the distance, was Nottingham territory.

In 1979, it was not common to wear a replica shirt to the match. I had my itchy replica Admiral lemon yellow shirt on, slightly too small for me, with yellow and blue striped flappy collar, the corners of which had been sucked and chewed to a shrivel (I was seven, okay?), with a blue stripe with Admiral logo dotted down each sleeve. However, this was covered with a number of layers that my Mum no doubt enforced on me before I left the house. Besides, the grown man did not wear a replica shirt to a match: they wore working man's clothes, with a rosette on one chest and the outline of a packet of fags on the other.

Rich primary colours could be seen from each end of the ground. To my right and across the pitch, there was a sea of waving yellow Saints flags. To my left a similar view, but red Nottingham Forest flags. I went to get my flag to join in and be a part of this yellow sea. I bent down, went to grab the flag, got the stick end caught in the cuff of my coat and snapped the stick clean in two. Holding up the flag in my arms, with my juvenile height was a fruitless exercise. I still have the un-waved flag, preserved no doubt because of the minimal amount of exercise that it had that day. I remember in 2003 I had a flag but didn't take it, so it dawns on me as I write this that I have never had the opportunity to wave a flag for my team at a cup final. What a closeted life I have led. I hope I have some spare change this year to change that.

In those days, the players came out of the tunnel from behind the goal, under the Saints fans this day. The manager leads out his team, followed by the captain, the goalkeeper, then the remaining players. Each player would have a stony face concentrating for the battle ahead, fiercely chewing on some gum. I always wondered why players didn't blow bubbles with their gum. Lawrie McMenemy marched out regally with the Saints players behind him. But, the Nottingham Forest manager, the legendary Brian Clough, wasn't leading out his team. He had passed that honour on to his assistant Peter Taylor. I was really sad about that. Lawrie McMenemy was a big name in the game, no doubt, but Brian Clough was the biggest, the brashest, and arguably the best.

I remember being so nervous that day, leading up to kick off. I wanted them to win so badly and I know Dad did too. He told me that as a kid himself he followed Arsenal, even though he was raised in St Mary's – just a stone's throw from the stadium today. That was until he made it into Southampton's youth team as a goalkeeper. He wasn't there long, a broken leg ended his association with the club. But whilst he was there he told me about how each youth player had a 'minder' from the first team. Dad's 'minder' was Sir Alf Ramsey who was a left-back at the time. Although an England International and playing for the Saints in the Second Division, Ramsey would be forced out of Southampton after losing his place in the team and being sold to Tottenham Hotspur. Ramsey would have a distinguished playing career blighted by being in the England team that lost 6-3 to Hungary in 1953. This was the first time a 'foreign' team had beaten England on home soil, and would be Ramsey's last cap for England.

Of course, Ramsey will be remembered as the England manager who won the World Cup in 1966, moulding a style of play that wasn't always agreeable with the public, but which got the best results of all. He presented on television as a very stiff individual, ill at ease with the public glare, with a clipped accent in the old, posh, BBC style.

Dad remembers him as a younger man, with a much rougher, common voice. According to Dad, Ramsey was a gypsy, born in Dagenham, and was evidentially not proud of it. Sometime after his association with Dad, it is thought he had taken elocution lessons to radically improve his speech. But Ramsey was good to Dad, and took an autograph book to each match, and had the book autographed by the opposition team. According to Dad he had dozens of signatures of some of the best players of the day. He kept the book for prosperity but in 1970 gave the book away to a neighbour who had a son. At the time, with two daughters, at 35, he had given up hope for a son. A year later, the Accident that is me turned up in the world.

That book, wherever it is – probably in some bullet proof glass mounted in a snooker room of some multi-millionaire somewhere hot and sunny – is mine. What was he thinking?

It's a nice story, but I believe his love for the team germinated from his time there. I don't have any philosophical or psychological reasoning as to why we have such an unhealthy thirst to see the team win, but imagine that was the start of it. He was part of the club. Part of the team in some way. Part of the town. Therefore, Southampton Football Club was his. And now, in 1979, on a bright spring day, it was mine too. We needed to win. We had to win.

We lost.

I remember that in the opening minutes Saints looked good. I know this because after about ten minutes Dad had had quite enough of lifting me up and was knackered. I told me to crouch on the bench seat instead and spring up and stand on it when we get close to goal.

Not long after, we scored.

David Peach ran through on goal, went around the mighty Peter Shilton in goal and placed the ball in the back of the net. That's what I saw through the fence down at the other end of the pitch. When I look back at the game on YouTube I was amazed I have it stored to memory so clearly. Alan Ball played a ball over the defenders perfectly into Peach's path who did coolly waltz past Shilton to score.

The noise when the goal went in was loud. But Dad had me in a bear hug that, frankly, I did well to survive. The noise might even have been just Dad if I think about it, given the fans in closest proximity to us went deathly quiet. Dad's chatter was then all about how he rounded the best goalkeeper in the world. Nobody does that. What a magnificent goal.

The rest of the first half played out in a similar way, through the tiny squares of the perimeter fencing. Saints were playing very well, and were having the better of it. At half-time we were still winning.

We were on our way.

I've always admired and been fascinated with Brian Clough. There are a number of excellent books about him, the best being Duncan Hamilton's glorious account of Clough in 'Provided You Don't Kiss Me'. Hamilton was the Nottingham Sports reporter and travelled with the team during Forest's glory years. In the book he emphasises

Clough's incredible man-management skills and how he made players feel bigger and better than perhaps they were. The night before the match in the team hotel, Clough was not satisfied with the team and felt they were edgy. He ordered two crates of bitter and demanded his team 'sup the lot' before bed. Forest's young striker back then was Garry Birtles, who passed out under the strain and had to be dragged to his bed. In this day and age of the professional athlete on a strict diet of boiled chicken, steamed broccoli and warm water, such a thing would spell certain doom for a team. However, these were different times, and in hindsight I wished I hadn't read about that.

I am sure it is the same with all football fans who get to a final. You think about the game ahead, what might happen, which players need to play well or step up. For a supporter of an underdog team, you also think about how the game could be won. You might think that it will be important to keep the game at 0-0 for as long as possible and nick a goal near the end, similar to Saints in 1976. Or you might think that your team will play the game of their lives and go toe-to-toe with your superior opponents and hope they have an off-day. It may surprise you to learn that this kind of thinking goes through the mind of a mad seven and three-quarters fan at Wembley for the first time. The bare minimum thought that pops into your head before the game, and which popped into mine was, to play well. Play a good game and don't get hammered. Don't make terrible mistakes. Don't mess up.

I've witnessed a number of torrid Saints matches where we've been hammered, well beaten, not given a kick, or tossed the game away. I've been to football horror shows in every shape and colour. Dad always used to go into an immediate rage when Match Of The Day or some other football programme would replay Dirty Leeds' 7-0 thrashing of Saints in 1972. It's torture. The second half of the League Cup Final in 1979 – my first ever real football match was also my first horror show. There were tears streaming down my face for much of the second half, as the crowd around us danced and jigged and bounced in celebration.

It was immediately clear that Brian Clough had worked his magic in the dressing room. His team came out with a purpose in the second half. Saints were being pinned back in their own half, which I thought was completely frustrating, given much of the game in the first half when Saints were on top was played at the same end, the end furthest away from me. Couldn't Forest have had their flurry of attacking football in the first half so I could have at least seen it a bit closer?

Things started to go horribly wrong. I remember our goalkeeper Terry Gennoe receiving a pass pack from a defender. He went to smother the ball and as he did so managed to squeeze the ball out of his backside, between his legs, whereupon the ball rolled slowly, agonisingly, along the goal line. Fortunately, the ball bobbled by the far post and the ball was smothered out before a Forest player could pounce. I had not seen anything like it. I would not have even dared allow this scenario to take place on the Subbuteo pitch as it was so absurd.

Shortly after Saints were rocking again, unable to clear the ball out of their penalty area. The ball ricocheted to our central defender, Chris Nicholl, who instead of booting the ball clear into row ZZ, decided to read the inscription on the match ball. Birtles (the one who passed out on his manager's instructions – remember him?) snatched the ball away and couldn't miss from about six yards.

But that was okay. It was only 1-1. Still plenty of time to win the game still.

The Wembley pitch was normally a fantastic sight; a perfect pitch with green stripes weaved across the pitch in all directions. Because of the bad weather in the preceding days, the pitch was in a bit of a mess, with huge clumps of grass lifting off the surface whenever a long pass or tackle was made. I never really saw the pitch in any form of detail of course, but I remember Dad being a bit miffed about the pitch. His outlook was about to turn into despair as Forest inevitably scored again.

The second goal was also scored by Birtles. He received the ball on the edge of the box and raced past Nicholl to blast the ball in the net. I thought about my played out matches in Subbuteo. This was actually going to plan so no need to panic, I thought. Saints will race back with two goals. But there was only 15 minutes to go now and Saints remained on the back foot. It seemed that, as soon as the second goal went in, Tony Woodcock, the other Forest striker thrashed the ball home from close range to make it 3-1. Saints were dead and buried, second best and well beaten in the end.

With about seven minutes to go Dad's mate wondered if we should leave. I didn't want to go, but Dad had had enough. There were joyous celebrations all around us by the Nottingham Forest fans. People were dancing and hugging and I suppose it was all too much for him. Ordinarily Dad would never entertain the idea that you should leave before the end of the match. At The Dell he would point out people leaving in other stands and shout out "Look at him! Where does he think he's going? The game's not over!" This would then be punctuated with an expletive such as "Prick!" or "Prat!" Sometimes Saints would be 4-1 down but would still bemoan any early leaver.

But on this day, with the excuse that we would get stuck in traffic if we didn't go right then, we set off, clambering around the Nottingham

Forest supporters around us. I imagine if I were Dad being around that kind of jubilation at your expense would have hurt so badly. That day I don't remember any bad behaviour from Dad, but in equivalent circumstances in later years his behaviour would become the stuff of legend.

When we got out of the ground we started to walk back round to Wembley Way. Suddenly we heard a huge cheer. Dad raced over to the nearest exit gate where he must have seen a steward who could have seen what happened. "It's 3-2!" he shouted. Typical! He was told we couldn't go back in (it wasn't even the gate we originally entered) and we didn't know what to do. Did we hang around here to find out the score? What if Saints equalised and there was thirty minutes extra time? If they had equalised I am certain my relationship with my Dad would not have been as good as it was over the years. In retrospect it is a conundrum that messes with your head. Do you want your team still to win even though you won't see it? Do you actually want them to lose so as to justify your decision for leaving early? What would I be like this year if I travel back to England, but don't get a ticket? Or worse, what if I get a ticket but find out at the turnstiles my ticket is a fake? Would I want Saints still to win? I am sure I would, but would I prefer to get a ticket, get into the ground and see them lose? I don't know. Of course, I realise his attitude (and of course mine) to early leavers was as a result of this particular match.

Within a couple of minutes, the game was over and we stopped milling around outside and set off for home down Wembley Way, my scarf draped over my bowed head, dragging forlornly across the concrete. It looked very different on the way out than from the way in. We had a head start over most of the remaining 99,996 supporters, so Wembley Way was almost empty. Suddenly, Dad grabbed my hand and told me not to move from his side. When I looked up we saw about six Nottingham Forest fans running towards us. Young Men. Teenagers. Hooligans?

Dad thought we were going to get a 'seeing to'. The group came up to me for some reason. Instead of punching our faces in, one of the gang said, "Chin up son, you'll win the other one!" He then threw his red and white striped scarf around my neck, patted me on the head and ran off with his mates celebrating. Dad was so relieved. The fan was referring to Saints' next game against Arsenal in the FA Cup. It was a nice thought to come back in two months' time and watch my team win the FA Cup instead. It cheered me up actually, up until we played Arsenal, when we got knocked out of the FA Cup in a replay.

When I saw the Forest fans inside the stadium I thought to myself – I want that, I want to be part of the winning team. There was no possible way that I could simply change teams, even though my sisters were responsible for getting me a Liverpool and Tottenham shirt when I was 5 or 6, just to push Dad's buttons. It was already ingrained, part of my DNA. It was a curse of sorts. I would just have to be patient.

That November, when the teams met again in the new season, with Nottingham Forest displaced as League Champions, but now European Champions, Saints annihilated them 4-1. Why couldn't they play like that in the Cup Final? By this time I had completed my football fan apprenticeship and was learning that as well as needing to be inhumanly patient to win a cup, I would have to get used to the sudden inexplicable highs and the predicable lows that would come with being a Southampton fan.

Going for it

"Saints may never get to another final in your lifetime. Go for it!" – Kellie.

An eight o'clock kick off for a midweek game during England's winter is nine o'clock in the morning in New Zealand, and I am at work.

Saints were playing Liverpool in the League Cup semi-final, this year branded as the EFL Cup. This Liverpool team were a shadow of their 1980's ancestors, and Saints had finished above them in the league last season, but this was a tough draw. Saints were having a disappointing season, and Liverpool had been rejuvenated by their charismatic German Manager Jürgen Klopp.

When the draw is made for the next round of a cup, you want to draw a 'lesser' team to give you a great chance of progressing into the next round. However, there aren't normally many lesser teams in a semi-final. I was particularly excited about the Liverpool draw though. I wanted Saints to play Liverpool. I wanted Saints to beat Liverpool badly. Last season, earlier in the same competition they beat us at St Mary's 6-1. It was a fluke result. Every time we attacked forward we got picked off and punished, exposing our reserve defender Steven Caulker doing impressions of a football imposter (we got rid of him that season, and his next club was Liverpool – work that one out!).

The League Cup semi-final takes place over two legs. Saints won the first leg against Liverpool at St Mary's 1-0. Normally this would have been an excellent result, but Saints had yet again failed to take their chances, spurning a number of great opportunities to win the game 2-0 or 3-0 which would have put us in an almost unassailable position. Squandering these chances kept Liverpool in the contest, even though I suspect that was their worst performance of the season to date. Under normal circumstances I would have been elated with the result, but I was disappointed. I'd felt we'd spurned our chance. I was nervous going into work that morning, the second leg was going to be a challenge.

I work in an office as a sub-contractor at Auckland airport. I am a Business Analyst supporting projects delivering IT solutions. I work at my desk and go to meetings and do all the unremarkable things that an office worker does.

The company I work for is a great company to be associated with, progressive and innovative. Being progressive and innovative means I can tune in to Radio Solent on my smartphone to listen to Dave Merrington and Adam Blackmore provide their excellent and accomplished commentary on each midweek game whilst I work. Me, Dave and Adam have spent many hours with each other, Dave and Adam commentating, me listening in alone.

When I listen to matches I have all the normal, nervous body twitches and arm actions as with any supporter listening on the radio or watching on TV. I could be jumping out of my seat, putting my head in my hands, and involuntarily swinging a leg as if I was playing and kicking the ball. But I'm working too. Well, a bit. I could leap up and punch the air for a goal, but no one at work would even bat an eyelid. A number of work mates know what's going on – it's no secret, and there is a lot of empathy as in my office of about thirty people there is a diverse range of nationalities: German (four of them no less, great guys, very funny – not at all like the tired stereotype), Swiss, Swedish, Indian, Malaysian, Tongan and a bunch of English. You may be surprised to know that there are also a couple of New Zealanders who have a genuine support for a team, over and above any rugby allegiance. In the office there are supporters of Newcastle United, Liverpool, Chelsea, Arsenal, Manchester City, Hammarby in Sweden and Borussia Monchengladbach in Germany, so there remains many opportunities to share banter and crow over a victory or wallow in a loss even though I am over the other side of the world. We also run a Premier League Fantasy Football league I which I seem doomed to lose.

At about eight thirty in the morning, I prepared my smartphone, got to the right web page, plugged in my headphones, made sure they were working and then went to my calendar on my computer to block out the next couple of hours so nobody could call me in for a meeting or disturb me.

When I looked at my calendar, to my horror I had realised I had a meeting that morning, all morning, at another site at the airport. This was a disaster. There would be no way I could get out of it, and after a few minutes plotting and scheming to remove myself from the meeting I came to the conclusion that I had to go.

So I closed the web page with a heavy heart, packed up the headphones and went for the meeting, popping my phone on silent.

At the end of the meeting, at midday, I was walking back to my car with a colleague, talking 'shop'. I had yet to glance at my phone at all until I sat in my car. When I looked, it said I had twenty-four new text messages. Without looking at any of them, I knew Saints had won the tie and were off to Wembley.

I calmly got out of the car then danced a well-rehearsed spastic jig of delight. I then got back in my car and calmly drove back to my office.

I tried to sit down at my desk and look professional but I was all over the place. It was lunch time so I went for a walk. I realised I had not looked at any of the twenty-four texts I had received. I didn't even know the score for that matter and had only assumed we were through to the final.

Shauna set me seven texts. She was watching the game at home and promised to update me with score news. Dad used to do that. But he would only send me texts if Saints scored. If Saints conceded a goal I didn't get to know about it. Shauna though, kept me well up to date.

"Fraser Forster save of the year. Just before ball crossed the line he hit it away. 0-0." This was at 10:12 a.m. about 15 minutes into the second half.

"Ward-Prowse is injured!". 10:16 a.m. about 25 minutes to go.

"WE'RE OFF TO WEMBLY!!!". She spelt Wembley wrong.

"1-0 to Saints!!!"

"Long, 90th minute!"

"You're off to the UK!"

Am I?

(Another text had all these emoji's which I thought were five penises which I didn't understand at all. Maybe that was meant for Shauna's boyfriend, Ryan, who was Liverpool through and through.)

I had obviously considered that if we got to the final that I would definitely want to go. But that is not the same thing as actually intending to go. I had decided that Saints were unlikely to reach the final, that a 1-0 first leg lead was insufficient to take back to Anfield and that this year Liverpool were superior and would overrun us. I had also considered how inconsiderate it was for Saints to get near a final this year after being generally poor this year and taking a considerable step backwards from recent years. Furthermore, I had been to England last year with Kellie for a month, and sent Sarah and Shauna to visit their Nanny for Christmas 2015. Our travel funds were less than zero. And finally, my work was ramping up with a new project – there would be no space for any extended time off, and I needed the money to buff up our savings.

So that was that then. Not going to the final. I'll watch it on the telly. Then I got a text from sister Debbie.

"Do you need a ticket?"

This was absurd. Still absorbing the enormity of the result and what that would mean for me, I needed to work this through with Kellie, so I rang her. She spelt it out for me. "Saints may never get to another final in your lifetime," she said. Harsh, I thought. "I want you to go. We made a deal. When we came to New Zealand we said these were the games you have to go back for". This was looking promising.

"We can't," I said, rolling off a bundle of excuses.

"You're going," she said with a tone of finality. "Go for it!" she said.

So I walked back into work and booked a return flight to London Heathrow right then and there. I managed to get a remarkably reasonable return flight fare for 2,300 dollars (1,150 pounds). I don't ever remember getting a long haul flight to London that cheap before, and I could have gone to just less than 2,000 dollars if I chose a non-refundable booking class. I'd be travelling to Los Angeles late on Friday, 24th of February, and would arrive in London Heathrow, on Saturday 25th of February, a full day before the game, at around 11:00 a.m. This would mean travelling back in time which I have found to be worse for jet lag.

Flying with the local carrier was the safe option. The flight I was on has a stop at Los Angeles, but it is the same flight to London, so if the flight was late into Los Angeles there would be no transiting issues on to another flight.

I booked to return on Friday 3rd of March in the afternoon, and would arrive home on Sunday 5th of March in time to go back to work the following day. Nine days total, six in England. It was going to be tough but worth it.

My manager was completely supportive and getting a week off work was no issue, although I knew up front that more than a week would be a problem. It wasn't long after Christmas, and New Zealand effectively shuts down for three weeks over that period, and we were kicking off a new project and further delays getting the project moving due to holidays was unreasonable.

That afternoon at work, I needed to find the Liverpool fans in the office (two of them) to offer my condolences for the result. In fact, I was going to do nothing of the sort and intended to gloat at them for the entire afternoon if I could. One of them was full of sanctimonious congratulations which stole my thunder and ruined my intended banter routine. The other one said he didn't know the score and would watch the game that evening. Don't bother, I said, we beat you! You're out! Much more satisfying.

I'd received a couple of texts from Ryan's Dad Niall (also a Liverpool fan). The first was a whinge about how Saints were defensively minded. Apparently, Saints had not just 'parked the bus', they'd built a car park ('park the bus' refers to our team being particularly defensively minded). Watching the game that night it was an unfair criticism. We were the better team in both matches, won both games and thoroughly deserved it. Actually, Liverpool were horrible, which merely added to my thrill. And in fairness he also said well done, unlike the previous year when Liverpool beat us 6-1.

He texted me when it was 5-1 back then: "A big High Five to you!" he put.

"A big piss off to you," I had replied. My congratulatory text at the end of that game was "Hope you get stuffed in the next round and Anfield burns down!" I am the sorest of losers. Niall and his family are from Dublin. He considers me the best Englishman he knows, and, proudly, the only Englishman at that. He thinks Kellie is one in a million and thinks I was won in a raffle. Once he said to me "You remind me of my brother. He's handicapped too." Nice.

At home, I watched the news intently for confirmation of Saints' success on New Zealand television. There are many peculiar aspects of the Kiwi (the human version, not the dumb bird), that really do bake my noodle. For example, in New Zealand the news is on at six o'clock, on two different channels, for an hour. There is another substantial bulletin run by both channels, TV1 and TV3 at around 10:30. After every programme in the evening there is a two minute bulletin to keep the viewer up-to-date.

Now, I realise that this is relatively comparable to the news bulletins in the UK. Except there is just not enough real news in New Zealand. The Kiwi has an insatiable appetite for current affairs, but there just isn't any, comparatively. New Zealand has the most radio stations per capita in the western world, all vomiting the same tiresome drivel all day and all night long.

The six o'clock news is so dull and benign, and when the bulletin is supplemented with news around the world, well I sometimes just want to stop the world and hop off. The sports bit is even worse. The football, usually from the Premier League is relegated to the 'and finally' slot, whilst New Zealand football stories only get on the news if the national team have been beaten badly. The rest of the sports section goes something like: rugby, rugby, rugby, rugby, rugby, rugby league, rugby, rugby, triathlon, and finally. Triathlon isn't even really a sport! It consists of people not good enough to run, cycle and swim on their own, so made up a sport to do all three! How does that get air time?

Anyway, suffice to say there was no news of Liverpool's demise (it could never be about Southampton's success). Instead there was a basketball story about a player in the New Zealand Breakers team, who play in the Australian NBL League, whose eye popped out of his socket whilst on court.

That night I did watch the game on record. I think Kellie is fascinated by this, because although I knew the result, I knew what happened, I still scream at the referee for giving Liverpool another 50-50 decision. I still jump out of my seat when Saints miss another chance, even though I know this was not the moment they scored.

Typically, Saints were guilty of missing two easy chances, by Dušan Tadić, our mercurial Serbian forward, and Steven Davis, our top Northern Ireland international midfielder. This could have put the tie beyond Liverpool's reach before half-time. Liverpool came back into it in the second half as you would expect, but were generally bereft of ideas. Fraser Forster's miracle save came from his own error, and Liverpool had two tenuous penalty appeals. Our winning goal came in the last minute, Josh Sims (a young forward player on as a substitute) ran at Liverpool in their half, sprayed the ball out to our Irish striker Shane Long to take a touch and thrash it into the goal. Cue mad jumping around again. Bring on Manchester United in the final!

I'd never warmed to Shane Long. Purchased from Hull City in August 2014, and previously at West Bromwich Albion and Reading, hardly football meccas, he had never set the Premier League alight. When Saints bought him, I wondered if this was a progressive signing. Sure, he is an extremely hard worker and harasses defences incessantly with his tireless running, and he is lightening quick and can draw defenders into a rash challenge. But he isn't a natural goal scorer and his best scoring record in the Premier League before joining Saints was only 11 goals. I also thought it crass to give him the number seven shirt. This shirt has belonged to club legends Ricky Lambert and before that Matt Le Tissier. I didn't think that was at all appropriate.

I'd admit that if he was a good goal scorer, Southampton certainly would not have been able to secure his services for the relatively paltry twelve million pounds, and would be unlikely to get a sniff of signing him for double the price. But I felt our signings at that time were, in general, pretty astute, and I thought that we could have done better to purchase someone with pace and skill, not just pace.

However, I am not a fan to bear any form of grudge to a new player, and hoped he would develop into a fine acquisition. His progress was slow, but in the second half of the 2016 season he enjoyed the best form of his career, running defences completely ragged, and matching the chaos he caused with goals too. I was mildly impressed.

But in 2017 his form dropped markedly and had only contributed one goal up to the semi-final against Liverpool. Clearly the year before was a peak of sorts, and I congratulated myself that my original assessment that he was not a good player and inferior to the team's needs was accurate.

I also did not warm to him as he tried to evade my attempts to get his autograph. Back for a holiday in England in May 2016, we got tickets to see Saints versus Crystal Palace on the final day of the season. It was a good game, we won 4-1 and finished the season in a magnificent sixth place. A few hours before the game we had congregated with many other Saints fans to wait for the players to drive into work. We were at the game with my niece Kate and her husband, Ian, with their two boys Luke and Ryan (Dad called them the Kray twins). I was helping Luke to secure some autographs on his Saints shirt that he had mounted on cardboard so it could be showed off at home, and which presumably offered decent purchase for any footballer wishing to sign it with an applicable black marker. As this was the final game of the season, Luke had many signatures already, but needed the Republic of Ireland international's Shane Long's scribble. He said he needed it really, really, bad. I'd also purchased a green Saints away shirt and hoped that Shane would sign it so I could give it to Shauna's boyfriend, the other Ryan.

Luke, as well as knowing all the strengths and weaknesses of the entire squad (as you would when you were seven – I certainly did), he also knew which car belonged to which player.

"Look!" he said as a giant Hummer with blacked out windows swept by into a car parking space, "it's Virgil Van Dyk!".

The players, to their great credit, patiently signed autographs and interacted with the supporters. I watched our forward Sadio Mané messing around with lots of kids – he pretended to steal the phone of a mother angling for a picture of him and her kids. The kids and I thought it was hilarious, the mother less so! But this certainly was a side of the modern football player that you never get to see. Mané was clearly enjoying it am I sure he was going beyond his designated duties there. Meanwhile Kellie was having fun too taking a selfie with Fraser Forster, our giant England goalkeeper, before asking me, "Who was that?" Cue eyes rolling in my sockets.

Luke was getting concerned but eventually Shane Long showed. But instead of walking to the end of the line of autograph hunters, he jumped in half way through, way beyond where we were standing. Thinking on my feet, I took Luke's ink-scrawled shirt, left him with

Kellie who was building a portfolio of selfies with handsome footballers who she didn't know, and set off to jump in and secure the signature.

I noticed there were a lot of other adults securing autographs for themselves which I thought was no good. This kind of thing is for the kids (says me with an extensive Subbuteo collection) and Shane would think I am getting the autograph for myself or maybe seek to make some money by selling it on eBay. I needed a different approach so I went for respectful politeness.

"Mr. Long?" I said.

"Mr. Long, sir?" I said, a little louder.

"May you please sign this for my nephew?" Technically Luke and Ryan are my great-nephews, but that makes me feel older than my Mum which won't do at all. Seriously, Kate could have been more considerate in their decision to have children.

Eventually I got Luke his signature. But I needed the shirt signed too, so persisted. However now Shane was ignoring me. Looking up at me, then ignoring me. I'm sure he was thinking, you've had your scribble ya ijit, now feck off.

Thankfully, Kate snatched the shirt, burrowed into the mass of people, and came out with a barely legible knot of ink on the back of the shirt.

So based on only a fair to middling contribution to the team and his inability to immediately respond to my multiple needs for a legible signature over the needs of all others, I hadn't warmed to Shane Long at all. But when he scored the winning goal at Anfield, to beat Liverpool in the League Cup semi-final in January, in the last minute of the match, against Liverpool in particular, to send us to Wembley, my opinion suddenly altered.

Shane Long is a legend.

Past opinions are also immediately revised. It was fantastic of him to get me two autographs – he didn't have to do that. And the signature on Ryan's shirt was perfect. He was brilliant last season and has not been given a fair run of games this year. We play him in the team to his strengths, unlike Hull and West Brom. He always gives 110% and is a great role model to youngsters in the way that he goes about his business.

It's totally irrational. It would be more credible for me to think, typical! This means I might need to spend thousands of dollars to go back for a match that we may not win, that I may not get into, and may not get time off work for. I've only been to England a year ago and it is an expensive, exhausting trip. I'm going to lose a week of glorious sunny summer and get a week behind in my work and lose a week's billable pay. Thank you very much (not) Mr. Bloody Long!

But absolutely no. That is not my thinking at all. Thank you, Shane Long. You are a hero to a pot-bellied bloke in his late-thirties (roughly), living 12,000 miles away who watches you play in the middle of the night. And you are yet another club legend to wear the coveted number seven shirt.

(As a footnote, Shane Long's green Saints shirt takes pride of place in Ryan's room, according to Shauna who also promises me that when she is in his room the door remains open and Ryan's parents are in the house. Also, when copying Shauna's texts into the book now, I realise they are actually party poppers not willy's at all and therefore nothing to do with Ryan.)

1982

The Second Season of Kevin Keegan.

Context: the England football team had failed to qualify for the World Cup in 1974. The World Cup winning generation had gone and their manager, Sir Alf Ramsey had been callously removed from his post, eventually to be replaced by Don Revie, the former Dirty Leeds manager. Calculating and conniving, Revie set about building the England team in the image of his Dirty Leeds team, particularly off the pitch. Despite a new breed of flamboyant football player in the English game, Revie couldn't settle on a team and continually chopped and changed his line ups. To nobody's surprise England missed out to Italy in qualifying for the 1978 World Cup tournament, but by that time, and to everyone's surprise, Revie had bunked off a tour of South America to agree a deal in Dubai to coach in the United Arab Emirates, and end his tenure prematurely.

In England, the hooligan problem continued to grow as we moved into the Eighties. Attendances at football matches continued to decline. The standard and quality of football started to stagnate. The flamboyant players of the Seventies were in decline, and defensive-first negative football prevailed.

The England team were showing signs of progression which would lead to qualification to the European Championships of 1980 and World Cup in 1982. Their best player was Kevin Keegan. Kevin was small, stocky, strong and a fearless player who, irrespective if he played in midfield or as a striker, was often a match winner. His tight Seventies perm and stretched '7' number on the back of his shirt was as recognisable then as a David Beckham shirt is today. He was often known as "King Kev" or "Mighty Mouse" for his indefatigable spirit.

He played for the great Liverpool team on the Seventies, under Bill Shankly initially, and had played time in the England team before Ramsey was sacked. In the Summer of 1977 he moved to Germany to play for SV Hamburg – a bold move for an Englishman to sign for a foreign team. In the Summer of 1979 he was voted European Footballer Of The Year. Since Kevin won it, only one other Englishman has won this award in the last 37 years. At which point I get a phone call.

In 1980, we lived in a new end of terrace house. The house was functional but soulless, one of hundreds on this new housing estate. Our house was one of the first blocks built and I had a fantastic first summer playing football with kids much older than me, on dirt land earmarked for building. The winter of 1979 was bitterly cold and had ended in us losing the League Cup final.

Eleven months later, on Thursday, the 7th of February 1980, my Dad called me from work. Dad never called me from work. Why would he? How many sons receive a matter-of-fact phone call from their Dad? Who would want to stop work, find a phone (no mobiles in 1980 remember), dial home to speak to their eight year old son? By this time me and my Dad were on the same page football-wise. I had dutifully collected football stickers for the Panini sticker collections Football '78 and Football '79, even though Saints' Ted MacDougall eluded me (I was convinced Panini never published a Ted MacDougall sticker and to this day have yet to find evidence to the contrary). My Subbuteo collection was also expanding, so I believed Dad and I could talk about the game 'man to man'.

Mum came to get me and brought me to the phone. I picked up our slender trim phone, off our low table opposite the front door, and said hello. I don't remember the exact wording of the call of course, it was too exciting to remember anything other than the feeling, which was elating: Southampton had signed Kevin Keegan for the start of the 1981 season. Dad was beside himself. I didn't believe him. He had to tell me again to re-enforce the news. I couldn't believe it. Dad was laughing. I eventually realised it must be true, then.

Southampton had signed England's best player.

How did that happen?

Lawrie McMenemy describes the events in his autobiography 'A Lifetime's Obsession'. He had sensed that Kevin was due to return to England and decided to call him (no agents or middle men to get in the way – this is definitely a story of the Eighties, it would be impossible for this to happen today for a number of reasons). He used the excuse of wanting a particular German lamp to set off his new house that he was building. Kevin agreed to bring the lamp, if he could get it, next time he was playing for England at Wembley.

With a connection made, McMenemy would call again when he noticed Barcelona and Real Madrid were interested in his signature (Barcelona, Real Madrid or Southampton – who would you pick? I am not making this up). He talked up the team, and by the time Kevin was next in England, they were talking contracts.

A press conference was called in the Potter's Heron hotel in Romsey, Hampshire. The day before the press had been tipped off about 'some news' at the club but the national newspapers had not cottoned on. On the day, the hotel was packed full. A door was opened and in walked Kevin to everyone's complete amazement.

And he also forgot to bring Lawrie his lamp.

It makes me chuckle that every so often, I read an article by the national press that paints a disingenuous version of these events, as if they have not, to this day, forgiven the club for mounting such a heist without their prior knowledge or endorsement. Indeed, Keegan's second season was arguably the best of his career, but his time with Saints seems to have been scrubbed from the record books.

When Kevin left SV Hamburg in May 1980, he had won the European Footballer Of The Year again. No Englishman has matched that since.

His first season for the Saints in 1981 was blighted by injury. But Southampton had set their stall out. They finished eighth in 1980 and started to transition from a solid mid-table Division One team, into a credible team who could challenge the top of the league. More internationals were added to the team. David Watson, England's regular centre back also came from Germany, Werder Bremen. Charlie George – one of those flamboyant players from the Seventies, joined the team, mainly to sit on the injury table during his time at The Dell, and Mick Channon was back from Manchester City. The team had experience (Ball, Keegan, Channon, Boyer, Holmes, George, Watson, Nicholl), youth (Williams, Graham Baker, who Dad introduced me to in a pub one time) and excitement (all of the above, plus Golac and fellow Yugoslav in goal Ivan Katalinić – akin to having an Eastern European Basil Fawlty in goal). In fact, on four occasions in 1981 Saints played with four past or present England captains in the same team: Keegan, Ball, Watson and Channon.

Saints finished sixth at the end of the 1981 season, above Nottingham Forest, above Manchester United, above Tottenham Hotspur and above Dirty Leeds. They had also qualified for the UEFA Cup (now known as the Europa League). They were an exciting team going forward, happy to win 3-2 rather than 1-0, an anathema to the league in many respects in those days. But they were suspect in defending, and frequently made me realise that the Terry Gennoe incident at Wembley was a perfectly ordinary occurrence where Southampton was concerned and not at all far-fetched.

I went to two games in the 1981 season – my first 'real' games at The Dell. I stood behind the goal at the Milton Road end of the ground and watched us beat Norwich City 2-1, then draw with West Bromwich Albion 2-2. Keegan played both games but didn't score.

But hooliganism was still a problem. In fact, general exposure of a nine year old boy to a bunch of smoky and drunk men effing and jeffing for ninety minutes did not constitute good parenting and Dad appreciated this fully. Many of the words I was hearing needed to be translated by some of the bigger boys on the building site, and it took me many years to work out what a quim was.

In the Summer of 1981, Southampton knocked down the Milton Road end of the ground, including the queer-looking 'chocolate boxes' – three small upper stands that seemed to be hanging off the back wall of the Milton Road end, seemingly elevated at different heights owing to the road running behind that end of the ground (Milton Road, coincidentally) at an angle to the pitch.

In its place they built a new two-tier terrace. The Effers and Jeffers would continue on the lower tier, whilst the upper tier was announced as the country's first 'Family Centre'. A simple concept, football related and nothing to do with family planning. The idea to put kids up in the stand away from all the fighting with the Dads had amazingly never been introduced anywhere before. Suddenly I had a safe place to go and watch the football, and Dad didn't miss a beat. He immediately got us both season tickets to the 1982 season. The season ticket was another treasure to me – which I still have. It cost Dad 45 pounds, and another 22 pounds for me. It was not at all splendid and refined like a cup final ticket, it was a small red wallet with a clear insert with a card that had my name on it. On the other side of the wallet was a number of coupons labelled 1 to 21, then A to P. The numbers corresponded to league matches, the letters for League Cup, FA Cup and UEFA Cup matches. You tore off the correct coupon (identified by a sign outside the turnstile) and gave it to the ticket officer inside the turnstile along with one pound for an adult, and 50p for me.

It promised to be an exciting season for me and Dad. It was fortunate that the Family Centre was standing room only; had Dad bought seats instead, we would have only used the edge of them.

Much of the side from the previous year remained intact. Dave Watson moved to Manchester City whilst Charlie George had also left, to the relief of the physiotherapist and club doctor, and a couple more youngsters were blossoming into first team players, including Rueben Agboola and Steve Moran. One of my favourite Saints players, David Armstrong, signed for this season. He was easy to pick out – his bald looks always made it look that we had a senior citizen in the team. He kindly came as guest of honour to Dad's Seventieth birthday. I enjoyed a great chat with him, and remember he graciously didn't flinch when I accidentally spat on his lapel as I was talking.

The first home match was against Wolverhampton Wanderers on a Tuesday night. As fortune turned, Dad was on a night shift, so Debbie's current man, Chris would have to fill in. No problem! Chris was great to hang around with. He would load me up with 10p pieces and send me off to the nearest arcade machine at the Eastleigh Working Men's Club. Fantastic! If I run out of coins, no problem, go and find Chris and get some more! Going to matches with Chris was a different experience. Instead of parking (what seemed like) ten miles away and enduring an endless walk to the ground to arrive two hours before kick-off, Chris's approach was a little more direct: drive directly to the ground, park in front of someone's communal garage in the next street, and get to the game right on kick off.

Although the ground, and the Family Centre was packed to capacity, there would be no doubt about whether I would see anything or not. This is because I had a stool. All kids took a stool to the matches (mine was a small, folded wooden variety), and would place them on a step on the terrace, stand on them, and hey presto! You were the same height as the adults. That was until a goal was scored, where a surge of noise and bodies would propel you forward away from your companions. Your stool would be lost until a kindly soul would reach out for it and present it back over to you. You would return to your spot of sorts (never exactly the same place, but generally so – depending on the volume of crowd) and off you go again.

I lost my stool four times that night! We won 4-1 and we were off and running. Keegan scored, as did Moran, and Mick Channon scored twice. His goal celebration was something of legend, his right arm swinging around like a windmill as he celebrated back toward the centre spot. That would be my goal celebration until I became a senior player, modelled on the great man. Chris returned to the substitute bench after the match (after popping into the Eastleigh Working Men's club again on the way home) and Dad returned for the next game.

In October, with all home games won easily, Ipswich Town came to The Dell. They were runners-up in the league in 1981 and current UEFA Cup holders, so this match would be a real test. Subbuteo previews went well (Southampton now had a new fetching, classy kit of red with a white broad stripe down the front, reference number 350), and I predicted that Saints would brush them aside as freely as we had all season. I've hunted high and low on YouTube to see any footage for this game but to no avail. However, I have it all upstairs, no need to look it up in the reference books.

I also had a new stool for this game. The wooden foldy number had wilted under the free-scoring exploits of the team and the subsequent surges that took me to all corners of the Family Centre. Now I had a custom made stool, painted in red and white stripes, with 'SAINTS' emblazoned on each side. Someone from Dad's work had built it for me and it stayed with me throughout all my standing youth days. I still have it today, and at 4 a.m. in the morning at kick off, I sometimes have it with me for matches. If I am not standing on it, I have a coke and some chocolate biscuits on it at least.

Ipswich scored within the first minute. I was shocked off my new stool. How could this be? I would look to Dad for reassurance. He would tell me there was plenty of time to get back in the game. And he was right. Keegan scored a penalty to equalise. But still in the first half, Ipswich scored twice in a couple of minutes. That was surely that, game over wasn't it? I'd never seen a team ever come back from two goals down to win on Match Of The Day. I turned to Dad to hear his wise words.

"I think we're bollocksed Russ," he said.

But this wasn't normal 1980's football. This was football that was, at the time, on a different level. David Armstrong made it 3-2, lashed in from inside the six-yard box. Steve Moran made it 3-3 after an hour. Armstrong made it 4-3 just after. I remember our three goals felt like every time we attacked we would score, like my matches on the building site with the bigger boys. The three goals were actually scored within eleven minutes. Ipswich fought back, but we hung on and won the match 4-3. It was incredible. I was as exhausted getting home as if I had just been playing for my local team on a Sunday, rather than watching a game. Although that day, I remember getting home at 7:15 after Dad decided to take one of his scenic routes. I'd suggested to him to ask someone for directions (after all, my sage observation regarding the diversion on the way to Wembley in 1979 would mean that my recommendation would be taken in good faith). I was told to shut up.

It didn't stop there. In early December we beat Manchester United 3-2. Manchester United scored first, but Steve Moran equalised and before half-time Keegan made it 2-1. United equalised in the second half before Kevin Keegan scored one of the best goals that I have ever seen. At this point I should add context because as a Southampton fan, I am spoilt for truly fantastic goals. Matt Le Tissier scored 25-30 goals that were beyond world class on his own. So, when I say that Keegan's goal was one of the best I have ever seen, that is high praise.

Alan Ball clipped a ball into the penalty area. A United defender tried to head clear, but merely directed the ball toward Keegan who crashed an incredible overhead kick into the back of the net.

Except the goal was disallowed. After a discussion between referee and linesman, David Armstrong was adjudged to be in an offside position. By the laws of today, the goal would have stood without an issue, but during the Eighties, this was interpreted within the law as being offside. I've watched this back on YouTube. It's an incredible (no) goal and in my bias, illogical view, should have stood for no other reason than it was absolutely brilliant.

But the match wasn't finished there, with one minute to play, Armstrong, atoning for his indiscretion burst through to score the winning goal.

Against Stoke City in March 1982, Saints stormed into a 3-0 lead (ex-boyfriend Waldron, Armstrong and Channon scored). In the second half, Stoke scored three times to make it 3-3. By now I was used to this kind of scenario. As I looked to the clock that sat on top of the East Stand intersecting the advertising hoarding there, showing the time of 4:40 p.m., i.e. five minutes to go, I felt confident that this team will once again come to the rescue, which they duly did, on cue to win 4-3 (Mark Whitlock, a young reserve defender with a Hitler-like moustache).

But the season had a few downs as well as ups. Although The Dell was a fortress, we lost too many away games, and we lost at home to Tottenham Hotspur 2-1. Ipswich had their revenge on us winning 5-2, with their striker Alan Brazil scoring all five goals. But at the end of January, for the first (and currently only) time in our history, Saints were top of Division One. Played 22, Won 12, Drew 4, Lost 5, Points 40, scored 1,999 goals, and conceded nearly as many.

It was at this time that Dad believes critical mistakes were made. And he was dead right. Our striker Steve Moran had become injured and had not been adequately replaced. We brought a replacement striker from Oxford United in the lower leagues, Keith Cassells, to fill the gap. But he failed to make the grade. In addition, defensively we sometimes struggled and really needed to replace Watson with an equivalent, skilful defender, but never did.

This was most evident during the UEFA Cup. We'd reached the Second Round to meet Sporting Lisbon of Portugal, who were a top European side. Oddly, they had Malcolm Allison as their manager, who had managed in England in the Seventies with varying degrees of success. They had a top Portuguese striker Jordão, and a Hungarian international goalkeeper Ferenc Mészáros.

This was an exciting night! Dad got to the ground extra early, before the turnstiles had even been opened. It was relatively early in the season and we were yet to find a regular place on the terrace. So when we were let in (Coupon D for this match), I took a spot right at the front of the upper terrace directly behind the goal – a fabulous viewpoint. Dad stood a few rows back to allow other kids to reach the front. No need for the stool that night, and it remained with Dad for the evening.

Jordão scored first in the second minute. Sporting's number 10 Oliveira raced down the right with no Saints defender within a mile of him. With all the time in the world he clipped a ball into Jordão who deflected it in off his head unchallenged.

Next, Nick Holmes scored a comical own goal. As Sporting charged in on the Southampton goal again, Holmes, playing out of position that night, swept the ball off the striker's foot and straight into his own net.

Next Manuel Fernandez had the freedom of The Dell, this time down the left hand side. This time, instead of the Saints players racing into a defensive position to make a tackle, they decided to race back and simply watch and admire Manuel Fernandez dribble the ball into the net. Nicholl, then Golac, then the goalkeeper Peter Wells, each ballet dancing their way over the ball until the striker, confused by this new tactic, fell on the ball, which then trickled into the net. The legendary Barry Davies' crotchety commentary said it all: "And I don't know which of the players has the greatest disbelief, the scorer or the defenders … I mean, this is really quite unreal. You wouldn't believe it even if it was in a comic! I mean look at this [replay]!" The video should be removed from YouTube.

So 3-0 down at half-time. Time for an amazing comeback? There were too many people between me and Dad to find out if this time we really were bollocksed. Not only did we have to find three goals to draw but in European competition, away goals count double in a two-legged match that ends in a tie. So we needed a minimum of four, and then go to Portugal and get a result.

The second half started well. Keegan scored a penalty. Next Mick Channon deflected a shot in for 3-2. The Sporting goalkeeper Mészáros made a number of fine saves, and became unsporting in equal measure as I saw for the first time some of the professional aspects of the game as he calmly wasted time and ran down the clock with slow goal kicks.

But at the end, Sporting drifted another simple ball over the top of our defenders who stumbled over Sporting's attack. The ball squirted to Manual Fernandez to fire his shot past the goalkeeper. 4-2 and we were out. And other than Sporting's fourth goal, it all happened right in front of me. What an awful night. It seemed that we played a 1-1-8 formation with no defensive cover at all. The second leg was almost academic, which ended in a 0-0 draw.

The season started to ebb away around March. Whilst our first 11 could match anyone in the League (after all we'd won at Anfield, beating the mighty Liverpool 1-0), our strength in our reserves was not so great. We only won three out of our last fourteen matches and ended up seventh. We even drew 5-5 with Coventry City. Melancholy had set in: I'd said to Dad I didn't want to go to this midweek game. He said he didn't either. I'm glad we didn't miss an eventful game!

Liverpool came to The Dell in April, with Saints needing a win to restart our season. This was the first time I had ever seen the legendary Liverpool team. They had all the stars, Bruce Grobbelaar, Kenny Dalglish, Ian Rush, Craig Johnston, and Ronnie Whelan. I was really excited to see these players, who you normally only get to see on the television. Yet what I saw in the flesh was very different to what I expected.

Liverpool always found it very difficult to play at The Dell and lost often, riled perhaps by Shankly's sore 'ale house brawlers' remark. Throughout this game the Liverpool players cajoled and harassed the referee at every opportunity. I remember Kenny Dalglish being the worst offender. Through the capacity crowd I could hear him bleating incessantly in his grating high pitched Glaswegian accent, often running away from the play to gesticulate to the officials. But despite their poor attitude, they were a great team, on the way to reclaiming their championship title.

That day, we lost 3-2, and this time we were on the end of a late winner by Liverpool. But our equalising goal at 1-1 was perhaps the best goal I have ever seen, better than all of Matt Le Tissier's goals, perhaps. It can be found on YouTube if you search for the "greatest goal of all time". I remember it really well and recall being ecstatic to what I had seen. In our own half, David Armstrong plays a short ball back to Nick Holmes, who plays it back to Armstrong, who plays it back to Holmes, who plays a long ball up to Keegan, just inside the Liverpool half, who heads back to Cassells, who passes to Ball, who plays it to Cassells, who plays it left to Keegan making inroads down Liverpool's left, who cuts inside to Ball, who plays a quick pass to Baker, who flicks it back to Keegan, who in turn flicks the ball on the edge of the box to Armstrong, who overhead kicks it back to Keegan, who heads it to Channon, who drags it off his right foot, on to his left foot, and smashed the ball into the net.

I was nearly eleven years old. Any wobbles of support, such as the Coventry City debacle, had gone. I was a fully-fledged fan, bordering on obsessive. Both me and Dad were stuck on a journey now, a ride we couldn't get off of no matter how much we tried. And in truth, we never tried very hard at all, it was all too intoxicating. The season I had just seen, even though ending in a bit of an anti-climax, was just sensational. It will never be repeated in my life time. Southampton had moved from possible challengers to absolute contenders, like the Chelsea's, Manchester City's or Arsenal's of today, we were the 'big boys'. Keegan ended up as Player Of The Year, and Steve Moran was Young Player Of The Year, even though he missed much of the second half of the season. Moran would thereafter be blighted with injury, but that season he and Keegan were the best strike force in the country, with Keegan the best player in the league, enjoying his best season.

England went to the 1982 World Cup in Spain with Keegan as their captain. But he had injured his back and was fighting to get fit. He travelled back to Germany in a borrowed car to get treatment from his trusted doctor whilst in Germany to get him fit. He returned to Spain to play the last 20 minutes in England's 0-0 draw with the hosts which eliminated us from the tournament. The decision by the England manager Ron Greenwood to not play Kevin from the start was a mistake. Even an eleven year old kid like me knew we needed at least a 2-0 win to qualify for the semi-finals. We had to go for it! Imagine in this day and age is someone like Lionel Messi sat farting around on the bench for Argentina when they needed to win 2-0? Keegan had to play! He didn't and England came home.

Meanwhile, during the Summer of 1982 back in England we filled a weak point of the team – the goalkeeper – with the world's best goalkeeper. We had signed none other than Peter Shilton. This was the final piece of the puzzle. There was no doubt in my mind, we would win the Division One title in 1983, and probably the FA Cup as well.

I could not wait for the 1983 season to begin.

(As an interesting coincidental footnote. I write this chapter exactly thirty-seven years to the day that Kevin Keegan's signing was announced, even taking into account New Zealand time.)

No Ticket

Your Seat Awaits!

So Debbie's text said, did I need a ticket. The use of the word 'need' implied to me that Debbie obviously had a stack of tickets either waiting to be distributed right then and there, or she was just a phone call away from an acquaintance who would able to supply any number of tickets to her in an instant. Dad was fantastic at this. He would have a network of people he could go to at work or in the pub to sort out two tickets for any game anywhere.

Working at the massive Ford Transit plant in Eastleigh meant that Dad had access to potentially 4,500 Saints fans from which to bum tickets from.

However these days, things are a little different. When the football club announced the details regarding how fans could secure a ticket, it became clear that tickets were going to be like gold dust, and that there were going to be a great many people begging for a ticket. Finding someone willing to assist would be a rarity.

Saints received around 31,500 tickets for the match, the same number as their opponents, Manchester United. Prices were between forty pounds and a hundred pounds. Tickets would be sold in priority order, and only through the web site, so no chance of queuing from four o'clock in the morning from outside the ground, then.

Sales between the 2nd and the 6th of February was for season ticket holders to secure their tickets, but only one ticket could be bought per season ticket. On the seventh and eighth, official members who had purchased tickets for eight home games, as registered within the ticket database, could buy their ticket. As a supporter, you could enrol as an official member, for twenty-five pounds, for priority access to tickets.

This meant that if you had been to eight matches, but had been given two tickets, or if they were purchased on someone else's membership card number, i.e. the computer didn't know you had been to eight games, you would have to wait. If you had been to eight games but were not an official member, you would need to register as an official member first before getting a ticket.

Even though in New Zealand, I bought an official membership for the 2016 season. Knowing I would be in England on holiday at the season's end, I would be able to catch some matches, and wanted to give myself the very best chance of getting a ticket. But, before I left for England, when I went to purchase my ticket, I found that I couldn't because the ticket office would only send me the tickets to my home address in New Zealand. This was absolutely no good to me at all when I would be in England to watch the game.

Fans who had a membership with seven matches could get their tickets on the 9th of February, and so it went on until on Saturday, the 11th of February, there were only 6,000 tickets left.

I partially agree with the club's logic. The fans who have been to the most games are the most deserving of a ticket. Someone like me, barging their way through on the pretence that coming from such a long way away is somehow cool and admirable, and therefore entitled to a ticket, is arrogant. For the FA Cup Final in 2003, I was a season ticket holder with Dad, and we were in agreement at the time that we hope the club control the ticket allocation such that 'hangers on' and 'part-time supporters' didn't get a ticket ahead of the regulars. Now, I don't believe I fit into the category of 'hanger on' or 'part-time supporter', but I didn't deserve a ticket ahead of season ticket holders or members who attended matches, nor did I deserve a ticket more than other family members in and around Southampton who would not be able to go.

But it seemed the wheels were in motion. Debbie had got determined, as she is wont to do, and put a few 'feelers' out. Kellie could see Facebook messages asking for spare tickets for a friend coming from New Zealand. However, it seemed that there was no Saints supporter who would be keen to give up their own entitlement to go to the match to give it to some nobody a million miles away. Funny, that.

If I got to go, I would be going with nephew Daniel. This was on the proviso that we could organise two tickets not one. But like me, he had no purchase history with the club that season.

Dan was Debbie's first child, in 1981. This meant I was an uncle from the age of nine, which gave me some very cool notoriety at school. Dan was like a little brother to me, and given I was generally an unpleasant child, this meant being mean to him. As he grew up, he also got the Saints bug, from Chris of course and also Dad. He was also a better Subbuteo player than me. There were countless occasions that I had to cheat to win or even draw matches with him. The easiest trick was to knock the entire goal out the way when his player took a shot. I'd also surreptitiously put my fingers across the goal line to keep the ball out. I'd lie about how much time was left in the second half and think nothing about ending the match a minute early if I was winning or extending the time if I was losing. I was a rotten uncle.

But, it appears, he bears me no ill will. It doesn't seem to have caused any lasting damage. When we go back to England we always spend some time with him and Sama in Bristol. It's a great place and they always show us a great time. Sometimes though, when I look back, I was a total shit to Dan.

I have always enjoyed going to the football with Dan though, both home and away games. I remember when he came with me and Kellie's brother, David, to a match. It was a gusty day, a walking back from the game, David had nudged Dan and said, "watch this…"

He then blew out from his mouth, like blowing out some candles. About fifty yards ahead a girl was walking on her own. David's timing was lucky: once David had blown, the girl's skirt wafted upward to expose a delight that I would imagine would have made his adolescent years worthwhile.

Then, when Dan was about fifteen we went to The Dell sitting in the Archers Road end of the ground (the loud, boisterous end). Before the match he was holding a pair of socks, each sock rolled up, one in each hand. I looked at him and asked why he had taken off his shoes and socks. He said he hadn't. They had fallen out of his trouser legs from the previous night.

In writing this I realise people will read this and conclude that I am still being a git to him, by exposing this kind of detail to a wider populous. To provide a bit of balance, I went to a match with Dad, around 1997, against Nottingham Forest. Dad had got us seat tickets in the main West Stand at The Dell. As the match reached half-time, both me and Dad carried out our normal half-time ritual. This consisted of standing up from our seats (if we were sitting), having a hot beef Bovril drink that Dad would have put together in his flask, reading the matchday programme, and having a general look around the stadium. During the half-time interval at this match, I was minding my own business, looking around the ground, when I saw, about ten rows behind me, Dan.

Have you have ever seen the Alan Partridge comedy sketch where Alan sees a colleague in the distance called Dan, and calls out to him? It's a classic sketch. Dan doesn't hear Alan, so Alan calls out louder, again and again. Dan still doesn't respond, but Alan, undeterred, keeps calling out, with each cry of "Dan" more hopeless than the last. It's much funnier on YouTube than it is in this paragraph.

When I saw Dan up in the stands behind me, I cried out, "Dan!?" He didn't hear me.

I cried out again, more loudly, over the hubbub of the crowd, "Dan! Daniel! Dan! Dan! Dan!" I would wave my arms at him trying to get his attention. I was positioned in the middle of our row so it wasn't practical for me to move out of my row and up the stairs to greet him, so I tried again.

"Dan!? Dan!? Dan!? Dan!? DAN!?" People around me started to stare.

Dad had been for a wee. When he came back, I pointed up into the stands and said to him, "Look, Dad! There's Dan sat up there."

"Where?" said Dad.

"Up there," I said, jabbing my finger up into the stands in Dan's direction.

"Oh yeah!" Dad realised. "Daniel!? Dan!? Danny!? Dan!? Dan!? Dan!?" Dad shouted out, in a much louder, booming voice.

"Dan!? Dan!? Dan!?" I continued with him forlornly. Dan didn't respond.

The teams came out for the second-half. Dan had ignored us completely, and me and Dad gave up and instead focussed back on the football.

When I caught up with Dan a couple of days later, he told us why he had ignored us.

He wasn't there. It wasn't Dan!

More recently, whilst back in England in 2013, we went to a match against West Bromwich Albion (the one with the swooning Shauna incident). The match was uneventful, but won 1-0, but it was noteworthy because Dan had brought his long term girlfriend Sama for the first time. Sama isn't in to football at all, and had brought a book to read. After being told in no uncertain terms you can't read a book at football match she duly fell asleep.

Me and Dan had agreed that we needn't get tickets co-located together for the cup final, after all beggars can't be choosers. We would get what we could and be grateful. If we could only get one, then I would have it as Auckland is a little further away than Bristol. We both set about some research for alternative methods of acquiring a ticket. After all, Wembley held 90,000 and the tickets issued to the two football clubs only totalled 63,000. Where were the other 27,000 tickets?

I took to the Internet. I found a site, a 'reliable and secure' site to pick up tickets. It had just over 1,000 tickets for sale, with informative notes on the web site such as '22 people have already purchased tickets for this event' or '7 people are currently looking at tickets'. The lowest price was 259 pounds. This, though, was for a Manchester United ticket. We would certainly not want to be seated in amongst them. The cheapest Saints ticket was 390 pounds, the disparity no doubt due to the demand for Saints tickets, for fans who get to cup final's once in twenty years, being much higher than for Manchester United fans who were last at Wembley eight months earlier in the 2016 FA Cup Final.

Dan and I had resigned ourselves to paying over the odds for the ticket from one of these secondary ticket outlets, even if Debbie could indeed find a friend or two to give up their ticket. For me, this was going to be an expensive venture come what may, so I needed to take this firmly on the chin.

The site looked good. It had copious ticket options, informative support and was modern looking. I sent the link to Dan and Debbie and decided to do a bit more digging.

Of course this was a dodgy site. At the time, they would have had no tickets and would bank on securing these kinds of tickets from their various sources, which would include player's agents, dignitaries who couldn't be bothered to go, and other crooked people from within the game. This would undoubtedly include fake tickets or tickets that simply did not arrive.

On the web site it said that tickets would be delivered as a courier service, but that in some circumstances the tickets would arrive on the day of the match. For me, this was cutting it way too fine. I couldn't possibly travel without the knowledge that I could get into the game. In other circumstances, the purchaser would need to attend a designated hotel, and acquire their tickets from a 'representative' there. Imagine getting to some dodgy hotel in grimy London somewhere only to find there was nobody with any knowledge of your ticket?

I researched on forums providing feedback on this site. Much of the contributors to the forum actually gave this site rave reviews. One read "I was extremely nervous about buying tickets from a secondary supplier. I looked at a few options on-line and was no more reassured. However, I came across [the web site]. Result? Tickets arrived at 7:30 a.m. the next morning. Great seats, all together, and my son had an amazing time with his three friends. Yes, it was very expensive, but I got the seats I wanted, the service was excellent and I would definitely use them again." Looks promising. This was the typical review of using this site.

Then, when I looked deeper, I found less complementary reviews. "We ordered tickets and have paid for delivery fee for tickets to be delivered to the hotel. I received an email that the tickets are dispatched but when we got to the hotel [it] was never there. Their support has accused me for being dishonest that I received the tickets but wanted to get refund. I requested proof from their end but never got them."

Or, "My tickets never arrived, I followed their procedure and waited three days before the match to chase. [The] match was on Saturday I called them on Wednesday to chase and was told my tickets will be posted on Thursday to [be] received Friday. Tickets never arrived, and have asked for a refund and they have completely ignored me."

How about, "Tried to purchase tickets and was asked to fax or email utility bill, photo ID and copy of credit card without reasonable explanation of why other than that credit card company regulations required it. This is a red flag for identity theft and my credit card company advised me not to proceed."

Digging further into these secondary ticket sites, they place an additional administration fee on tickets purchased, plus a booking fee, and purchasers found that additional money was taken from the credit card than originally agreed. Worse, the credit card payment portal did not have any form of security around it, meaning your credit card details can be seen and used by the unscrupulous. And worst of all, one of the review sites where you can comment about their service, was actually hosted at the same address as the secondary ticket company web site, i.e. it was the same company.

They were not the only site like this. There were many other secondary ticket outlets with similar suspicious dealings. All with the same tales of woe from supporters desperate to see their team play. One site had their own message board that had been taken down supposedly because a competitor was adding fake reviews of their service. A likely story.

This was not looking good. I'd been smart and obtained cancellable flights, but even so, that incurred a fee on each leg of the flight, and it was two legs to London via Los Angeles. I'd still lose 600 dollars if I backed out, about 300 pounds.

We were going to have to hang in there for a ticket and take our chances day by day. A few days passed, and Debbie messaged Kellie on Facebook to say it wasn't looking good.

Seriously, what was I thinking here? What an earth was I doing? This was pure folly, chasing my team around the world at significant cost, trying to muscle my way in for a ticket that was, whilst not underserved, perhaps unwarranted, and trying to do this across nine days, of which only six will be in England.

About two and a half weeks before the match, we found a web site that we believed we could trust. It was a site that deals with tickets belonging to people who can no longer go to an event. We had found on the official Premier League web site a list of 'unauthorised' web sites, including the sites we'd previously identified, which had helped us identify if this web site was trustworthy or not. It was not listed on this web site so were satisfied to proceed on this basis.

Daniel had been doing his own research about Club Wembley. This was a concept similar to a season ticket, where supporters can go to all events at the national stadium. The privilege to do so costs many thousands of pounds, and is essentially hospitality seating for the rich and richer.

Club Wembley includes a concept regarding transferring tickets for an event. If a member does not want to go to particular event (I'm thinking rugby league or rugby union here) they can formally transfer ownership of the ticket to someone else, for that event only.

Neither me nor Daniel knew anyone with a Club Wembley ticket, but this web site did. It was commonplace for Club Wembley members to sell the rights to transfer a ticket to a buyer on the site. This is absolutely not permitted in the Club Wembley small print, but no matter – this was effectively our best chance, and as it would turn out, our only chance to get a ticket.

We found a pair of Club Wembley tickets, at the Southampton end of the ground. The cost was 486 pounds (900 dollars) each. We had a discussion over email, and decided to go for it. In for a penny, in for a pound, well for me about 1,500 pounds including air fare. It had been costly, but these were prime seats in the ground with hospitality access. We would be able to do lunch in some of the restaurants inside the stadium. Would we go to The Venue and Arc buffet restaurant, or would we go the Atrium Lounge or The Bench Brasserie? A little bit posher than a KFC before the game, I think.

Our tickets arrived the next day as e-tickets with the large slogan 'Your Seat Awaits'. I undertook some forensic analysis to make sure they were not forgeries and came to the conclusion that I had no idea if they were or weren't. One thing Dan noticed was both the tickets were made out to him, and according to Club Wembley rules each ticket must have the transferee details. So he went back to the web site to ask if the tickets could be reissued in the correct names. We then received a personal email from the Club Wembley ticket owner, not the web site broker, with the corrected details. This was important because it was from his work address. I was able to find out who he was and what he was all about. He had his own painting and decorating firm and was one of the directors of the company. This reduced the risk of forgery, I thought. If the ticket was fake, it would mean that I could nobble him with Club Wembley who would surely confiscate his ticket.

In the interests of being able to sleep at night with the transaction done, we decided to agree that the tickets were 100 percent legitimate. There's nothing we could do about it now anyway, we'll find out when we enter the ground if the tickets are real or not.

The tickets allocated to the football club sold out on the 16th of February, and Chris, Kate and Ian had been unable to secure a ticket for them and the boys. At the start of that week, there had been 5,000 tickets available, but were snapped up by fans with the requisite membership and purchase history. Ian and the boys had been to matches, but only one match was against their purchase history. They would have gone to more games except many of Saints games this season were on Sunday because of live television and European matches not taking place until Thursday nights, and Sunday was when the boys played football. That sums up the modern game for me, young boys unable to watch their team play because the national and European television audience must take precedence: it is a wonder that any kid in this day and age grows up to support a team.

An extra 600 tickets were awarded to Saints for sale later in the week, but it would make no difference; the sold out sign would go up on the web site before they were given an opportunity to purchase. They weren't the only ones though, many Saints fans who had been to Inter Milan in Italy, to Sparta Prague in the Czech Republic, and Premier League away fixtures, were not considered priority to the club unless they had the right number of home games. No doubt this was because the football club don't actually control the selling tickets for matches at other grounds.

Reading the forums, there were many fans pleading their case for a ticket without the right number of matches to qualify. Fans from yesteryear trying to jump on the bandwagon, fans who would have gone to games but had been ill or injured all season, fans who work long hours and weekends, fans from overseas – like me. Some fans took umbrage at having to be a member to qualify to buy a ticket for the final. It cost twenty-five pounds for a membership, but the football club were still allowing fans to purchase memberships first, meaning that a fifty quid ticket would effectively cost them seventy-five. Clearly, the football club were using the cup final to be opportunistic, but I would certainly see past that in my desire to get a ticket if that what it took – to throw a strop over the membership 'levy' and miss out on principal was absurd. However, for Kate and Ian, whose family of four only had one membership between them, then 200 pounds for tickets would have suddenly become 275 pounds. If I were in their scenario, with young kids part of the deal, I would suddenly be thinking very hard if we could afford to go. In some respects, it doesn't matter if you go through the legitimate means or illegitimate means for ticket purchase, you still end up getting stung in the pocket.

It was sad, I really wanted Chris, Kate, Ian and the boys to go too. They would certainly have deserved it more than me and are more credible supporters because they are local. I felt awkward shelling out a not insignificant sum to go whilst those guys could only watch on the television. I hoped they would be friendly to me when I saw them. I knew Luke and Ryan wouldn't – they would still give me the normal child to relatively-unknown-uncle abuse which I receive whenever I go over to visit, such as "you're a wee hole," or "you smell like Nanny's poo," or the rather lyrical "you're a bum bum poo hole head."

Meanwhile, I'd packed my match ticket, plane ticket, Saints beanie, fingerless gloves, Saints scarf, Saints tracksuit top, Saints shirt, Saints waterproof jacket, extra strong mints, New Zealand to UK plug adapters, phone charger and headphones. I don't have a jacket because I have never needed a jacket in New Zealand, so might have to blag one or buy one. My passport is up to date, my ETSA visa for travelling through the United States for two hours, has been authorised, my travel insurance has been purchased, I'm up to date with my latest business bills, I've sorted out roaming on my phone and I've cleared the credit card. I am ready to go.

Raring to go. Come On You Saints!

1984

FA Cup Semi-Final 1984, Southampton versus Everton. Highbury, London, Saturday, 14th of April.

My excitement over the 1983 season disintegrated completely during a holiday at Butlins Minehead, with Debbie and Chris. The 19th of August 1982 was a bad day all round. Chris had brought me my first ever cheeseburger which I found to be disgusting: the cheese made me gag much to Chris' annoyance. And as well as going hungry that night, Kevin Keegan signed for Newcastle United.

It transpires that towards the end of the 1982 season, as Saints started to flounder, he began to get cold feet. Ironically, he felt that Saints lacked the ambition to win trophies (he must surely have known that the signing of Shilton was imminent – they were in the same England squad for the World Cup for crying out loud!). Moving to a Second Division team was not going to increase his chances of silverware whatsoever, and I felt personally let down. Dad thereafter referred to him as a rat.

The 1983 season was an anti-climax and the best we could finish was twelfth. Our nadir for the season once again came in European competition when the farmers, postmen and accountants that made up the Swedish team IFK Norrköping beat us over two legs in the first round. Saints have always been rubbish in European football: even last season, when we reached the group stages of the Europa League, we somehow managed to squander qualification to the next round even though we had beaten Inter Milan and Sparta Prague. The big positive for 1983 therefore was that we didn't qualify for European football in 1984.

But when 1984 came around the team had developed. By now Mick Channon, Alan Ball, Ivan Golac and Chris Nicholl had left, in addition to Keegan, and the only major new reinforcements from 1982 was Frank Worthington, another one of those Seventies showmen, and

Mick Mills, another former England Captain. Crucially additional players were developing through the club to be international class players. Mark Wright, a gangly ginger central defender was years ahead of his time as a 'cultured' defender, and Danny Wallace, a small pocket-dynamo winger who sometimes used to keep me and Dad busy in the Family Centre by ducking from his wayward crosses, but was also capable of top class goals, like the one he scored against Liverpool (another Saints victory).

It was evident early on in the season that Saints were in business. In their first six games, Nottingham Forest, Arsenal and Manchester United were all beaten by Saints, with a creditable 1-1 draw at Liverpool.

The Manchester United game was an interesting one. Dad had purchased an old yellow Triumph as opposed to the Ford Cortina's or Capris that Dad normally had. He had decided that the vehicle was not capable of getting all the way from Colden Common to Southampton (all of 10 miles), so decided that we should travel to games by going in completely the opposite direction toward Winchester, stopping in Shawford to catch the train into Southampton Central. Shawford was one of those sparse train stations where you would never see a passenger nor a train. There was no electronic board informing you when the next train was. There was just track, and concrete. I would be beside myself with worry every week wondering if a) the car would reach Shawford; b) the train would actually arrive at a rough approximation of the arrival time; and c) get us into Southampton Central by 2:45 p.m. latest so we could get to the game. One match, against Luton Town, we arrived just on half-time; it was 2-2 at the time and there were no further goals. The whole situation traumatised me. When a dilapidated train finally arrived, the feeling of relief that washed over me was like a bomb disposal expert cutting the correct coloured wire.

We got to the Manchester United game with no issues as far as I can remember, but it was leaving the match that was the problem. On the way back to Southampton Central, we somehow ended up in the channel of Manchester United fans being escorted by police to their trains returning north. At one point, I started to get a little crushed by a barrier due to the volume of people. Inexplicably, Dad punched the bloke next to him in the head making him stagger backwards into the herd of people. These were the days that hooliganism was at its absolute peak and I wondered had Dad lost his mind? We were surrounded by Manchester United fans, I had a Saints shirt on, and he started a fight. We were going to die, I was sure of it.

Remarkably there was no reaction from anyone. Sure, the guy he hit wasn't very happy and argued with Dad about why he had hit him, but we got away without any further aggro. On the train Dad was very remorseful, realising the danger he had put us in and his inexplicable behaviour (we'd won the game handsomely 3-0 too). The Manchester United fan had contributed nothing to deserve what he got other than being one of hundreds of people contributing to my lack of room. Nothing like that had ever happened before, and it never happened again.

Chelsea fans, early the following season, would be banned from The Dell after incredible scenes of fighting and vandalism inside and outside the ground. Me and Dad stayed in the ground until about 8:30 p.m., some three hours after the end of the match. Chelsea, who had filled the entire Archers Road end of the ground were spilling into other terraced areas and were fighting with unsuspecting Saints fans. Normally, at the end of the game, the away fans are penned in the ground by a police cordon, unable to leave until all the home fans have disappeared. Sometimes away fans would be locked in for more than an hour after the end of the match. This game was so wretched, an announcement came over the ground near to the end of the game. Instead of Chelsea fans remaining behind, the announcer told all the Southampton fans to remain in the ground, to give the police an opportunity to remove the Chelsea collective. At the end of the match (won 1-0) I could see the doors at the back of the Archers Road end open for the Chelsea fans to be led away by police.

Not one Chelsea fan left the ground at the final whistle; I would never forget it. The whole ground was in a stand-off as the announcer frantically tried to convince Chelsea fans to leave. Eventually Saints fans started to leave: as soon as they stepped out of the ground the Chelsea fans disappeared en-masse. It was unbelievable just how organised this was. In seemingly just a few moments, the Archers Road end emptied.

There were two junctions close to The Dell on Hill Lane, one at the end of Archers Road and the other at the end of Milton Road. Hill Lane would take fans back towards the city or the train station. Both of these junctions were blocked by Chelsea fans entirely. I could see the mass of people fighting at the end of the Milton Road. Next to Milton Road was Springhill Primary School. From our elevated position at the top of the Family Centre, we could see the Chelsea fans enter the school, and rampage classrooms for tables and chairs that they smashed into weapons. Bits of school furniture would be thrown by the masses at the junction towards Saints fans as they tried to leave. I don't remember seeing many police.

It seemed me and Dad were in the safest place in the city. The fighting finally died down, and Dad decided we had to make a run for it. I pleaded with him not to punch anyone again. He kept his promise.

We thoroughly enjoyed the season. We beat Coventry City 8-2 and in our very next home game beat Tottenham Hotspur 5-0. Saints finished second in the league, runner up for the title behind Liverpool by three points. I remember losing a home game to Notts County 2-0 – points that we tossed away. If only we got it right that day we could have been League Champions. In truth though, we had a great run in to the end of the season unlike 1982, and never really threatened Liverpool at the top.

The FA Cup was a different matter. We'd won away at Nottingham Forest in the third round of the competition and had been drawn away to our fierce rivals, Portsmouth, at Fratton Park. Radio Solent carried radio commentary. Listening to football on the radio is exhilarating and exhausting. The descriptive commentary required for such a medium has an urgent, frenzied quality about it as the commentator tries to keep up with the game whilst providing the detailed verbal picture of events whose outlines and colours are completed in your mind.

As a kid, when Saints were playing away I would normally be home with Dad listening to the away matches on the radio, through Dad's over large, louder than it should be, booming hi fi system. Originally in the Eighties, full radio commentaries were occasional. When there wasn't one, there would be a radio DJ filling in until a goal had been scored in 'one of our featured games'. The featured games would be those involving Bournemouth, Portsmouth and Southampton. If a goal was scored there would be a jingle, similar to the sound from Who Wants To Be A Millionaire when a contestant begins their round. Then the DJ would say, "There has been a goal at …" followed by a dramatic pause, and then the name of the ground that goal had been scored at. Then, the reporter at the game would come on the line to deliver the news to the listener. Because I only listened to away games, I soon got to know where all our opponents played.

The only thing was, Saints were never that great at winning away games, so invariably the reported goal was one that was conceded. You could tell immediately: a lot of noise and cheering and a reporter shouting to be heard over the noise meant a home goal to the other team; a muffled noise and a reporter broadcasting in a slightly surprised tone as if he found five pounds down the sofa, meant Saints had scored.

It went something like this.

"That was 'Fly Me To The Moon' by the inimitable Frank Sinatra!" The DJ would always be softly spoken and normally called Duncan.

Doof Doof! Diddly-dum!

"Um, yes. There has been a goal in one of our featured games!" At this point I am thinking, please be Fratton Park! Please be Dean Court! Anywhere except where Saints are playing!

"Let's go to Hillsborough and our reporter, John Hughes!" Dad would suddenly move to the edge of his sofa. My stomach would clench.

"Yes, it's Sheffield Wednesday one, Southampton nil ..."

"BOLLOCKS!" Dad would shout.

"Imre Varadi scored. Slightly unfortunate for Southampton, the ball ricocheting off the referee into the path of Varadi who raced in on goal to lob the Southampton goalkeeper!"

"Oh dear," the DJ would say, in a condescending tone, even though he would know nothing at all about football. "Let's hope the Saints can kick the ball into the goal soon. Next, here on Solent Sports Special, the Brotherhood Of Man with 'Save All Your Kisses For Me'."

Later – Doof Doof! Diddly-dum! I would suddenly prick my ears up and my fog of doom would dissipate. Dad would jump out of his seat, startled like a meerkat. Come on Saints, come on!

"Let's go back to Hillsborough, where it's Sheffield Wednesday one, Saints, nil!"

"Penalty here, Duncan!" A penalty? Who to?

"Penalty to Sheffield Wednesday!"

"BOLLOCKS!" Dad would collapse in his chair again.

"Hand ball by Mark Wright, no doubt about that one! Mel Sterland ready to step up and take the penalty to make it 2-0! Here he comes ..." Please, please, please miss!

"SAVED! Saved by Shilton!!! Great save to his right!"

Did he say saved? Saved? Cue mad dancing around the living room, as if we were riding on invisible space hoppers. I am absolutely convinced that celebrations like these would be comparable to a multi-million pound lottery win, without doubt. Dad would punch the air and go on to say, "Right then, go on and bloody win it now!" Sometimes we did, mostly we didn't with the cruel twist of football fate pointing in our opponents favour. By the end of the game we would both descend into melancholy, with Dad taking the dog up the pub.

Games that had full commentary were much more intense. My favourite ever radio commentary was when Saints played Portsmouth at Fratton Park in the FA Cup fourth round in 1984. This was a local derby that didn't occur very often, mainly because Portsmouth were always rubbish and in a lower league than us. They were then in

Division Two (second tier) and Saints were one of the best teams in the country. But an away fixture in the FA Cup was never easy and these kind of cup matches are always incredibly close as the lower team raise themselves for the contest whilst the better team could get easily complacent and edgy. The game was all the more intense and hostile given the hatred between the fans in an era of hooliganism where Portsmouth were one of the most feared and notorious supporters.

I was nervous. Dad was nervous. I had never experienced a local derby before and Portsmouth had nothing to lose. And they gave it a really good go, dominating the match for long spells and keeping the contest physical that did not suit Saints' style of play.

Portsmouth pressed forward followed by a crescendo of noise. The commentator struggled to have himself heard. With each Portsmouth attack the more nervous we became. Dad would cry out "Bloody hell!" in a resigned tone of voice when Alan Biley, Portsmouth's long, blond haired striker, headed over the bar from about three yards. It was an easy chance, a bad miss, but this was not looking good, and we were getting an ominous sinking feeling.

We struggled through to half-time and kept the game at 0-0. Dad was puffing his cheeks, pacing the room. I was meant to be updating my 'Football '84 Sticker Album' but couldn't concentrate on matching the players with the correct position in the album. We didn't fancy this at all, and didn't much like the idea of a replay either. The second half continued to the same script as the first half. With each attack, the tension became tighter and tighter, the commentators voice louder and more urgent. The crowd sung their 'Pompey Chimes' louder and louder. Saints players were pelted with coins when they neared the touchline. Our left back, Mark Dennis (quality player, should have played for England, mad as a hatter), was hit on the head by a coin and was helped to his feet by the police. This sent Dad into a stir. Both linesmen were also hit by coins during the game. The commentator would relay the information with dismay.

Saints started to gain a footing in the game, and Dad edged forward on his chair, but then Portsmouth missed another chance and he slunk back into it. Another shot went across the face of the goal, the commentator screamed, it must be a goal, but no Portsmouth player could poke the ball into the net. I don't think I had ever felt so nervous and Dad wasn't helping. He'd prophesise doom and gloom such as "I don't like this, Russ", or "Here they bloody come again" or "they're going to bloody nick it!" punctured with Tourette's like reactions to Portsmouth players ("prick!", "twat!") or Portsmouth fans ("bastards!", "animals!").

The game swung back Portsmouth's way and were finishing the game the stronger. The commentary volume started to rise again. With two minutes to go Alan Biley got the ball in the clear just six yards out. The commentator sounded as if he was out of his seat, beside himself with excitement. The noise reached a maximum, both crowd and commentator, but I couldn't hear what he said. Was it a goal? Did he score? He must have scored? We had to wait a few moments for the crowd to die down. Finally, my brain could piece together what had happened. With the goal gaping, Biley had blasted the ball over the bar. He was a solid player but on this day, Alan Biley shot for goal as if he had never played the game in his life. It was beautiful!

Into injury time, Saints bald midfielder, David Armstrong received the ball down the right and burst into the Portsmouth penalty area. He clipped the ball across the goal and with the goalkeeper scrambling to get across his goal, Steve Moran ran in to volley the ball into the net from close range.

We went bonkers, dancing round the house as if the carpet was red hot, the dog trying to get involved without understanding what he was supposed to be doing. I would bet that a multi-million pound lottery win would not generate celebrations quite like a Southampton goal in the last minute of the game that beat Portsmouth that day.

There was hardly any time left to go, and the game was duly won. The Saints players raced off the pitch fearing the home supporters. I was knackered. Dad went off to make stew for dinner. The Saints manager, Lawrie McMenemy cheekily said afterwards, "We got a good result and four pounds fifty in small change!"

In the next rounds we won away at Blackburn Rovers, then in the quarter final, beat Sheffield Wednesday 5-1 at The Dell after drawing at Hillsborough. People were hugging me that night! I really did not like that at all. There were people who, like me and Dad, had found their preferred spot in the Family Centre. We'd never spoken, they had never spoken to Dad, and Dad had never spoken to them. But they were grabbing me and hugging me (in celebration you understand, there was nothing Operation Yewtree about it).

It is true to point out that some fans would find another spot once they had irritated Dad. He didn't like moaners. He understood the quality of football we watched and was grateful for it. But some fans seem to have a singular objective of whinging and moaning from minute one to minute ninety, and this was like a red rag to a bull for Dad. People would be told to shut their trap, or be invited to piss off to Fratton Park if they weren't happy with the football on offer here. He'd even argue with the BBC or ITV commentators who would be climbing up a gantry adjacent to where we stood, to begin their work.

BBC's Barry Davies and John Motson would be informed, in no uncertain terms, that they should bloody well bring the cameras here every week. Brian Moore, David Bobin and Gerald Sinstadt, on the other hand, and on the other channel ITV, would be told unceremoniously that the BBC coverage was better.

Saints had earned a semi-final against Everton, who were a resurgent team and who, the following season would win the League title. However, they were an inferior team to Southampton at that time. In fact, with the other semi-final being between Plymouth Argyle and Watford, the Saints were clear favourites to win the cup.

To me there was no doubt. If Saints played well, we would win – and we were playing very well. We would have a near full strength team to pick, with Steve Williams, who was now in his prime at the heart of the Southampton midfield, the only doubt. Dad had purchased some decorations from the puny Saints shop on Milton Road and the house was decorated with red and white balloons.

As a season ticket holder, getting semi-final tickets was not a problem. This would be only my second match away from The Dell, the first being at Wembley in 1979. This match would be at Arsenal's Highbury Stadium.

Dad outdid his previous eccentric travel arrangements to get to a game, by going on a coach to the match. This was not an official football club coach, but a hired coach trip, probably through Dad's work.

He warned me before we set off for the day, that I might learn a few new words on the coach, but that I was to keep my head down and not listen to any of it. This was fine by me, but I had not realised that Dad had booked us on a Tourette's sufferers day excursion to North London.

I had never heard so much effing and jeffing in my life! It was a completely different language where a series of the worst swear words in human history were occasionally punctuated with a real word. Looking back on it I should not have been on that coach. Once a couple of beers had been downed, the singing started, some of which weren't sweary but incredibly dumb. One song I remember word-for-word – not much of an achievement given the standard of song: "Goodbye horse, goodbye horse / I was saying goodbye to my horse / And as I was saying goodbye to my horse / I was saying goodbye to my horse". What the hell was that about? Another song consisted of saying the words "I had a wheelbarrow, the front wheel was bent," repeated indefinitely until we reached Fleet Services. Dad would laugh along to the songs and a little bit more nervously to the banter, and I considered that if this was what adulthood would be like I wasn't having any of it; just leave me to my Subbuteo, Lego and ZX Spectrum thank you very much.

Reaching the ground was a total relief. Dad was traumatised just as much as me I think. He didn't realise it was going to be that bad. Someone showed him a picture of a naked lady with legs at more than ninety degrees apart – right in front of me (I actually do remember thinking, that was quite a lot of hair), and he was hit on the head by an empty beer can. We were overjoyed to reach the stadium, which seemed to be entirely hidden by rows of terraced houses.

Our tickets were in a standing area in the Lower West Stand, and we positioned ourselves near the front, close to the half way line. The pitch was directly in front of me, and level with my chest which, at the time I thought was unusual and great, but in retrospect not ideal, standing effectively below pitch level. Opposite me was the Art Deco East Stand, which I think is a listed building. To my right was the smallest stand, the Clock End, complete with a clock on it, as you'd expect. To my left was the North Bank, that looked to me like the biggest stand I had ever seen. By kick off this stand would be a sea of Everton blue, going back into the darkness underneath the roof.

Dad and I were confident. Steve Williams was fit to play and I felt sure that we would get the job done. The Everton team had good players, but had weaknesses. For example, Tony Curran, who you will recall played one season for Saints in 1979 managed to get a game for them.

Saints started well, as did the Everton goalkeeper, Neville Southall. There were one or two goalkeepers down the years who always played a blinder at The Dell. Southall was one of those goalkeepers, and you always wondered if there would be any way past him. Unfortunately for us, he was having an equally fine game at Highbury this day. He saved from Steve Moran early on, and then from Danny Wallace. Saints were on top at half-time, but Everton had snuck back into the match in the last few minutes of the half. Not to worry, I thought, plenty of time to get in front.

In the second half Wallace drove through only to see his shot tipped round the post by Southall. Frank Worthington blazed a shot over the bar, then soon after juggled the ball calmly before looping a cross to Mark Wright who headed over. But Everton were right back in it, Adrian Heath, Everton's forward who looked about seven years old, shot wide when clean through. Mick Mills had to sweep a ball off the line from a Terry Curran cross. Saints were suddenly on the back foot and Everton started to dominate. It was incredibly tense and we were hanging on. In the last twenty minutes we could hardly get out of our half. This was suddenly not going at all to plan. I remember David Armstrong missing a chance in the last minute of the match, blazing the ball over the bar. How I needed that shot to go in to relieve the anguish.

The game ended 0-0 and extra time was required. We suddenly had been given a lifeline to get off the ropes, re-group, and re-take the game by the scruff of the neck.

Everton scored the winning goal three minutes from the end of extra time. A free kick near the corner flag was curled in for Heath to nudge the ball with his head over Peter Shilton and destroy my dreams.

I was in total disbelief. Dad was crestfallen. I just stared at the Everton fans in the North Bank, jubilant, bouncing and hysterical. I wanted that to be me but we had blown it.

This is the match that has hurt the most. Much of it had to do with the expectation that me and Dad had. Certainly, I had never considered being beaten in this match, and this complacency left me ill prepared to be as disappointed as I was. It was like grief. I had been gutted in 1979, but was still very young. At this match I was twelve and much more cognisant as to what was at stake. I was shocked, but I was also disturbed by Dad's reaction. You never saw Dad really upset, but he was this day, most likely thinking along the same lines as me, that this was meant to be our year.

When the final whistle blew, the Everton fans invaded the pitch and made straight for the Saints fans at the Clock End of the ground. We watched as pitch battles ensued between the fans. Right in front of me, not three yards away I saw a Saints fan grapple with an Everton fan, roll him over on the ground and punch him in the face. I saw a splash of blood and his nose depress into his face. Deep down I thought, good. But I kept that nasty thought to myself. To cap off a horrible day we had to go home on the coach with the menagerie of mongs again. Fortunately, most of the coach was as disappointed as us and it was a much quieter trip home.

Somewhere during the trip home, the coach had stopped to pick up some fish and chips. I remember sitting next to Dad on the remaining journey home, near the front of the coach, eating our fish and chips (or in my case, deep-fried battered beef burger and chips, soaked in vinegar), with hardly a word spoken on the coach, let alone a moronic song being sung. He turned to me and simply said "Sorry, Russ," as if the day and result was his fault, his responsibility. As a parent, I get where he was coming from: the coach and the hooliganism in front of a twelve year old kid was not a good look – even for the Eighties. But I reckon somewhere in that apology was the result itself, and perhaps an acknowledgement that the team that I had been brought up to support was going to be more tortuous compared to supporting a Liverpool or Manchester United team.

Once home, the balloons came off the wall. Dad was cross as in my anger I'd pulled off the paint as well as the blu tac. Three days later, our next home match was against Everton, a cruel twist. Saints won 3-1 and Everton hardly had a kick. It felt like a hollow victory though. Was it too much to ask to play like that the previous Saturday? Evidentially so. Everton won the final easily against a tepid Watford team. That should have been us. Dad didn't even shout down the neighbours for mowing the lawn on that cup final day.

Do you know, this match still hurts today? I needed to watch it back on YouTube to help with my recollection of what happened, and I couldn't bring myself to watch the goal or the end of the game.

It's fair to say that when I was twelve years old, Everton ruined my life.

1986

FA Cup Semi-Final 1986, Liverpool versus Southampton. White Hart Lane, London, Saturday, 5th of April.

For the 1986 season, Lawrie McMenemy had left Southampton, much to Dad's dismay. He was replaced by former player Chris Nicholl, who was told by the club that he would have to 'cut his cloth' accordingly and the 'extravagant' spending by his predecessor had to stop. This marked the beginning of a turn of fortunes for the Saints, who had been accustomed to finishing in the top seven or eight teams each year.

From 1984, Frank Worthington, Steve Williams and Mick Mills had gone. In had come Jimmy Case, an experienced, uncompromising midfielder, part of the top Liverpool team of the Seventies and Eighties, who had replaced Williams. George Lawrence, a tall winger, had returned for a second spell. I used to enjoy watching Lawrence play – I had no idea what he was going to do next, and I suspect neither did he. He had the nickname 'Chicken George', supposedly because he looked similar to the character in the Roots mini-series on the television; the slave who trained chickens. In retrospect, the nickname is crass at best, but at the time it stuck.

But we still had Peter Shilton, and Mark Wright, both regulars for England. Nick Holmes and David Armstrong were also still there. But it was clear that Saints had turned in a downward direction, and we would finish fourteenth from twenty-two teams that season. In one game, away to Luton Town, we lost 7-0.

But we had made it back to the FA Cup semi-final, this time to play Liverpool, and this time to be played at Tottenham Hotspur's ground White Hart Lane. Dad came through with the tickets, but as we set off for London, our expectations weren't high. Whereas in 1984 we expected to win the semi-final and for that matter the cup itself, this year we were hoping rather than expecting.

Liverpool were the best team in the land during the Eighties, but Saints knew how to beat them. In those days, I had no problem with Liverpool and followed their exploits as they won trophy after trophy in England and in Europe. Dad even got us tickets to the FA Cup Final in 1988 at Wembley as a neutral to watch Liverpool versus Wimbledon. Wimbledon won in a big surprise 1-0 and John Aldridge of Liverpool missed the first penalty in an FA Cup Final at Wembley since 1923. It was a thoroughly enjoyable day.

Dad had a problem with Liverpool in those days. If unemployment in Liverpool is so bad, he argued, how is it that so many fans get to every single game home and away? Liverpool had huge home game gates exceeding 44,000, and at The Dell they brought as many fans down as the London teams did. Normally, away fans would be held in the corner of the Archers Road end of the ground, caged in. But London and Liverpool fans had the entire Archers Road end of the ground to themselves.

To understand the answer to such a complex question, you would need to deduce the answer through careful research of the socio-economic fabric of Merseyside and understanding the intrinsic value and positivity football brings to that industrial region. You would have also need to considered similar cities and spoken to the local Scouse people to paint a fair and balanced picture of area. Dad's approach was a little less considered, perhaps. When Liverpool were playing, he'd shout out "Look at 'em all! They nick the money for the tickets or they climb over the wall! Bloody Scousers!" I was not sure about this, but as a kid you go along with such vignettes of wisdom from your father, don't you?

There was no doubt Dad loathed Liverpool. On television, he was adamant that every TV show had to have the "obligatory Scouser" in it (this will start to mess with your head now when you watch telly). And the Scouse accent drove him round the bend. They were the only people who could gob and talk at the same time, according to Dad.

Then in 1985 came the Heysel disaster. Before the European Cup Final in 1985, Liverpool fans at one end of the ground stampeded Juventus fans who were poorly segregated. This was known as 'running' and hooligans would do this to other fans regularly inside and out of grounds in those days. The stadium was poorly maintained and a wall collapsed, killing thirty-nine Juventus supporters. This sent Dad apoplectic as we tuned in to watch the final only to see a disaster unfold live on television. There, of course, can be no excuse as to the primary cause of the incident but Liverpool never had a track record of hooligans, whose fans were generally thought to be benign, unlike

Millwall, Chelsea, Portsmouth or Cardiff fans who had a scandalous reputation. I found that strange.

The outcome was seismic for English football. All English clubs were banned from playing in Europe indefinitely. Saints had again qualified for Europe the following year but found themselves thrown out of the tournament along with Everton, Norwich City, Liverpool, Arsenal, Manchester United and Tottenham Hotspur. Clubs were re-instated in 1992, but Saints would not get another opportunity until 2004. Dad would never forgive Liverpool for having Saints tossed out of European competition. It was an added edge for this game to us.

And it proved to have consequence for the good people of Liverpool too. In 1989 came the worst disaster in English football's history. There are a bunch of books on the subject, of which Pat Scraton's 'Hillsborough: The Truth' is the definitive account. This is where ninety-six Liverpool fans were sent to their death at an FA Cup semi-final between Liverpool and Nottingham Forest at the Hillsborough ground in Sheffield. After South Yorkshire Police failed to put in place an adequate crowd control operation around the ground, an enormous number of Liverpool fans were left trying to enter the stadium. The crush that ensued was alleviated by the Chief Superintendent ordering the opening of an exit gate which saw the fans surge into the ground. Because there was insufficient signage all the fans went to the same two caged pens of supporters. Fans already inside the pens anticipating watching a football match started to be crushed, and then asphyxiated. The game was abandoned after six minutes as fans spilled on to the pitch, climbing over the six foot cages penning them in, as they fought for their lives. This was seen by the police as a pitch invasion, with all the hooligan history of English football's past and the Heysel disaster coming into sharp focus. As people started to die inside the stadium, ambulances and Fire Brigade services were denied access on the basis that the supporters were 'still fighting'. Even the Chief Superintendent changed his story about his decision to open the gate. He told the FA Secretary not ten minutes after the game had been abandoned that the Liverpool fans had charged the gate open.

As if that wasn't enough, a cover up was painted by both South Yorkshire Police and latterly the West Midlands Police to discredit the fans and spin a new story where fans were drunk (police even tested blood alcohol levels on the dead), fans attacked police, urinated on them, stole from the dead who were dragged on to the pitch. None of which was ever corroborated by the mountain of video and CCTV evidence of the day. The impact on the lives of Liverpudlians was profound. Ignorance, bungled inquests and government inquiries over the next twenty-five years took its toll on the city; one MP even shamefully referred to Liverpool as the 'self-pity city'. Finally, in 2015 a new inquest delivered a verdict of unlawful death on the ninety-six, and apportioned blame directly to the police, ambulance service, safety engineers at Hillsborough, and Sheffield Wednesday Football Club, owners of the Hillsborough stadium. Sadly, even though the police stories had long since been discredited, the police still peddled the same inept and callous stories at the inquest as they did twenty-five years earlier. The results of the inquest had brought into question the viability of the South Yorkshire Police force. It's a desperately sad story which, at least has started to form some sort of closure for the families of the ninety-six and the people of Liverpool.

Of course, for days and weeks afterwards, the reports in the newspapers around the incident, fuelled with the lies of the police painted a terrible picture of Liverpool Football Club. And despite the efforts down the years to tell the true story of the incident, the mud stuck. And it has stuck with many people even to this day. It certainly didn't improve relations between Dad and Liverpool.

I didn't much like White Hart Lane, and I didn't much like the match. We were sat high up at the North Stand end of the ground. A huge post holding the roof up obscured our view a little.

Peter Shilton had to make a smart save at the start of the match. It was a preview for what was to come. A series of Liverpool attacks, punctuated by an attack of sorts by Saints, would be the order of the day. The Liverpool goalkeeper, Bruce Grobbelaar would be a virtual spectator throughout the match.

At half-time we were still at 0-0. But it had been a difficult match to watch. Liverpool were dominant, but Saints stood firm. And it had come at a cost. Our imperious defender Mark Wright had collided with Peter Shilton in stopping Craig Johnstone getting in on goal. Wright had broken his leg, and we could see it clearly. It was awful. It meant Wright missed to upcoming World Cup in Mexico, and we had a much more immediate problem in trying to keep Liverpool out.

Dad's assessment of the first half was short and precise. "Not looking good, Russ," he told me. Even if we clung on for a draw we'd go to extra time, and even if we could hold on then, we had to do it all again in a replay. There wasn't much to smile about.

The second half continued to the same tune. Ronnie Whelan blazed wide of the post for Liverpool, Shilton had to save at the feet of Jim Beglin, and then tipped the ball round the post from another Whelan shot. Shilton was superb and the make-shift defence clung on for extra time. The closest Saints came to score was when George Lawrence headed well wide from close range under pressure from the Liverpool defence.

In extra time it all went horribly wrong. Kevin Bond, our other central defender, attempted a header back to the goalkeeper Peter Shilton. It lacked power and was never going to reach the goalkeeper. Ian Rush, the prolific Welsh goal scorer pounced on the ball and swept it past Shilton into the goal. It was harsh on our defender, who had been immense, but tiredness got the better of him and Liverpool had finally struck. Moments later, Rush had another goal, almost out of nothing, from a tight angle from the left. And in just a couple of minutes the dream was dead yet again.

This wasn't as hard to take as 1984, but I sensed that it might be some time before we get an opportunity like this again.

Saints had been robbed from playing in Europe in 1986, which I was unhappy about. But losing in 1986 to Liverpool put them on notice as far as I was concerned. They then beat us in the 1987 League Cup semi-final 3-0 after two legs to further stoke my dislike. Thereafter as we moved into the Nineties it pleased me that Liverpool's influence on the game started to fade as they could not recreate their success in the Eighties. Even today they are miles away from ever winning the Premier League again, and each year when their supporters have sensed this could be their year, there is always a wry smile to be had when they are beaten at home again in January to end any lingering Liverpudlian thoughts of triumph.

But they have had occasional success in the cups to wipe the smile off my face, and even won the European Cup in 2005, beating AC Milan on penalties, after being 3-0 down, charging back to draw 3-3. I remember that morning at work in New Zealand managing to avoid the chatter about the match and somehow getting home to watch the match that evening without knowing the score. I sat down to watch the repeat on the American ESPN Sports channel. Before the match started, an advert came up with one of those pumped up American announcers. "Welcome to the replay of Liverpool versus AC Milan," pronounced Mee-larn. "Congratulations to Liverpool Football Club on their amazing success!" I couldn't believe it! Why were they showing me this? Pictures of Steven Gerrard lifting the giant European trophy? Did America not have a concept of spoilers? ESPN completely ruined that match for me. Idiots.

In modern times, I think Liverpool football club has become a bit of a parody. During the semi-final I saw an advertisement on the touchline about Liverpool's youth system. That's ironic, I thought. It seems to me that Liverpool didn't bother with a youth team – they just purchased the next big talent from Southampton rather than bother to nurture talent themselves (the club have also been banned from signing youth players for illegally approaching a youngster at another football club). Perhaps it was actually an advertisement for Southampton's revered youth set up?

Liverpool have a habit of buying Southampton players, and Southampton have an equally irritating habit of allowing our players to join Liverpool. In days gone by this wasn't the case. I remember Peter Crouch moving to Liverpool in 2005, but it was a rare thing.

When Saints returned to the Premier League for the 2013 season, no one really knew about our team. The lazy journalists had Saints as favourites to go straight back down again which was hilarious to me. Our team had been rebuilt with Premier League-class players, from before we had made it back there. Our team was young, hungry, skilful and strong. And so it proved, after a rocky start with some tough matches we held our own admirably and stuffed Liverpool 3-1 along the way.

After an even stronger season in 2014, where Saints won away at Liverpool, they put a bid in for our star striker Ricky Lambert. Lambert joined us from Bristol Rovers for one million pounds in 2009 when we had plummeted into the third division, now known as League One. Lambert was a great striker, another great number 7 for the club. He was a prolific scorer of goals, and as we rose through the leagues he continued to put the ball in the net. He was a big guy, an excellent target man, but much more than that, skilful and with the vision to pick out a pass. We had been in the Premier League and in his thirties now, Ricky Lambert was now an England player. But he was a Scouser, so the lure to join his home town team was too great. It was a shame, but he left as a true Saints legend, and Liverpool had a 4.5 million pound bargain. Unfortunately, Lambert's time at Liverpool was not successful. When I saw him play they never played to his strengths at all. In retrospect it was a pointless signing for them and a waste of a season for Lambert, and I felt aggrieved for him.

Liverpool also bid for our clever, talented midfielder Adam Lallana, who had been at Saints since as a youth player, that same summer. It was said there was some disruption from the player behind the scenes and was sold for twenty-five million pounds. I'm not convinced about Lallana's behaviour in agitating for the move, and am appalled the way he gets booed by Saints fans. I'd love to see him back at the club one day and was a great servant to us.

Liverpool then came back again for Dejan Lovren, our high quality Croatian centre back. He'd only been with us a single season, but hotfooted it north for a cool twenty million pounds. Certainly, Lovren did agitate for a move and behaved appallingly to get what he wanted.

The next summer, in 2015, Liverpool were back again, this time for Nathaniel Clyne, our left back we had bought by Crystal Palace and turned into an England left back. Another 12.5 million pounds added to our coffers.

Signing number five was Sadio Mané, in the summer of 2016, for 34 million pounds. That was more than 125 million pounds on five players in three years.

Other players have been rumoured too, such as Shane Long, Fraser Forster and Virgil Van Dyk. It has become a real problem, and Southampton have helped perpetuate growing animosity between the fans, including me. If Liverpool have any ambition to be a properly big club and win championships or cups, they would be competing to buy players from Real Madrid, Barcelona, Bayern Munich or Paris Saint Germain – just like other big clubs that win trophies do. Liverpool buy the potential that Southampton have cultivated over a long time in the hope they turn into world beaters.

To my mind the situation has become a joke and the club should actively come out and say, no more, and perhaps start to report some of the rumoured shady methods that undermine and unsettle our players, to the Premier League. It's got so bad, when we buy a player, Liverpool fans look on to see who they will be getting in a year or two's time. When Mother Theresa became a saint, I wondered how long it would be before Liverpool made an inquiry about her.

I dislike Liverpool as I do Everton. But the truth is, I dislike many football teams. Teams I want to see beat every week. Teams I want to see relegated and disintegrate into a nothingness at the arse-end of football's pyramid system. Liverpool because of 1986, Everton because of 1984, Portsmouth because, well they are Portsmouth. I'm not a supporter who can sit down and enjoy the merits of a 0-0 draw between Liverpool and Everton. I'm far too partisan. I want both teams to lose so badly and I know I can't have that so the match becomes meaningless to me.

Beating Liverpool in the semi-final this year was special. It made up for 1986 I think. I regret missing the second leg and I suppose that dulls it a bit but I feel I can watch that winning Shane Long goal on repeat for ever.

The Long Haul

NZ2, Auckland to London Heathrow, departing 11:10 p.m. Friday 24th of February, arriving 10:20 a.m. Saturday 25th of February. Flight duration 24 hours, 30 minutes. Economy service class.

With one week to go before I was due to travel, Kellie told me plainly that I was now getting on her nerves. The topic of discussion from me was all about the match. What if we win? Who will play in defence? Will we get a goal? Will I get in with my ticket? She had been very, very patient and humoured me way beyond the threshold that any normal person would humour another. But at some point I would undoubtedly cross the line, and one further assessment of José Mourinho's first season in charge of Manchester United had sent her over the edge.

I'd also not behaved well, seemingly pushing her buttons whenever I could. She said flatly that because I was going away for the match there was no need to decorate the house in red and white balloons, banners and flags. I had done this on numerous occasions, the last time when Saints were promoted back to the Premier League for the 2012 season. Approximately three weeks prior to the cup final I had sneakily got out my Subbuteo League Cup replica trophy and placed red and white paper ribbons on it and put it by the television quietly. This was noticed by Kellie and noted. I received a verbal warning, in the same way a boxer might for a low punch. Then, a week out, I carefully and quietly removed my giant flags and banners from under the bed in the spare room, charged up my cold hard ball of blu tac, there especially for occasions such as this, and decorated the house beautifully, carefully placing flags and banners on the window, being extra careful not to knock over our beloved porcelain Mickey and Mouse couple, a treasure from our early years that sat on top of both our wedding cake and our wedding renewal cake. Kellie was asleep from a night shift and I was deathly quiet. I was sure that when she woke up she would see past the garish red colour illuminating our lounge through the sunlight like a brothel's waiting room (apparently, I wouldn't know), and she would see the clever angles I had used for the banners and think it an enhancement to the house for the time being. Maybe it would make her feel more part of it and connected to my adventure. Kellie gets me (about 95% at least when it comes to football) and it is to her immense credit and patience that she lets me go off at a footballing tangent from time to time. She also enjoys the football and gets excited by it, so I feel very blessed to have her as my wife.

But as with chuntering on and on about the match day after day, there is a limit. I was taking a risk with Kellie here – this could tip her over the edge. I could be in big trouble. After waking up half way through the afternoon she wandered around the house with blurry eyes at first not noticing. When she did, she was calmness personified. She questioned what was going on. I explained about the cup final, again. I was told not to be flippant, but could tell she was waning and eventually yielded when I explained the blu tac was only on the window glass not the wall (previous decorative pieces of mine had tendency to rip a chunk out of the wall if it fell off or was pulled off). She relented. Surrendered more like.

That evening, after Kellie had gone to work, one of the flags peeled off the window and fell on the floor, taking with it Mickey and Minnie Mouse. Minnie survived unscathed, but Mickey landed on top of Minnie, and smashed in two. Those two ornaments were priceless to us. I didn't need to be told – I immediately took down the decorations entirely, and took the shame the following evening with Kellie. Sometimes it takes something as jarring as this to realise just what an idiot you are.

Two nights before I was due to leave, I received a text from Debbie. The Southern Daily Echo were trying to get into contact with me. It was apparent that out of 90,000 fans I would be the one travelling the furthest. Or at least, out of all the Saints fans attending, I was the one prepared to make the most song and dance about it. There had been some problem getting hold of me, either incorrectly attempting an international call (honestly, it is easy – to call New Zealand, dial 0, followed by 64, followed by the telephone number, remembering to drop the initial 0), or misspelling my email (typically Russel rather than Russell – seriously I have never met a Russel with one 'L', have you? It's an urban myth). Eventually, after calling me and texting me close to midnight, there was success and I received an email with a set of questions.

These included: "What was so special about this game that made you fork out the probable huge cost of flights and tickets?".

My response: "I always said I would come back for Cup Finals. (Actually, this upset my other sister Tracey because she told me if that was the case being a Saints fan she would never see me again!)." My original response bragging how cheap the flights were, was I think, unnecessary. I'm glad I deleted it.

Question two: "How do you think the game will go? What's your prediction?" This is, of course, something that I have thought much about. In fact, I am convinced that I would be in the top ten Saints fans cogitating on if Saints could win, and how they could win. So the start of my response was "I haven't thought about it." In truth, I'd even completed a 'pros' and 'cons' chart. I listed all the positives on one side of a notepad, and the negatives on the other. It didn't help. Saints were the first ever team to get to the final without conceding a goal, except now Virgil Van Dyk, our supreme defender is injured and our other centre back José Fonte had been sold to West Ham United. Saints are an organised side though, they'll deny space to the Manchester United attacking players, but our defence had suddenly gone leaky with a reserve and youth team player filling the centre of defence. Our form was poor – seven defeats in the last nine games, whilst Manchester United are unbeaten since the previous October. Saints do have pedigree against the top teams though and had beaten Manchester United at Old Trafford twice in the last three years, but no pedigree in big games like this. Overall Saints had undoubtedly gone backwards in form and talent in 2017 from their sixth place finish in 2016, whilst Manchester United were improving all the time under José Mourinho's tutelage. This season Saints had been missing chance after chance – at times some of the misses had been incredible and defied the laws of probability and physics simultaneously, were as accurate as a scud missile, and were rarely able to score more than one goal in a game. Yet in January they purchased a new striker from Napoli, Manolo Gabbiadini, who although looked like a skinny glue sniffer whom you might find hanging outside a pub in Portsmouth trying to bum a fag or some money, had scored three impressive goals in two matches. But Manchester United had the aging but world class Zlatan Ibrahimović who seemed to be scoring a hat trick every week. Perhaps though, things were changing; Saints had won their last match 4-0 at Sunderland, although Sunderland are bottom of the league. Saints had been playing twice a week almost all season and suddenly had a welcome two week break to recharge and plan how to win the cup, whilst Manchester United were swotting Saint Etienne twice and Blackburn Rovers and so were in the groove. The list went on, and on, and on, with more 'cons' than 'pros'. The biggest plus I could find was that Saints had drawn the 'lucky' west dressing room at Wembley, although I remember in 1979 Saints were the first team for years to have the lucky dressing room and lose the match.

So in the end I bottled the answer, I said "1-1, with Saints to win on penalties." If this happens I would not be confident that my body, mind or spirit could cope.

Another question was, "For all the costs of flights etc., is this worth it for you, to see Saints potentially win a major trophy?"

My initial response was "duh!" On reflection, I thought that a little juvenile so deleted this and said "It would be amazing. I'm like any other fan desperate to see us get our hands on a trophy. I just live a bit further away. It's turning into a bit of an adventure though, and I'll get to spend some time with my extended family too so it will be totally worth it." In fact, if we lost it would be the most miserable week of my life.

When Debbie was in communication with the reporter she said my age was 66. Cow! So I couldn't resist remarking that whilst providing my correct age of thirty-nine my sister was actually thirty-five years older than me. If that made it into the Echo, it would be hilarious.

I'd also sent a picture of me outside my house holding a Saints flag, in front of the windows that were adorned with flags and banners.

I considered my responses would fuel a rip-roaring article and that the reporter couldn't possibly fail in curating a tale that the earnest Echo Reader would devour with interest. So it was a slight surprise when he emailed me the next night to inform me that he didn't know if it would make the Echo at any stage before or after the final, and that he was handing off his report to a colleague as he was pushing off on holiday. This did not sound promising.

There was another article that the Echo had published, titled 'Lucky Saints mascot brought out of retirement ahead of EFL Cup final against Man United'. Snappy title I thought. It was about a guy living in Singapore who travelled 'thousands of miles' to get his mascot from 1976 out of his loft and ready for Wembley. The mascot was this huge smiling teddy bear wearing the Saints shirt of the day. This guy was travelling back for the Final, and had also travelled to support Saints in their European exploits in Israel, Czech Republic and Italy this season. So what? Singapore is only 6,813 miles (10,841 km) from Wembley, merely a stroll compared to my intended gargantuan effort. I would be travelling 11,388 miles (18,327 km), some 4,525 miles further, but without a bloody three-foot blob in a Saints shirt. This guy's brother was also meant to go with him from Australia, but couldn't. Ha! No doubt he did not want to be seen with a bloke cradling a giant soft toy.

If they could publish that tat, surely my story would make the front page?

I kept checking the Echo web site before I left to see if the article about me was there. I checked again once in Los Angeles but could not find it published.

Debbie was still on a mission for tickets. The Saints allocation had been sold out for days, but she was still scheming with ideas on how to acquire some. Most fans without tickets were doing the same. I heard a story about an employee of Southampton Football Club urgently needing some work done to fix a leak. The plumber was a Saints fan and his quotation for the work was either: a) two adult and two concession tickets for the League Cup Final at Wembley on the 26th of February 2017, with no money changing hands; or b) no work being able to commence until the week after the cup final. Unsurprisingly, this innovative approach to accounting practise was unsuccessful.

I had worries about the cup final. In the Premier League Saints had beaten Bournemouth 3-1 before Christmas and went a creditable seventh in the table. We were then mullered at home by Tottenham Hotspur 4-1, then beaten at home by a dreadful West Bromwich Albion team 2-1, well beaten at Everton 3-0 (that one was a sickener). Even lowly Burnley had beaten us 1-0.

It was only in the cups that we had been getting any kind of result. We had beaten Liverpool in the League Cup semi-final of course, 1-0 both home and away. In the FA Cup, we had also beaten Championship side Norwich City 1-0 in a replay after a 2-2 draw. But our manager made the dreadful decision to rest almost our entire first team in the next FA Cup match at home to Arsenal, owing to the volume of games we were playing, and effectively threw the game. We lost 5-0.

Out of nothing we then beat Leicester City, the reigning Premier League champions 3-0. It seemed that we had turned a corner. But then it got worse again. Swansea City, primed for relegation, beat us 2-1, and West Ham United beat us 3-1 at St Mary's. You would be hard pressed to find a more appalling set of results since Harry Redknapp had us relegated in 2005.

This wasn't good form to be going into a cup final with. In fact, this was no form to be going into a cup final with. In twelve games we had shipped 24 goals, exactly two a game. In the Leicester game Jamie Vardy, Leicester's star striker who was in the midst of having a movie made about him and his team's exploits from the previous season, left an ugly kick on our best defender (and in all likelihood the best defender in the league this season) Virgil Van Dyk. Van Dyk left the field and was diagnosed with a foot injury that would keep him out of the team for three months, including the cup final. This was a bitter blow. He was a towering presence in our defence but also drove us forward. In our biggest games he was our biggest player and as such would be irreplaceable.

Around the same time José Fonte left for West Ham United. Since winning the European Championships with Portugal the previous summer, the media had reported he was wanting to move. José Mourinho, the Portuguese Manchester United manager was said to be interested in the purchase but no offer was forthcoming. Apparently, Saints were unwilling to extend his contract beyond the 2018 season, when he would be 34 going on 35, and were therefore open to receiving offers for the player.

This was a shame, I thought. Fonte had been a brilliant servant to the football club – a true legend. He joined us from Crystal Palace in 2010 when we were in League One – the third tier of English football. He went with us all the way back to the Premier League, found his way into the Portuguese national squad, until eventually becoming a European Championship winner. Quite a story actually – I'd rather see a movie about Fonte rather than Vardy.

But during this season, whilst still our Captain and first-choice defender, Fonte found himself rested for European matches. I didn't like this: I am sure a player like this who you would describe in a cliché as 'Southampton through-and-through' was not given an opportunity to play in a tournament that, in some ways, defined where we are as a club: six years before playing Rochdale, six years later playing in the San Siro in Italy against Inter Milan. It also meant not playing European matches would mean if he left for another club involved in European competition, he would be allowed to participate for his new club.

So somewhere along the line a rift developed and Fonte was allowed to leave in the January transfer window. But not for a bigger club as he probably wanted, and was probably deserved, but for West Ham United of all teams! That London shower! Couldn't the club and the player reached some kind of middle ground to keep him until the end of the season? After all there was the massive games against Liverpool in the semi-final of the League Cup coming up and the promise of Wembley beyond that? Word on the street with fans is that Fonte did not behave particularly well and that led to his demise. I sense, however, that the club may have made some bad decisions with the player and were not whiter-than-white as they would have you believe.

In fact, overall, I was sensing Saints, as a club who prided themselves on making good decision after good decision, were starting to make a few bad ones. Certainly, offloading Fonte to expose our lack of depth in defenders was definitely not smart. But also I was yet to be convinced with the manager they had brought in in the summer, Claude Puel. I don't think he had done a great job in the league, and set us up to fail in Europe when it seemed impossible not to progress (we were in the top two qualifying positions throughout the six-game league, up until the last ten minutes of our last match). Of course, his record in the League Cup was without question. But after meekly surrendering at the FA Cup match against Arsenal, blowing the Europa League spectacularly and finding ourselves plummeting down the league, amongst many un-entertaining matches where Saints seemed to be incapable of scoring more than one goal in a match, I didn't think he was proving to be a good appointment.

And we had not purchased players particularly well in the Summer. Saints are renowned for selling their best talent (normally to Liverpool, irritatingly) but also replenishing their stocks with the next big thing. We lose classy defender Toby Alderweireld to Tottenham Hotspur, we bring in Virgil van Dijk. We lose club legend Ricky Lambert, we bring in Graziano Pellè. We lose Adam Lallana, we bring in Sadio Mané. But last summer we lost both Pellè and Mané, worth 30 goals to us in 2016, and replaced both with Nathan Redmond who had managed two up until Christmas. Redmond was young and may become a good player, but this season was lightweight and did not contribute enough to the team.

Meanwhile, since Manchester United had been beaten by Chelsea 4-0 in October, their record in all competitions was played 28, won 19, drawn 7, lost 2, and the two losses were either in two legged matches or Europa League group stages, which they won overall. Their danger man was Zlatan Ibrahimović who had scored five goals in the last three matches he had played in.

So the final had arguably come at the worst possible time.

But I had decided: we still had a great chance to win.

I'd organised with Debbie and Dan a full itinerary for my stay. I'd get to London and go straight to the stadium. Me and Dan would stay in the nearby Hilton hotel on the Saturday night. Dan would travel on the Saturday by car and park in the hotel. After the match we would travel (in jubilant mood after winning the match) to Debs and stay over. We'd probably drive into Southampton and join the celebrations and have Deb try to find us in the early hours.

Kellie went to work on Thursday night. Her last words to me before she left for work was to make sure I was better company when I came home. By eight o'clock I was packed, the dogs were walked, I was bored with writing this rubbish and was at a loss. Maybe I should play FIFA17 on the PlayStation 4 and act out the match on Sunday? My superstitious cells in my brain started working overtime. Would this have a bearing on the game? What if we lose? Perhaps I ought to adjust the difficulty to 'Amateur' just to assure victory? But if I did that, would that count? My brain was now suffering from dumb thought fatigue, it had been going on like this for days.

I satisfied myself that if I did lose the match I could find a reason to make the match obsolete, so picked up my red and white Saints controller (I kid you not) and pressed 'X' to play.

I decided to go for realism and not pick Van Dyk who was injured, and I inhibited the computer from picking Rooney for Manchester United for the same reason. I played a 4-2-3-1, in a format slightly wider and more progressive than our manager Claude Puel tends to play. I picked the back four as expected, Bertrand – England full back, Yoshida – Japanese international central defender, Stephens – a young central defender drafted into the first team owing to our lack of central defensive options and Cédric – Portuguese international and European Championship winner last summer, with Forster in goal. There was no place for the new defender who had signed, Martín Cáceres: his pedigree was high but was not match fit and could not be risked. I had Oriel Romeu and Steven Davis (Captain) in the holding midfield positions, and Gabbiadini up front. Behind him I sprung a surprise and played Tadić in the middle with Ward-Prowse and Shane Long either side, at the expense of Nathan Redmond who, for me, has been lucky to get such a consistent run in the team. Other than Redmond for Long, I think this is the side that will play in the final for real.

The game loaded, supported ably by Martin Tyler and Alan Smith (former gangly Arsenal striker, big nose). Wembley was breath-taking, even on a PlayStation game on my 55-inch Sony TV. I could just about make out where I would be sitting. Nice seats.

Saints started well, keeping possession for long spells thanks to my ponderous abilities using a PlayStation controller. Manchester United's Chris Smalling was booked for a clumsy foul on Gabbiadini. Ward-Prowse's shot was straight at De Gea in the United goal. Saints pressed again, meticulously, cautiously, with Tadić forcing a second routine save out of De Gea. So far so good.

After twenty-five minutes, the game changed. United maintained a concerted spell of pressure as if they had suddenly woken to the task. Fraser Forster had to save down to his left to beat out a Juan Mata shot. Saints got penned in, unable to clear their lines. A cross came in that evaded Yoshida, and Ibrahimović struck like lightening to score. In the second half Saints huffed and puffed but created little. I replaced

Long with Redmond who did better, and brought on Jay Rodriguez for James Ward-Prowse. I pushed my team into a more attacking mindset. Martin Tyler mused that Manchester United were well on top. Alan Smith agreed. I suggested to them that they should perhaps go elsewhere and sew their seeds.

Tadić was ineffective and largely anonymous. The full backs Cédric, and particularly Bertrand were struggling to push forward. Davis and Romeu were overworked in midfield. These were real problems that Saints needed to solve on Sunday. If they could get Tadić on the ball in space, preferably centrally rather than out wide, we'd be more constructive and incisive. I often feel that if we can push Bertrand on, we tend to play better, and Cédric can put in a wicked cross. But neither was happening under my control and the second goal was inevitable, even though Forster had saved gamely from multiple United players. A second goal was scored by Mata with ten minutes to go. United won, and at a canter, and even though Saints were game in their application, had too little to question the United defence.

I could not help but think that this scenario could very well play out on the day. I do hope not. We'll only get once chance at this; I'll only have one chance at this. At least with FIFA17 I could replay the match again and again until I won, on the 'Amateur' skill level at that.

My flight was on the Friday, late at night. Kellie had come home from her work at 7:30 a.m. (working as officially the best Midwife in New Zealand) and we went for a cooked breakfast with Shauna, proudly wearing her new black Saints away shirt. They would be watching the game at home on the Monday, a 5:30 a.m. kick off for the poor souls left back in New Zealand.

The day at work was boring. I had lots to do to keep my excited mind occupied. By about 4:30 p.m. I was clock watching. I worked up to 7:00 then bimbled over to the International Terminal in my Saints shirt to drop my bags off (I checked-in online – it's the only way to travel in this day and age). I had purchased access to the airport lounge. There was no way I was going to rough it with riff-raff, and settled down. Time slowed. I was missing Kellie and the girls already. The stay in the airport was uneventful. By 11:10 p.m. I was sat in seat 55A, and was off to the Cup Final.

Playing the Game

The 1987 season was the last one that me and Dad were season ticket holders for a while. This was because I was moving from kid's football on Sundays to senior men's football on Saturdays.

From the age of eight I played in eleven-aside kids teams in the Southampton Tyro League. Many players came through the Southampton Tyro system including the likes of Steve Moran and Darren Anderton (formerly of Portsmouth and Tottenham Hotspur, I played against him when I was ten – he was rubbish!). I played Centre Forward, the number nine. I wasn't particularly good, I couldn't tackle, I wasn't a quick sprinter, my first touch wasn't always the best and there were always other players who were more skilful than me. But I had this knack of scoring goals, between the ages of nine and sixteen – lots of them. I was very quick when I received the ball, as fast as a whippet, could turn with the ball 'on a sixpence' and I just had an instinct for getting in the right positions, losing my marker, making runs across defences, and scoring goals. My goal celebration was always the Mick Channon windmill. Irrespective that we were winning 1-0 or losing 9-1, when I scored the celebration and joy was always the same.

I was always very distinctive when I played. I was tall but slight, my hair was blonde – opposition players and managers would always shout "Get hold of Blondie!" I had this lolloping gait that people told me reminded them of Chris Waddle, the former England, Newcastle United, Tottenham Hotspur and Marseille winger, hunched forward, arms dangling by my side or hands on my hips like some form of underdeveloped sub-human species, always looking completely knackered. But I would run and run and run and be a complete pain in the backside to opposition defences. I would pick the ball off of the defender's foot, harass them incessantly, and never give up. One guy who I played with said I had elbows like razor blades.

Dad placed me in teams that he called 'bum sides'. They weren't terrible teams, but they were never top of the table teams. This meant I never won anything (except the 1981 Southampton Tyro Six Aside Consolation Cup Runner Up medal, thank you very much), but importantly I played in every match and it was fun. I was never hanging about waiting to play as a substitute. Playing football in the seniors was never as much fun and I always longed to turn the clock back to my childhood matches.

Dad and our Old English Sheepdog Dougal would attend all matches. He would take up a position next to the opposition goalkeeper on the by-line away from the other supporters who would typically gather around the half way line. He told me I was a rubbish shot and said if I aimed at him and the dog, the ball was bound to go in. He wouldn't admit it, but as I got older and moved into the seniors, he would call out to the opposition goalkeeper, "Hey, 'keep? See blondie out there? That scrawny little bleeder? Well, he's going to sit you on your arse today. Mind your back picking the ball out of the net." Many, many times he would go back to the keeper after the match and tell him, "I told you so, didn't I?"

I wasn't a particularly nice kid, but as I got older the more unpleasant I became. On the 9th of January 1985, my inseparable best friend Mark was killed in a car accident on his way to school. I was devastated, as was Dad, as one of his very best mates was Mark's dad. I decided right then and there that friends were a waste of time, and I proceeded to extract myself from groups of people and alienate myself a little bit. My school work went downhill fast and my one escape was playing football. But I was becoming a right little prima donna, selfish both on and off the field – I'd even swear on the pitch at my team mates. I was fourteen, furious and a fool.

The coach at the time, of course another friend of Dad, took Dad to one side and said what I was doing could not go on. Dad just shrugged and said that he should go ahead and throw the book at me. On a Saturday morning after training, I was told about the way I was behaving and it shocked me. The coach threw me out of the team for a bit, and it became a catalyst for me to repair myself. I sorted my attitude, my school work, my relationships. I got everything straight. So much so that, in one game, a team mate, Michael, the coach's son and a friend of mine, shot for goal. It was deflected and dribbled along the goal line. All I had to do was to tap it in the goal, except when I got there, I held it up and beckoned Michael over to tap the ball in himself.

In my last junior season I was getting noticed. Opposition coaches would come over to my team and ask to talk to Blondie. They would shake my hand or pat me on the back and say things like "we just couldn't deal with you today", or "you were just too good", or "blimey you were a pain in the backside to us", or "you're going to go far". There was never any chance of me being good enough to be a professional – I knew I was never even close to being good enough. But it did mean that perhaps I could get a look in, in the Southampton Senior League set up, or even the Hampshire League.

When Dad left Saints, he went into Hampshire League football. It was a very high standard. The Saints third team, the 'A' team also played in that league up until the Eighties or Nineties. Above that was the Southern League, and above that the actual Football League. In my time, the Hampshire League's standing had diminished. The Football Conference now sat below the Football League as a feeder league, below that multiple Southern Leagues, and below that the Wessex League. But it was still a good quality league to kick about in. After talking to Dad about it, he said to just join in with the seniors at the local Colden Common football club during pre-season. He said, just do what I do and I'll get noticed. I did and I signed on with them before I was sixteen.

I loved being part of that club. I would go up on Saturday mornings and help get the pitches organised, mow some of the grass and put up the rope barriers around the ground. When I was playing, I'd see my name in the football programme. Some of the senior players looked after me and would look out for me. Ian Steele, although a Portsmouth fan, also helped out on a Saturday, as did others including Mr. King (Mark's dad) who owned the post-match boozer, the Black Horse and was chairman of the club (I always referred to him as Mr. King). At sixteen, the club put me on a diet of steak and Guinness to build me up. The steak was stolen out of the meat raffle prizes on each Sunday night, and I would hide in the pub in the corner with pint after pint of Guinness. By the time I was legally able to be in a pub, I was over going into them.

I was at Colden Common for about three years. In the first year they looked after me and brought me on as substitute for games, and travelled with the first team. When I wasn't in the team they farmed me out to Twyford to play in the low standard Winchester League. Whilst still sixteen, I equalled my Dad's record in playing in the Hampshire League when he was sixteen. I tried to gloat at him, but Dad had the perfect put down, "Listen, son – come back to me when you can keep your place in the Hampshire League for a season or two," he said, flatly. I scored my first goal in the Hampshire League against Blackfield and Langley with my willy. A cross came in that completely evaded the goalkeeper and I poked it in with my nob on the goal line, my eyes watering in pain. That season, I seemed to bag the goals for the first team in all the friendly matches they called me up for.

In the second and third seasons there, I settled in with the Reserve side, in the Southampton League. The Colden Common first team was improving, and in a few years they would be Hampshire League Champions – at that level at seventeen was beyond me. I'd scored some goals but found myself being a 'confidence' player. If I felt good and was doing well, I would do well. If things were not going well, I sometimes struggled. Dad never, ever said that I had a bad game. I always played well according to him.

I remember in my second season, we were joined in pre-season by a new kid Steve Guppy. He looked a bit like me, and we would always get paired together and hit it off well. He would be my strike partner in the team. The main difference between him and I was that he was good and I wasn't. At the start of pre-season he was pretty non-descript. But his rate of improvement started to accelerate. At the start of pre-season I could beat him in sprints, by the time the season started he was leaving me and everyone else at the club for dead. He stayed with the second team with me for about two months of the season, then was off with the first team. By Christmas, nobody could get the ball off him. Later that season he had a trial with Southampton, which Saints were foolish to reject him, then signed for Wycombe Wanderers in the Football League, managed by the legendary Nottingham Forest and Northern Ireland manager Martin O'Neill (and who played against Saints in the 1979 Cup Final). He went on to play for Leicester City for many seasons and Celtic, and played for England too and had a first class career.

In one match when both of us were playing, I got substituted towards the end. This bloke came over to me. "Are you Steve Guppy?" he asked. I don't know why I did this but I responded, "Yes I am!"

The scout told me he was from Exeter City, another Football League team, and expressed how impressed he was with me/Steve, and whether I would like to go for a trial. I told him sure, that would be great. I don't know who was the biggest idiot me or him; he marched back to me after the match demanding I give him the card back. As it happened he'd been talking to a scout of another club, Coventry City, who put him straight. That's how close I got to the big time – off someone else's talent! Dad said I was a prick.

At the start of the next season, Colden Common organised a charity match against the Lord Taverners XI. The Lord Taverners are a registered charity to play football and cricket all around the country. The team is normally filled with famous people from stage and screen. I got in the team that day, in front of hundreds and hundreds of people, and scored a great volleyed goal too.

It wasn't a great day though, all in all. The Taverners' goalkeeper was Ray Winstone, a famous tough guy actor who, at the time wasn't that famous but still doing the hard-man routine. He spent the match being abusive to his team mates who he thought were inferior. It was awkward for the supporters. Dad could be heard telling Winstone to "settle down" from his normal position beside the goal. There were complaints after the event because it was felt that the Lord Taverners players weren't all that well known.

In the third season things went wrong. My season started fantastically well, confident, playing well, lots of goals, getting lots of plaudits and pats on the backs from other players, I felt ten feet tall. "Bloody marvellous!" my Dad would keep saying, proud as punch. Then I got a kick on the knee that side-lined me for two weeks. When I was fit again I only played once more. The club had invested in a youth team and I was getting in the way of players in the new youth team progressing, so I had to go. It didn't go down well with certain people at the club, but it was what it was and I had to move on.

My nephew Dan also got to play for Colden Common. He was a much better player than me. He jumped straight into the Colden Common's first team midfield and stayed there for a few years. Me and Dad were really proud of Dan for this, but only Dad could go and see him play. I refused to set foot back at Colden Common again as I had felt I had been treated very badly and in fairness a lot of others at the club felt the same. I never did see Daniel play.

I'd also been playing Sunday for Totten Youth for a season. I played at some great semi-professional grounds, even against a United States representative team (scored a very good goal that day too). But I was relieved when I got a call one Friday night saying I wouldn't be playing the following Sunday. Two games in a week end was too tough for me and frankly, the other players at Totten were simply much better than I was.

I played for Otterbourne for couple of seasons in the Hampshire League and then West End. I was struggling with my knee however. I would play a couple of games then it would get sore. I'd need two weeks to recuperate, then fight my way back in the team, get settled in the team, only for my knee to go again. It was now 1993 and I was twenty-two. I felt it was time to walk away from it all. So I did, and never went back. The Saints had been waiting patiently for me.

(Incidentally, I found out from Dad a few years ago, that the Colden Common football programme was running a 'where are they now?'

column. Apparently, I was the subject matter one week and apparently, I am held in high regard still. That's nice.)

Dad was really disappointed. He could not understand how I could just walk away from playing. But I did, and whilst I do regret it from time to time, it was the right thing to do. Sarah came along three years later and I was a family man now with no time for such nonsense – even going to watch the Saints became limited to only a few times a season because of cost and higher priorities.

Saints had continued to decline from their heyday in 1984 when we finished runners-up to Liverpool. In 1987 they had finished twelfth, and as well as me and Dad they had lost the services of some of their best ever servants, Steve Moran to Leicester City, the legendary Peter Shilton left for Derby County, David Armstrong left for Bournemouth, Mark Dennis went to Queens Park Rangers, and Nick Holmes retired. The following year they finished twelfth again and in 1989 thirteenth.

Then, in 1990, Saints enjoyed a bit of a renaissance. Their well-regarded youth policy continued to provide players. Joining Danny Wallace was brother Rodney and brother Ray. All three played against Sheffield Wednesday during the previous season, making some sort of record. Saints had also brought through the combative defender Francis Benali, and cheaply purchased soon-to-be England goalkeeper Tim Flowers and defender Jason Dodd. In 1988, Alan Shearer made his debut for Saints in a 4-2 thrashing of Arsenal. Shearer scored a hat-trick that day, but it wasn't until 1990 that he became a solid fixture in the side. Danny Wallace, Tim Flowers and Alan Shearer would all go on to play for England. (Incidentally, Danny Wallace scored on his one and only appearance for England against Egypt in 1986. He remains to this day, according to The Guardian, the last player to represent England in a moustache.)

The team came of age in a 4-1 thrashing of Liverpool who that season would reclaim the league title (and to this day, their last). But things seemed to go south after that. Saints finished only fourteenth in 1991 and Chris Nicholl was sacked, replaced by Ian Branfoot who ushered in a new style of football, hoof-it-up-front-and-kick-anything-that-moves style of football that appealed to no one – certainly not the supporters who stayed away in their droves. Branfoot 'guided' Saints to a sixteenth place finish in 1992, close to the relegation zone, and bettered that in the newly formed Premier League in 1993 with Saints finishing eighteenth, just two places shy of the relegation zone. Branfoot was rewarded for the poor football and declining attendances with a new three-year contract.

This may seem like the most oddest of times to re-acquaint myself with my team, but re-acquaint myself I did for the 1994 season.

However, I went with friends, not Dad. He did go to some games too, but he would sit in the West Stand of the Dell whilst I stood with mates in the Milton Road end.

Saints were on the downward slope heading out of the Premier League. However, there was a shining jewel in Southampton's crown (or halo?), Matthew Le Tissier.

2001

*The Premier League, Southampton versus Arsenal. The Dell, Southampton,
Saturday, 15th of May, 2001.*

Matt Le Tissier was the most sensational footballer I ever had the
privilege of watching. There were world class players kicking around
the Premier League during the Nineties such as Thierry Henry, Dennis
Bergkamp and Eric Cantona, but none of them came near to the sheer
poetry, creativity, beauty, drama and skill of Le Tissier. Best of all
though Le Tissier played for Saints, and amazingly stayed there
throughout his career.

I recall a pre-season friendly at the start of the 1987 season when
Saints played Benfica of Portugal. I think it was for Nick Holmes'
testimonial (benefit matches such as these were awarded to players with
ten years of service to the same club, and afforded the player the
opportunity to take home the gate receipts. In this day and age when
players earn a million pounds a minute, the concept of a testimonial has
become almost defunct and vulgar). Le Tissier was named as one of
many substitutes. Because it was a friendly, teams could nominate as
many substitutes as they liked and teams usually agreed to make
unlimited substitutions during such matches. I remember there were
too many substitutes to fit into the dugout with the manager so a bench
was set up next to the dugout. Throughout the first half I could not
help noticing this young kid fidget on the bench, evidentially keen to
play. When he got an opportunity to play in the second half, both me
and Dad thought he was sensational.

Sensational doesn't even begin to describe him. In his first four
seasons as he was gradually introduced into the team he scored 47
goals.

Le Tissier was six feet one inch and thin in those early years, with a
languid style that confused casual onlookers and press. He would drift
past defenders as if they weren't there, leaving them scratching their

heads or flat on their backside. He could cross the ball with pinpoint accuracy and with extreme pace. He could play a perfect pass over ten metres, twenty, thirty, forty or fifty. Against champions Blackburn Rovers at the beginning of the 1995 season he played the most sublimely accurate pass of about seventy metres, to play in our striker to score. His vision and intelligence in the game meant he could simply see things that no other player could. His close control was incredible, as if the ball was literally glued to his feet. At other times, he could coerce the ball under control as if it were tied to him by elastic. He was a prolific goal scorer and was only the sixth player to reach 100 goals in the Premier League. He could score goals direct from the corner, something he did on multiple occasions, ferociously whipping the ball in from the corner flag, arcing level with the six-yard area and bending back in to the corner of the goal, the goalkeeper always floundering aimlessly on the goal line. Against Wimbledon in the 1999 season, his goal from the corner was later awarded to a defender as an own goal. If you see the goal on YouTube, judge for yourself – I don't think anyone got anywhere close to it.

Best of all, his goals were incredible. There is this thing in England that if an English player scored a great goal, journalists or commentators would say that it was a goal befitting a Brazilian. Le Tissier scored 209 goals in 541 matches for Southampton; an excellent record for a striker – except he normally played in midfield. I think about seventy percent of those goals would be equivalent or better than what a Brazilian could do.

If Saints got a penalty, we always celebrated it like a goal because it was a near certainty he would score. His record was 47 penalties scored out of 48. In the one match that he missed a penalty, against Nottingham Forest in 1993, he scored a wonder goal by volleying in from 30 yards from the apex of the penalty box, just to make up for the miss. Dad would cheer "Never bloody misses!" at anyone who would listen as Le Tissier would invariably score from the spot.

Such was his standing in the game, if a match didn't have a moment of brilliance or magic from him it would be reported on. In some matches I would watch in total awe as to what I had seen, thinking to myself that'll be on the telly no doubt, only to find it not shown nor reported on. Against Queens Park Rangers one year he took a shot from the kick off at the start of the second half that sent the goalkeeper scrambling to save it. I wasn't sure if the goalkeeper stopped the shot or it hit the bar. I do remember even the referee applauded it, but it didn't get on the TV. In a match against Everton I saw him pick up the ball in his own half, wander past two Everton players, cut inside and unleashed an astonishing low shot from about thirty-five yards out that bent like a banana from right to left and smacked the base of the post, with the Everton goalkeeper Southall with no hope to save the shot. It was a breathless effort that, despite waiting until late on the Saturday night to see again on TV, never got air time. And this was part of the problem with Le Tissier. With any normal mortal player, this action would be shown again and again. With Le Tissier it was simply expected, almost par for the course. But whilst the tabloid hacks and tired television journalists used to take him for granted, preferring to wallow in the clichéd non-stories of the top four teams in the Premier League, we never took it for granted and enjoyed every moment of it knowing full well that we would never see a player like this ever again.

It was a crime that Le Tissier obtained only eight England caps (yes, you read that right, only eight caps). Instead of building a national team around Le Tissier, managers were just too afraid to pick him. He wasn't particularly a difficult player to manage, wasn't the type to have tantrums, wasn't particularly controversial, but he didn't fit into the perceived mould of what an English player should be. It seems certain that had Le Tissier been Brazilian, Spanish or French, he would have enjoyed a glittering international career. But because he was English and didn't defend or kick players, he couldn't play for his country.

It wasn't just Le Tissier who couldn't get a game for England. For most England teams, it has been pretty stock standard behaviour for the manager to omit their best players and populate their teams with nondescript triers. Just think of James Milner (61 caps), Phil Neville (59 caps), Glen Johnson (54 caps), David Batty (42 caps), Steve McManaman (37 caps), Trevor Steven (36 caps), Stewart Downing (35 caps), Steve Hodge (24 caps), Darius Vassell (22 caps), Carlton Palmer (18 caps) and Andy Sinton (12 caps). How on earth did these players have such a far more fulfilling career in an England shirt than Le Tissier?

Then how about those flamboyant or high-quality players from down the years that also didn't get the recognition at international level; Frank Worthington (8 caps), Stan Bowles (5 caps), Peter Osgood (4 caps), Alan Hudson (2 caps), Jimmy Greenhoff (0 caps), Jimmy Case (0 caps). I noticed when researching this that other top-class Englishmen Ian Wright only managed 33 caps and Glenn Hoddle, possibly the only player to hold a candle to Le Tissier, only managed 53 caps – six less than what Phil Neville managed.

Le Tissier had a reputation as a lazy player, one who doesn't track back and defend and tackle. It was all nonsense of course. Britain must be the only place on the planet where technical ability and vision is secondary to hard work and disciplined tough defending. The fact that successful managers of England were fearful of building a team around

Le Tissier says more about the inadequacies of the English game than it does about the perceived inadequacies of Le Tissier. Nobody complains about Lionel Messi's or Cristiano Ronaldo's work rate. Nobody ever raged about Diego Maradona not being so great in a tackle. Each of these players had teams built around them, and won top trophies.

The fact of the matter was, Le Tissier played for Southampton, and journalists didn't like coming all the way down Southampton. They liked to stay in London and Lancashire, at the bigger grounds, that offered the press a better food selection at half-time. The journalists preferred to be complacent and absorb what was happening at the big clubs. Eric Cantona was playing for Manchester United at the time, and was trumpeted as the Premier League's finest player. Cantona also scored great goals, although not at the same regularity or with the same spectacle as Le Tissier. Cantona also made goals too, and made things happen out of nothing, just like Le Tissier did too, except Le Tissier created more chances and goals for Southampton at the bottom of the league, than Cantona did for Manchester United at the top of the league. Yet the ordinary fan in the armchair got to see Cantona each week, as Manchester United were always paraded live on the television, whereas Le Tissier would pop up on TV three or four times a season, his goals consigned to Saturday late night Match Of The Day. As a result, history records the likes of Cantona were better than Le Tissier. The advantage I have is that I saw Le Tissier play live every week, as well as seeing Cantona on the television, and with this much better balanced perspective I feel qualified to say that Le Tissier was far the superior.

I recall listening to Liverpool versus Saints on BBC Five Live in the 1994 season. Saints lost the match 4-2 but Le Tissier scored both our goals. The commentator, the whingy Irishman Alan Greene said during the first half that it was the first time he had seen Le Tissier play and couldn't understand why there was such a fuss about his talent (context: Greene was BBC Five Live's top radio commentator and Le Tissier had been playing for Saints for eight years – and this was the *first time* he had seen him play). He went on to say that yes, he had scored a fantastic goal (separately looping the ball over former Saint and now Liverpool defender Mark Wright twice, before crashing the volley past the goalkeeper Grobbelaar at close range), and that, yes he had struck a fantastic shot that hit the post that brought a crescendo of applause even from the home fans and was – I quote "worth the entry money alone", but other than that, Le Tissier had done precious little in that half to warrant all the talk about him. I was listening with Dad that day and we were floored by the stupidity of the comments. I so wish I had that recorded but I never forgot it: right there was the problem with English football. And boy did we chuckle about it.

Football attitudes in Britain have always been very backward-thinking. Even in the 1880's the English football team used to refuse to take corners or pass to an opponent, because it was felt unchivalrous, unsporting and cowardly. In the 1930's England refused to enter the World Cup and proclaimed they were the true champions of the world when in fact the average English player was beginning to fall behind many other countries in Europe and South America.

In the 1950's England were beaten 6-3 and 7-1 by Hungary in the space of a year. Much head scratching and soul searching was performed to try and understand how Johnny Foreigner had beaten them. The fact that Hungary were tactically better, wore lighter boots, were fitter and more tactically aware seemed to miss the English hierarchy altogether. As far as we were concerned the approach of a couple of pints of stout before a match before sticking it up 'em was only the right and proper way to play. Carl Linde, a notable Swedish writer lamented, "The sorriest feature in this drama is that the English, with very few exceptions, cannot get themselves to recognise what has happened. In their self-satisfaction and conceit they still fancy themselves as first in the world and their defeats sheer accidents".

An English mindset of blood and thunder football, heart on the sleeve stuff, boot the ball forward, and boot the opponent upward hasn't really changed to this day. Understanding this starts to explain why Le Tissier did not get the chance he richly deserved. For instance, today, at the very top level it is obvious that tackling is no longer the most viable way to obtain the ball from your opponent. A tackle means the defender has to commit themselves to a challenge, often off their feet with no control of where the ball goes until after the challenge is made. Top modern teams like Real Madrid and Barcelona don't tend to tackle because it risks their player being momentarily out of the game, getting a yellow card or a foul, getting injured, or simply it gives the ball away. Instead they work hard at jockeying and harrying opposition players and denying them space until an opposition player ends up giving the ball away to an upright player in control of the ball. Yet, listening in on the Internet to pundits and ex-players on TalkSport and BBC Five Live, we still covet the tackle and demand that players tackle more. It's plain stupid and backwards. The English mentality remains decades behind and the national team will remain a bit of a joke for decades to come.

You can't argue that Le Tissier's laid back style and his decision to stay with Saints rather than pocket a giant pay cheque with a London team, affected his opportunities with England. Le Tissier's English nadir was the 1998 World Cup. He'd been injured the previous summer and pulled out of the summer English friendlies, and he had to work extra hard on his form to get close to the squad again, given that he was in a team in the lower, not upper, reaches of the Premier League. Prior to the World Cup a match was organised with all the fringe players for England against some of the fringe players for Russia (England B versus Russia B). Me and Dad watched the match together at me and Kellie's mid-terrace home in Eastleigh, and we marvelled as Le Tissier scored a hat-trick in excellent overall performance where he simply ran the show from the first minute to the last, like a conductor in an orchestra. The Daily Mail reported the next morning that his performance was "perhaps the finest ever performance by any player in an England shirt". However, that was still not sufficient to warrant a call up to the squad. More confusing still, the English manager was Glenn Hoddle, a like-minded player from a previous generation who was also mistrusted by the England manager of the day because he was talented.

I wonder in the modern game today whether a Le Tissier could exist as a player. The athletic nature of the game today, and the demands placed on players from such a young age, I doubt that such a player could be allowed to be cultivated.

And he's a thoroughly nice bloke too. I had my stag night at his and comedian's Mike Osman's bar in Southampton. I was invited to his table and Mike Osman bought me a bottle of champagne. I recall I was going to buy Matt a drink, he asked for a Malibu and Coke, but in my drunken stupor I forgot. In 2002, after the start-up company I was with went bust, I took the family to Disneyland Paris. On the first day there, me, Kellie and the kids were having a wonderful time minding our own business when an official from Disney came up to me. I was wearing my red and white Saints top with 'Le Tissier – 7' on the back. The official advised me that Mr. Le Tissier was in the park today and that it was not appropriate for me to wear the shirt. Very shortly after we were in a shop with the kids when this guy came up behind me.

"Don't think much of your shirt, mate!" he said. I looked round and it was Mr. Le Tissier himself. I remember we had a little chat (I was sure I was a bumbling idiot) and I recall he asked me if I wanted a photo. I told him that was not necessary and that I didn't want to intrude on his family's holiday. Can you believe I did that? What a nob head I was.

In 2011, I reached a birthday milestone around my late thirties-ish. Mum acquired Matt's phone number somehow and simply called him to ask if he would sign a shirt and address it to me. Matt happily agreed (in return for a charity donation) and the shirt has pride of place in my house: "To Russell. Happy Birthday. All the best, mate."

One of Dad's best stories was when he found himself in the same pub as Ian Porterfield. Ian Porterfield was a former Scottish professional player who, at the time Dad met him, was the Bolton Wanderers assistant manager, and had previously been manager for a time at Chelsea where he publicly sacked goalkeeper Dave Beasant (who coincidentally would be at Southampton by the time this meeting happened). Saints had beaten Bolton Wanderers 1-0 that day and consigned Bolton to relegation. Dad had gone to watch the match with friends and they had found themselves in the same pub that night as the assistant manager of the team that had just been relegated. Inevitably, the winning goal was from Le Tissier, and so Dad moved in for some conversation.

Porterfield was old school: discipline and tough defending, tick; blood and thunder football, tick; boot the ball forward, tick. Matt Le Tissier? No thank you. Porterfield had no time for the type of player Le Tissier was. His argument was that when the going got tough where would Le Tissier be?

"He'd be scoring a bloody wonder goal out of nothing to win the match!" Dad argued.

Porterfield disagreed completely. "The lad would go missing," was the counter-argument.

"Bollocks!" Dad pressed on, "You're wrong about Le Tissier, mate! Completely wrong!". And Dad pressed on further, demanding to know why he had publicly fired his goalkeeper at Chelsea. Why did he do that? What did it prove? If a 'keeper was having a bad time of it, castigating him in public was not the way to do it. Porterfield got relegated and a king-size flea in his ear for his trouble that evening. Not even the pros were immune from Dad.

Both little Luke and Ryan have met Le Tissier in the last year or so, but they were not impressed. They said he looked too fat and too old to be a footballer. He did retire fifteen years ago, to be fair boys.

You can't really do Le Tissier justice on the page. Just go to YouTube and watch the goals for yourself. I have his video, 'Unbelievable' with all his goals on it. It has been loaned to many Kiwis over the years to enrich their footballing education.

In the 1994 season, incredibly Branfoot dropped Le Tissier and left him to fester in the reserves. It was an inspired move from the manager, as Saints lost four and drew two whilst Le Tissier was away from the first team. He was brought back for the home match against Newcastle United, who were being managed by Kevin Keegan and were taking the Premier League by storm.

Newcastle United battered us that night. Saints barely had a kick and it was the kind of match you watched through your hands, almost unable to look. Newcastle missed chance after chance after chance. After an hour it was, incredibly, still 0-0. In a rare attempt at an attack, Le Tissier received a difficult ball that was delivered behind him. With the heel of his left leg he flicked the pass back over his own head, took a touch with his right leg that hooked the ball past a first Newcastle defender, looped the ball high over another defender with his next touch, collected the ball ten yards out and stroked the ball along the ground in to the far corner of the net. It was an unbelievable goal. What a privilege it was to see it.

Newcastle equalised ten minutes later and threatened again to go on and win which, in truth, they fully deserved. But Le Tissier wasn't done. With three minutes to go, a hopeful cross into the Newcastle penalty area was only half headed clear, the ball came back to Saints midfielder Neil Maddison, who nudged it with his head to Le Tissier. Le Tissier, receiving the ball with his back to goal, twenty yards out, popped the ball on to his right thigh, juggled the ball up and unleashed an unstoppable dipping shot into the back of the net to win the game. It was absolute daylight robbery, but combined, the two best goals you will ever see in a game of football. Dad missed this match. He was having a dirty weekend with Mum.

Le Tissier's magic couldn't paper over the cracks. Saints were dire and pretty much unsalvageable half way through the season. At Christmas, we only had fourteen points. Normally you need forty points to stay up by the season's end. With attendances dropping to nearly 11,000, the club finally removed Branfoot and brought in Alan Ball, who had been managing in the lower leagues, and Lawrie McMenemy returned to act as support as Director of Football.

Everything changed overnight. Ball modified the approach: he told the players that there was one world class player in the team, and that their job was to give the ball to Le Tissier. The quality of football improved – it was like watching a different team. With Le Tissier at the fulcrum of the team he blossomed into by far the best player in the league bar none.

Results immediately improved, beating Coventry and Newcastle again (thanks to Le Tissier in both games). Liverpool came to a snowy Dell on Valentine's Day to what became known as the Valentine's Day Massacre. I went to the match but also recorded it on TV and loved watching it back. That night the pundits were Mick Channon and Phil Thompson, former Liverpool player. Both were asked what they thought about Le Tissier. Channon, the only player in Saints' history to have scored more goals for the club than Le Tissier, waxed lyrical about his talents in his country accent. There was, according to Channon 'no better player around'. Phil Thompson, in the fear talent/blood and thunder camp, said that Le Tissier 'wasn't his type of player' and if he had the money would "keep his money in his pockets".

Le Tissier had his first goal in that match after twenty-eight-seconds, from about twenty-eight yards which went past Grobbelaar like a bullet: the ball hit the back of the net and bounced back on to the pitch before Grobbelaar had even finished his dive. A Le Tissier corner was headed in to make it 2-0 after just six minutes. And Le Tissier scored two penalties either side of half-time to make it 4-0.

At half-time, Mick Channon had a grin on like a Cheshire cat, whilst Thompson was decidedly uncomfortable. Le Tissier had run the show completely and Channon was only too pleased to crow about it. "He said, keep yer money in yer pockets!" he raved, pointing at the squirming Thompson who looked as though he wanted to be anywhere else but at The Dell with a camera pointed at him.

Next up, Wimbledon. In a hard-fought game, with fifteen minutes left, Saints had a free kick, twenty yards from goal, dead centre to it. Le Tissier stood a couple of yards back from the free kick taker, who rolled the ball to him. Le Tissier flicked the ball up with his right foot to juggle, and blasted a devastating shot past the Wimbledon goalkeeper. Another three points won by Le Tissier and suddenly we looked in good shape to stay up. Every game seemed to have incredible breath-taking moments of brilliance. As an asthmatic, I was needing to take my inhaler to games!

Then the team hit a bit of a blip and started to sink back down the table into real trouble again. Saints went to Norwich City needing to win. At half-time it was 1-1. Norwich sped into a 3-1 lead early in the second half, only for Le Tissier to score twice to equalise at 3-3. Norwich went ahead again 4-3 in the very next minute. But this whole Southampton team had a steely resolve: Le Tissier scored his hat-trick third with fifteen minutes to go to make it 4-4 and Saints won the game in the final minute 5-4 when defender Ken Monkou headed in from a Le Tissier corner. The Great Escape was back on. Le Tissier then inspired Saints to two magnificent victories against top teams Blackburn Rovers 3-1, and Aston Villa 4-1. Le Tissier was either the provider or scorer of every goal in those matches.

The fans were in total hero worship of Le Tissier by now. Every time he came near the touch line, for instance to take a corner, fans would stand their arms aloft, and bow to him. He had acquired the nickname Le God, and the Daily Echo placed posters on the edge of the city saying, 'You Are Now Entering [Le] God's Country', on a par with the Seventies graffiti 'Jesus Saves – but Channon scores the rebound'.

Survival in the Premier League came down to the final match of the season away at West Ham United. Permutations were complicated: two from Everton, Ipswich Town, Oldham Athletic and Sheffield United, as well as Saints could still go down along with the already relegated Swindon Town. As Saints were outside the relegation zone by the final day, they needed a result that was better than two of their competing teams to stay up. A win would guarantee their safety.

A Saturday in May in London was a great way to end the season. I was there with friends that day, with Dad listening from home. Saints conceded a goal early and struggled for much of the first half. Then, right on half-time Saints gained a free kick, twenty-yards out. The action was at the other end of the ground from us but we could see where Le Tissier was going to put it. The top left of the goal was gaping – we knew the ball was going in before he had taken his kick. The fact that he put it in the top right to score mattered not.

A goal right on half-time changes things and Saints came out in the second half hungry. Le Tissier completely bamboozled the West Ham defence before crossing for Maddison to score, right in front of us. Saints then conceded a bad goal to make it 2-2. Nerves were frayed. Elsewhere Everton had come from behind 2-0 to lead Wimbledon 3-2 and Sheffield United were winning at Chelsea. We all had radios so we could keep up with the scores from other grounds. Murmurs and mutterings would filter around the ground and cheers would go up during open play when a result would go our way. Once again, Le Tissier took control, juggling the ball and eluding West Ham players to lift the ball over the defence for our striker Iain Dowie to score. He was pulled down before he had chance to shoot so Le Tissier took the penalty to put us 3-2 up with twenty-five minutes to play. Saints held on until the last few minutes when the West Ham fans invaded the pitch. The game was delayed a few minutes and by that time we knew the scores in the other matches. Everton had won (shame) but Sheffield United had lost. Saints would stay up provided when the game restarted they did not concede three goals. They did concede one and the game was eventually drawn. It was an unforgettable season, which ended with hundreds of West Ham fans charging across the pitch seemingly to engage with Saints fans in a fight. As they reached the penalty box, they stopped, and en masse applauded the Saints away contingent. That was a relief, I was right near the front!

Saints progressed brilliantly under Alan Ball in the 1995 season and finished in the top ten. They purchased and sold within their means, and Liverpool's goalkeeper Bruce Grobbelaar joined us. Speculation around Le Tissier's future was inevitable but thankfully, he stayed put. The quality of football was much improved, the style of football was much improved and even Le Tissier got even better, despite only sporadic appearances in an England shirt. Highlights included home wins against Ipswich Town, Everton, Arsenal, Newcastle United and Tottenham Hotspur.

Le Tissier's top moments were plentiful. Against Blackburn Rovers home (seventy-yard pass assist), Aston Villa (last minute wonder goal), Tottenham Hotspur away (ran the show, scored both goals), and four goals against Huddersfield Town. At Coventry City away, Ipswich Town and Everton at home (scored and ran the show in wins). Le Tissier scored an incredible goal in an away loss at Blackburn Rovers where he received the ball around half way sauntered past three Blackburn defenders and lashed a swinging shot in from thirty yards. At home to Aston Villa he scored a last minute free kick to win the game, another wonder goal at home to Wimbledon on Boxing Day, scored a hat-trick in a 6-0 win over Luton Town, ran the show in yet another win over Newcastle, scored two and ran the show in a 4-3 home win against Tottenham Hotspur, scored in a 2-0 away win at Chelsea (great night, that one!), orchestrated victory at Wimbledon with a goal, and then at home to Crystal Palace. Overall, he scored 30 goals in 49 appearances.

Alan Ball was allowed to leave for Manchester City the following summer. It was sad because the entertainment he produced was off the scale and he was the manager, more than any other manager, that brought the absolute best out of Le Tissier. I just wonder, had Ball been allowed to continue, whether Saints continued improvement would have enhanced Le Tissier's reputation. As it was, Saints reverted back to their struggling ways in the seasons to come.

In the 1996 season, Saints again had to fight to stay in the league on the final day. They had given themselves a platform to survive by beating Manchester United 3-1 at home. This was the match that United players changed their kit at half-time, citing an inability to see each other in their fancy grey away strip. Saints led 3-0 by half-time, Le Tissier contributing one goal, and everything that was good about Saints play that day. Again, the permutations were endless but the same: get a better result than Coventry City or Manchester City to survive. All three teams drew, Saints 0-0 at home to Wimbledon, meaning that Manchester City, managed by Alan Ball sadly, were relegated.

It was the same the next season. Although unlikely, a series of results could have conspired to send Saints down. They didn't and Saints survived again. That season was the year we beat Manchester United 6-3. A memorable game, including another superlative goal from Le Tissier, chipping the giant Manchester United goalkeeper Peter Schmeichel from only twenty yards, after beating two players. On YouTube, watch goal number five for Saints, scored by Saints' Norwegian striker Egil Østenstad. Watch how he goes into the crowd to celebrate. Watch the nob head in the black and white jacket bouncing around and knocking his brother-in-law's hat off. That nob head is me.

At this point it was time for me to bow out of regular Saints watching. Sarah had been born and frankly I wanted to be around her just a bit more than I wanted to be at the football. I listened on the radio, saved pockets of cash at a time when money was tight, and hung out with her instead. Then Kellie squeezed out Shauna in April 1998 in between long chats with the paediatrician about Ronan Keating. Now I had two daughters to share my bed time stories with - not the normal bed time stories babies and toddlers get, more football orientated ones. I'd pop both girls in the same bed and settle them down to recite a story. One of my particular favourites was Saints beating Manchester United 6-3.

"Poor old Alex Ferguson. He didn't look very happy and was very red in the face. United's Roy Keane had been sent off for a terrible, terrible foul – he was very naughty, and Saints were winning 1-0. Then, Matty received the ball on the edge of the box, beat one man, beat another man, and from the edge of the box, hooked the ball high up in to the air. So high in fact that the goalie couldn't reach it and the ball came down into the goal to make it 2-0 to Saints! Hooray!" Proper bed time stories.

As babies and toddlers, they would get decked out in mini shirts and cuddly Saints toys. They even had bibs with 'Saints best dribbler' on them. Whether Saints were on the radio or on TV, I'd have one of them cuddled up into my arms, snoozing happily, until we scored, or conceded, or went close, or a bad refereeing decision was made, at which point poor Shauna or Sarah would wake up startled.

Saints again flirted with the drop in the 1999 season. With four games to go things were looking very grim indeed. What was worse, me and Kellie had to go to a wedding that day. Fortunately, Saints were playing away, at Derby County. After the church service, I snuck out to listen to the match in my car, whilst the photographs were being taken. Half way through the second half, it was still 0-0 and very, very tense. I had been joined by a number of other guys from the wedding service. The car doors were open and radio turned up so all who had gathered round could hear. The bride was furious, but to be fair, I hadn't noticed that the groom was sitting in the back seat listening on too.

On the final day of the 1999 season, Saints needed a win against Everton. Le Tissier inspired them to it, with Saints' small, new Latvian striker Marians Pahars scoring both goals. Pahars was another great acquisition for the team. At the time we signed him it looked like one of those dubious unknown signings from the backwaters of European football, but he was a diminutive, quick player and a natural goal scorer, and was a great servant to the Saints. In the 2000 season Glenn Hoddle became Saints new manager. His relationship with Le Tissier remained frosty. But Le Tissier was beginning to suffer from niggling injuries and an ongoing Achilles problem, so his presence in the team started to fade. By the end of the following 2001 season, Hoddle had smelt a better offer from Tottenham Hotspur – his former club, and left Saints to play their final ever game at The Dell without him.

Since the Hillsborough disaster, the Taylor Report demanded that all clubs needed to abandon standing areas and ensure all stadia were seating only. This reduced The Dell capacity from 25,000 in 1982 when I started going, to 15,000 in its last few seasons. This wasn't sustainable for the financial demands of Premier League football. So eventually, Saints built a new home back in St Mary's, a stone's throw from the place they were formed by the St Mary's Young Men Association, and where Dad grew up.

The penultimate match at The Dell was against Manchester United. Dad was able to source tickets from a bloke up the pub, but we knew with The Dell holding so few people now, it was unlikely we could get two tickets for both matches. The word on the street was we could only have one for both matches. So we agreed I'd take the United ticket, and Dad could have the ticket for the final match against Arsenal. So oddly, I went to the United match on my own. It was a good game too, Saints winning splendidly 2-1. I said my goodbyes to the old place, but then, as luck would have it, Dad came up with two tickets to see the last match at The Dell against Arsenal. (I knew he would!)

Dad had loads of odd ball friends that he could collude with in the pub, scrounge tickets or find out which player drinks where. Whenever a player was in the Black Horse pub, I'd be sent for to come and meet them. I remember a magnificent frame containing all the FA Cup Final programmes from, I think, 1970 until 1978, including Saints' triumph in 1976. As a kid I would spend much of the time behind the bar and in the house, playing and hanging out with Mark over a game of Subbuteo, but after he died, and as I grew up I would be at the bar as part of my senior football, building my weight with Guinness.

My favourite of Dad's best chums was Keith Bennett, or Mr. Bennett as I would always have to call him. He was the feared Deputy Headmaster at my primary school. Such was the friendship between them, I would be at school when Mr. Bennett would burst in to class, then apologise to the class teacher and demand to have a word with me. He was a large rounded man, with a balding head who would tower over the children. The class would gasp in fear as he entered the room, and as I walked out of the classroom the other kids would mumble to themselves.

Once outside the classroom, Mr. Bennett would close the classroom door and bellow, "Now then, Budden!" I would, however, be totally calm – having been through this routine many times.

Mr. Bennett would make sure the door to the classroom was closed and then crouch down to my level, placing his hands on his knees and talking in a much softer voice.

"I was just wondering, young Russell. Is your Dad on nights or days at work this week?" he would ask.

"Days." I'd reply.

"What?"

"Day's, Mr. Bennett," I'd correct myself.

"That's better. Excellent. Would you be kind enough to ask your father if he would come out for a drink this Thursday? You may get him to ring me, or you should drop by my office before 8:45 a.m. tomorrow to tell me if he is available."

"Yes, Mr. Bennett."

"Excellent. Thank you very much young Russell. You are a good boy, even if you do support Southampton. Now back to class and—"

Suddenly Mr. Bennett's voice would rise sharply again. "—Don't do it again!" He'd always sign off with a wink.

Back to class I'd go, with classmates desperate to find out what I had done. Of course, I was sworn to absolute secrecy so I had to tell people that I wasn't allowed to say. This seemed to make what I had done even worse, and that bit more impressive.

He was a dominating character and feared by the kids, but he was brilliant. I was in his class for a year, and at the end of the first day he called me over and told me that, because of his close friendship with my Dad, it would be twice as hard for me in his class. He explained to me that he couldn't be seen to carry me any favours and therefore he would be far tougher on me than with any pupil. It was the best year of school I had in my life. He was a brilliant teacher.

He wasn't perfect though. He was a Portsmouth supporter, at a time when Portsmouth were in the third or fourth tier of English football, much like they are today. Although a Portsmouth fan, he liked to get the kids out for game of football. Have you seen the movie Kes? It's an old movie based on the book 'A Kestrel for a Knave'. It's about a poor northern kid who befriends a kestrel. It's a masterpiece really, but that's not the point. One of the characters is called Mr. Sugden, played by Brian Glover, a dominating PE teacher who organises a game of football with his pupils only to take the match too seriously and competes in the match less like a coach, more like a player. Being so much bigger than the kids, Mr. Sugden could push them out the way and generally run rings round them to his own amusement. Mr. Bennett was I think the real-life version of Mr. Sugden, as he joined in rather than coach, dribbling round kids a third of his size, and blasting the ball into the top corner, before running away, his arms aloft, waving to the imaginary crowd. I loved these sessions because I would get stuck in to him, and if I could, give him a sly kick or send him flying with a naughty tackle. I never once got pulled up for it even when on occasion his large rotund body landed on the deck. In fact, the only time he did send me off was for no other reason than I nutmegged him (pushed the ball between his legs, collected the ball and dribbled away with it).

Dad certainly wouldn't have got the tickets from Mr. Bennett, that's for sure. Funnily enough there wasn't much demand to go and see Portsmouth play. But there were many others in the Black Horse he could do business with, for tickets, plumbing, purchasing a motor bike, anything. It was like the 'Star Wars' Cantina, with all kinds of weirdos, drunks and hard-cases, mixing with the likes of deputy headmasters and Dad. Mum was forever tearing her hair out after Dad had met a bloke in the pub, who would come do a job around the house, and invariably stuff it up. However, this time Dad had come up trumps: we would be both going to the last game at The Dell. It was like a cup final in some ways, not that I'd been to many to understand what that was like.

The last game at The Dell was on the 19th of May, 2001, about twenty-two years after I had started going with Dad. We sat together, behind the goal at the Milton Road end of the ground. I had spent much of my youth on my stool, standing in the Family Centre with Dad in the upper tier of the Milton Road end. In 2001, there was no upper tier, there was just one tier of seating which would go as far back as the road outside would allow. Because the road wasn't parallel with the ground, it meant that on one side the seats would go back, deep into the stand, whilst on the other side there would only be half a dozen rows of seats where the stand would meet a towering wall. It was good though that the tickets that Dad was able to blag was at this end. It felt right.

It was a good game. Saints fought hard against far superior opponents who, that day, had nothing specific to play for and who, in truth, played in a lower gear than normal. Arsenal scored first and led 1-0 at half-time, but early in the second half a sloppy defensive clearance put our energetic Moroccan international Hassan Kachloul through on goal to score and make it 1-1, right in front of us. Arsenal then scored a well worked goal on the counter attack. Robert Pirès, Thierry Henry and Freddie Ljungberg charged forward and it was Ljungberg who stroked the ball home. But Saint's grabbed an equaliser through Kachloul again. A hopeful ball was looped high into the penalty area, and when the Arsenal goalkeeper didn't deal with it, Kachloul prodded home.

With about fifteen minutes to go, Saints made a substitution, and Le Tissier trotted on the field to a huge reception. He was immediately in his stride and you just felt he was in the mood.

Le Tissier had already sprayed a couple of world class passes around the pitch when, in the last minute, he received the ball just inside the penalty area from a flick on. A defender tried to get in a tackle but could only flick the ball up. Le Tissier allowed the ball to bounce and shot on the spin. From our position, both me and Dad knew the ball was in the back of the net as soon as the ball left his left foot. There was no way the goalkeeper was going to get anywhere near it. Had there not been a goal net, the ball may well have hit us. It was a glorious goal, another Le Tissier special, and it was a perfect ending to the game, the season, for us and for Saints' 103 year stay at The Dell. Le Tissier would play on for one more season at our new home, so for him must have been a wonderful to end his career at The Dell.

That wasn't quite the end of the matter. Chris Marsden, a seasoned pro enjoying a superb last few seasons in the game for the Saints, then shot from outside of the box, and required an agile save from the goalkeeper to tip it over the bar. Deep down, I admit that I didn't want that goal to go in. A 3-2 win with Le Tissier scoring the winning goal in the last minute, was the perfect ending – Chris Marsden nearly spoiled it.

That wasn't the last match at The Dell though. The very last match at The Dell was a friendly against Brighton And Hove Albion. The Saints first ever opponents at The Dell in 1898 were Brighton United, who are now defunct. Brighton and Hove Albion were the chosen opponents for this final send-off game because they are the closest fit to the original team, and they were from a lower league, so beatable (a loss in a game such as this would not do). I managed to purchase me and Dad a ticket from the ticket office for this, what was for me, a third send off for The Dell.

It was another bright, sunny day. The groundsmen had painted 'The Dell – 1898-2001' into the grass, which set the tone for a party atmosphere. Fans were allowed to stand on the gantry's above the West and East Stands – almost certainly a no-no under normal circumstances. The game was low key, and for the record Saints won 1-

0, and there were two female streakers. Where the Arsenal match had been a joyous, happy occasion, this was a little melancholy.

With about fifteen minutes of the match to go, we could hear thudding noises coming from all sides of the ground. It took us a while to work out what was going on. Then a guy in front of us stood up and started kicking his fold-down seat. He was trying, like hundreds of others, to free his seat and take it home as a souvenir. It was an eerie sound and Dad didn't approve.

"Hey, don't do that! Leave it alone," he was calling out to people. It was like the old girl was being stripped bare. I didn't like it either. Some people had come prepared with tools, screwdrivers and wrenches, and shared them around other supporters once they had disconnected their seats. At the end of the match, the fans charged on to the pitch in celebration, the seats that they had retrieved in their arms, whilst the players ran for the dressing rooms, the noise of other seats being retrieved ongoing.

We took a little wander on the pitch for a little while, and took a bit of turf, as did everyone else. We could see gaps in the seated terracing where fans had got their seats, as if The Dell had some missing teeth. Eventually we left and slowly made our last trip back up Hill Lane. As we were walking back, we saw fans with some of the advertising hoardings, two guys were holding a McDonalds board, another had 'Draper Tools'. It was the end of an era for us.

That evening I took Kellie to the movies in Southampton. There were still fans milling around with seats or advertising hoardings. It made for a surreal evening, eating a meal and watching a gentleman with a huge 'Young's Sc' advertising hoarding under his arm, followed by another fella with 'affolding Tel 01962...' under his.

The new St Mary's stadium was bigger, with a capacity of more than 32,000. It may have less character and may be more functional, but it is a good place to go and watch football. The views are better from wherever you are, it's more comfortable and has more amenities.

But the Dell was a home to me. When I sleep and dream of football, it is The Dell where I dream, not St Mary's. I think I must have watched matches from every single stand, from every vantage point. It was small, a bit dilapidated and it had a miniscule shop, but I miss it terribly. I miss the pre-match rituals and build up to the match. I miss Dad paying the turnstile operator extra to let me take a friend into the ground without a ticket. I miss Dad heckling the commentators as they went up to take their position in the gantry. I miss staring at the clock on top of the East Stand when matches were close, willing for the minute hand to move toward 4:45 p.m. and the end of the match. I miss peering over the side of the stand to see the players come out of the dressing rooms in the corner, so I could be the first person to know the teams were coming out. I miss Dad shouting over to the West Stand, demanding the fans there to get behind the team and not to be so quiet. I miss people coming up to Dad asking where I got my stool from. I miss the half-time scoreboard where you had to decode the scores that were placed next to letters on the scoreboard, to matches against the corresponding letters in the matchday programme. I miss couples coming on to the pitch at half-time where the bloke gets down on one knee to ask his girlfriend if she would marry him. I miss the crescendos of "No! Don't do it!" by the fans just before she said 'yes'. I miss the scolding hot Bovril drink. I miss The Dell announcer urging a supporter to go to her wife right away because she has gone into labour. I miss the announcer urging the supporter much later in the game that he really ought to go (they never do, I wouldn't – she can hold on for ninety minutes, can't she?). I miss the long walk from Hill Lane to the game. I miss The Dell.

2003

FA Cup Final 2003, Arsenal versus Southampton. The Millennium Stadium, Cardiff, Saturday, 17th of May.

Tensions were high. Saints were at home in the quarter final of the FA Cup to Wolverhampton Wanderers, a Championship team (formerly Division Two – a second tier team).

Saints had moved to their new 32,000 all seater stadium and had developed a fair team after a bumpy start at the new ground. The manager, Gordon Strachan had forged a team, post the retirement of Matt Le Tissier, that was not reliant on one man. They were fit and physical, but their endeavour was honest. Their organised play may not have been ideal for the purest, but for the Saints fans, going toe-to-toe with the best teams in the Premier League and on a regular basis, was a new experience for the fans used to floundering at the bottom end of the table and flirting with relegation.

They had some good players too. In Anti Niemi from Finland, Saints had their best goalkeeper since Peter Shilton. Another top-class Scandinavian stood at centre-back; Michael Svensson was a rock in defence that season, who unfortunately would obtain a career-ending injury the next season. In attack we had the strong, bustling James Beattie – who would also go on to represent England.

This match was a big opportunity to progress in another cup competition against limited opponents. The crowd were charged up from the cup fever that had engulfed the town. Me and Dad were nervous too. We had had season tickets since the opening season two years before. Our seats were in the Itchen Stand, Block 10, Row G, Seat 292 and 293 (it's funny how you remember such stuff), near to the front, in line with the edge of the penalty box. There were no bad views at St Mary's stadium. Whilst the stadium itself lacked character and charm, it made up with in spades with modern space and comfort.

Fortunately, there were no large people to obscure my view or encroach on to my expensive seat. But there was a gentleman who sat in the row in front of us that got under Dad's skin. This bloke – and there are carbon copies of such a fella in every ground up and down the country – would bark out his opinions out load as if the entire Itchen Stand was hanging on his every word (they weren't).

Fortunately, Dad was on hand to keep him in check.

"Referee – you're bent! And I don't mean you're a cheat!" I remember this idiot shouting at the start of a match.

"Bloody hell, he's started already!" Dad shouted back. The idiot, although undoubtedly able to hear Dad would never turn his back and argue with him.

When an opposition player was laid injured in front of us, the idiot shouted "Hey, physio! Let him die!"

"We wish you'd die!" said Dad, much to the amusement of others. This would go on all season. The next season, when this guy went off on one again, Dad would say, "Got to put up with you again this year, have we, brother?" Sometimes, if the opposition had missed a shot at goal, the guy would jump up and spread his arms wide, like an umpire calling a wide in cricket. Dad would shout, "Sit down, prick!" and the guy would immediately sit down. Unfortunately, this guy was at the quarter-final.

Both me and Dad were nervous going into the game. Although we were playing a poorer team, you never can tell how a cup match can go, and Saints were unmatched for experience in losing badly to lesser teams.

Dad, in particular, did not feel comfortable about this game. To help us through the nerves, Dad had his normal trusty pack of Trebor Extra Strong Mints that he would always pick up from a newsagent (a dairy) near to the ground. As was normal when the game kicked off, we gave the team a roar of encouragement and Dad then passed me a mint. We both concentrated on the game hard, and sucked on our mints harder still.

After a couple of minutes, there was a foul just in front of us.

"Come on Ref!" Dad shouted, exasperated, as the free kick was not awarded.

As he shouted, his Extra Strong Mint expectorated out of his mouth and flew into the air. The trajectory of the mint was such that it landed on our friend in front of us. Right in the middle of the back of his head. Dad's saliva had made the mint stick fast on to this guy's hair. And there this brilliant white dot stayed unmoved, like some strange white shotgun wound or on/off switch.

I said to Dad quietly that he ought to inform the bloke about it.

"No I bloody will not!" Dad said.

I told him he couldn't just leave the white disc mint there on the back of his head.

"Can't I? Watch me!" Dad said.

It was hilarious. There was no way that Dad was going to mention anything to this guy, and there was no way that anyone else would be tapping him on the shoulder to tell him the gentleman behind spat his sweet on to him. And there was absolutely no way that the mint was moving from the back of this guy's head. Titters from the crowed broke out throughout the first half, our gobby friend oblivious.

At half-time the game was 0-0 and was on a knife-edge: it could go in any direction. The mint wasn't going anywhere, though. The guy went off for a bit, probably a pee, a pint and a pie, and returned at the start of the second half, mint still attached.

On the field, Saints were on the move. With nearly an hour gone, Saints won a corner. Michael Svensson won a header in an ungainly fashion at the near post, the ball squirting up into the air. Chris Marsden latched on to the looping ball and hooked it back over his head and into the net. From that moment Saints never looked like losing. A second goal came about ten minutes from time when a Saints cross was deflected in by a Wolves defender. Cue celebrations and a date in the semi-final of the FA Cup.

As with 1976, Saints avoided the top team left in the competition, Arsenal, and again drew a team from a division below them, this time Watford. The game was due to be played at Aston Villa's Villa Park neutral ground. This would be a new ground for me and Dad to visit.

It was a sunny day in Birmingham, a city I'd never been to. We got to the match early and pitched up in a pub, the Cap 'n Crown, according to a photo that I still have. There were masses of fans outside of the pub, spilling on to the streets, cordoned by police officers. There was no trouble anymore, just a volume of people having a drink before the match. We were able to negotiate the crowd and get into the pub to order. The unseasonably warm weather for April meant we could sit in the beer garden and watch the Saints fans sing and cheer over a nice cold Fosters, well known as the Finest Beer In The World. Dad sat on the ground, his back up against a wall. I stood, too nervous and too fidgety to sit down.

There were a group of guys chatting away, standing to Dad's right whilst he was sat down. The nearest bloke to Dad, who had his back to him suddenly farted the ugliest and dirtiest fart imaginable, right in Dad's face. Dad jumped up as if he had sat on a pin, horror on his face.

"HE JUST SHAT ON ME!" Dad shouted, shell shocked and incredulous, pointing at the guy who farted.

The bloke turned around startled. "Are you all right, mate?" he asked, agitated.

"YOU. JUST. SHIT. IN-MY-FACE!" Dad argued with him, eyes bulging, red faced.

"Sorry mate, I didn't know you were down there!" the guy said, half smiling.

"You dirty shit!" Dad carried on. Then there was a pause.

"AND IT BLOODY STINKS!" he started again in despair completely over-reacting to the pungent aroma making its way round the beer garden. "Jesus Christ!" Dad said, as if he had just had acid poured on him. He was hysterical. It was hysterical.

I was beside myself with laughter and that irked Dad even more. "You wouldn't like it if someone shat on your face," Dad admonished me. "I can still smell it, the dirty bastard!" It took Dad until kick off to get over the shame of someone inadvertently and accidentally farting in his face.

At the ground I met Super Saint, the Southampton club mascot, basically a bloke sweating like a United States over stayer inside a giant foam puppy costume. He didn't say anything to me except pat me on the back and stick his thumbs up at me. Dad wanted me to ask him why didn't the guy inside the outfit get a proper job, which I thought was a bit naughty, so I did. Super Saint walked off. I could swear I was getting a look from a giant puppy.

Before the start of the match we were distracted by two young girls taking their places to our left. It appeared they were topless except for a small Saints flag expertly positioned on the bosom. Not something you see every day.

The nerves had started to dig in again, so the respite of the girls, the mascot and the farter on the father helped take the edge off. We were playing against another seemingly inferior team. Watford, if anything, were more mediocre than Wolves. But if anyone was going to balls it up, it was certainly going to be Saints. The semi-final in 1984 had hurt the most. That was a game I don't think I have ever got over. And 1986 was hardly any better: a semi-final is no place to lose. There is a saying that no one remembers losing semi-finalists. That might well be true, but the bitterness doesn't half linger if you are a fan of the losing team.

The atmosphere was electric, one of the best I can remember. Two sides of the ground were a sea of red and white, whilst the other two sides of the ground were painted yellow – Watford's colours.

The game started and it seemed almost immediately Watford were going to score. I remember a hopeful free kick being floated into the Saints penalty area and thought that a Watford player had headed the ball into the net. Fortunately, our goalkeeper, Paul Jones – in for the injured Niemi – parried it away.

There were hardly any other chances in the half. Just before half-time though, Chris Marsden popped in a cross which was met by our other striker Brett Ormerod, another journeyman player, who rose to head home. Saints had scored a goal in the semi-final of the cup for the first time since 1976, and this was the first semi-final goal I remember seeing, at the tender age of 31. Dad retained a silly grin throughout half-time, as if high on the fart-wind breathed in at the pub before the match.

I was still wrecked with nerves. How would I feel if we lost this game, from this position, against this team? The possibility was unbearable to me. I spent the second half frantic, in an uncomfortable, pessimistic stupor, whilst Dad was in a confident, bullish mood.

"Nothing to beat here, eh Russ?" he told me. I wasn't so sure, and the second half of this match was possibly the most nerve-wrecking 45 minutes of my life.

The tension for me was at DefCon Four. Despite however angry, cross, excitable, tense, moody or frustrated that Dad was at a game, he would never drop the f- bomb at a football match. He would go through the gamut of other swear words, each of the b- words, 'bastard', 'bollocks' and 'bugger' would get a good run out at a game, and so would 'sod', 'piss', or 'shit' – these were all fair game, but the f-bomb was not permitted. That is not to say that Dad didn't put the f-bomb about a bit, but never normally at a match. He confided in me once that at a match, to always have a look around you and check to see if there are any kids nearby. If there is, then it is important to 'button it' as Dad would say. I learnt this from a very young age when Notts County beat Saints at home in a massive surprise loss in 1984. County's second goal, in the last minute caused me, at the tender age of thirteen, to drop the f- bomb in front of Dad. I soon learnt to associate the sudden outcry of the f- bomb to be followed by a sharp pain to the head. So to stop myself swearing I learned to substitute the f- bomb with another word. Originally I used 'fiddlesticks' which was very uncool and juvenile to take as aggressive voice armoury at a football match. So for football, I settled on the word 'faggot' which in 1984 did not have the same connotations as it does today. A faggot was a ball of meat and onions. As I grew up, I heeded Dad's advice to the letter, ensuring that when the f- bomb was swelling up inside me, 'faggot' came out.

However as 1984 became 2003, 'faggot' had a different meaning. I had spat out one too many faggots (there's a double-entendre right there for its latest meaning) during the last few minutes for the liking of a nearby steward. He took me by the arm and admonished me into my ear. Whilst of course I knew what meaning faggot now had, I had honestly not put two-and-two together and realised what a potty mouth I had become. This was the only time I had been pulled up by a steward at a Saints match (although there was one shameful occasion in New Zealand when David Beckham's LA Galaxy came over for an exhibition game, and I was mucking around with Shauna and her mates in the football team. I was told if I didn't stop mucking around – the game was dreadful – I'd be gone. Jobsworth prick!).

The game continued to be cat-and-mouse, a game of few chances. I just sensed something bad was waiting for us. As the game wore on the feeling got worse and worse. Watford hit the bar with a header and Dad became miffed with me because I had eaten almost the entire packet of mints. By contrast Dad was enjoying the match almost too much. Every so often he would nudge me and say, "Hey, Russ? Still winning!"

Maybe this was his way of telling me that everything was going to be okay, just like matches at The Dell in my first season when I would look to Dad for some inspiration and wisdom if we had conceded a goal.

And of course, he was right. With about ten minutes to go, Ormerod charged into the Watford penalty box, pursued by two Watford defenders. He screwed the ball across the face of the goal, away from the despairing goalkeeper, and James Beattie, sandwiched between two more Watford players bundled the ball into the net. On replay it showed that the crucial touch came from a Watford defender – another own goal to help our cause.

We celebrated the goal. Dad continued to celebrate after the game restarted, chatting away with other fans believing the match was won. He joined in the massive chorus of 'Que Sera Sera' adopted by fans whose team looks set to make it to Wembley. There he was, in his seventy-fourth year, standing like a five year old, bouncing around, his arms swinging in the air. Meanwhile, there I am, half his age, sat on my seat trying to peer through the arms of the waving, standing fans in front of me, elbows on thighs, my head perched on my hands, still not certain of the result and taking nothing for granted.

"Sing up, Russ!" Dad said.

"No chance," said I. "Not yet."

With four minutes to go, Watford scored with a long, looping header drifting over Paul Jones and into the net. I was beside myself with worry, and cross with Dad.

I ripped into him. "I told you that this could happen!!!"

Dad took the bollocking like a child told off at school. All celebrations stopped, and he sat down in his seat bolt upright. "Bugger!" he said.

The game time suddenly slowed. There were only a couple of minutes left to go, plus whatever time the referee decided to add on, but now it seemed like it was taking hours! As a kid, in really close matches I would stare at the clock on the top of the East Stand of The Dell and count out each remaining minute in my mind, using the word 'elephant' to space the seconds out accurately. I don't remember doing it at this match, but I bet I did, I've done it plenty of times as an adult. The assistant referee signalled four minutes of added time. Watford suddenly had a surge of confidence and a second wind, and Saints were retreating back to their own goal. This was becoming purgatory! There were loud whistles from the Saints fans for the referee to blow his whistle. I've never been able to whistle as a kid, it just comes out like a fart sound like the one Dad copped in the face.

Finally the match was over. We celebrated of course, but so much of it was sheer relief. We were exhausted, but safe in the knowledge we were off to the cup final!

On the way home we were hungry so stopped at a service station and ordered a big dinner each. Oddly however, neither of us could bring ourselves to eat so much as a mouthful.

Dad was reflective. I remember him telling me that he'd never experienced this feeling before. Neither had I. It all felt so strange. It really hadn't hit home that we were in the final of the FA Cup. Neither of us knew how to process this information and we did not know what to do with ourselves. We were exhausted and not thinking straight. It had all caught up with us.

The Daily Echo on the following Monday made merry on Southampton's achievement. It included a large picture of the two girls who were wrapped in the Saints flag, with Dad's head poking out looking at them with his mouth wide open aghast. I actually believe Dad was watching the match in this photo not the girls, but the picture paints a different story!

In 1976 Saints played Manchester United in the cup final – a top three team from the top division, and so it certainly was one of the biggest surprises ever that Saints won the cup that year. In the League Cup in 1979 they played Nottingham Forest who were undoubtedly at the time the best team in the country (and shortly to become the best team in Europe). Once again, Southampton's opponents in 2003 would be yet another top, top side, Arsenal on this occasion. Arsenal had won the Premier League and the FA Cup in 2002 – the double. In 2003, they finished runners-up to Manchester United. The following year after the cup final in 2004, Arsenal won the Premier League again, but this time without losing any of their thirty-eight matches, a monumental achievement in the modern era, earning them the nickname of The Invincibles. Once again, Saints would have to mix it with the very, very best if they had any chance of winning the competition.

Arsenal were formidable under the stewardship of Arsène Wenger, the French professor of the game. He had some of the best talent that Arsenal had ever had such as top French internationals Patrick Vieira, Robert Pirès and their superstar goal scorer Thierry Henry. France had won the 1998 World Cup, 2000 European Championships and would reach the World Cup final again 2006. They also had Denis Bergkamp, an absolutely beautiful player to watch, one of my all-time favourite players that I have had the privilege of watching.

With the normal twists of fate that accompany Saints in these situations, Saints' penultimate game of the Premier League season, a mere ten days before the final, was against Arsenal away. The Premier League crown was out of Arsenal's reach but nonetheless they wanted to finish the season on a high in front of their own fans. Although the final represented the toughest of assignments, Saints were a good solid side and this match would be a good indication of how things might turn out. After thirty minutes in this 'warm up' Saints were losing 5-0. It was a humbling experience. The final score was 6-1 and included a hat-trick for Arsenal's Robert Pirès. As much as Arsenal were unstoppable during this match, Saints were abject. At 4-0 down, the manager, Gordon Strachan, removed our ineffective French midfielder Fabrice Fernandes and brought on another defender, a young debutant Chris Baird, just to avoid the massacre. The ramifications of this result and the performance, and the way Arsenal seemed to be able to cut open Saints at will, had profound consequences on the way Saints would play the final. All you could do when listening to the radio, was to hope the torture would end soon. Goodness knew what was going to happen in the final, now.

Undeterred, we embraced the cup fever. I decorated our small house in Hook, near Basingstoke with balloons and flags with Kellie's blessing. She was expecting it, I had done the same in the semi-final, including dressing the kids up in Saints shirts and getting them to wear silly jester-style hats. The only difference was that the house was decorated in red and white for the semi-final, and yellow and blue for the final as Arsenal would be wearing their red. Mum and Dad's house was also not immune to my decorating skills. I stayed over on the Friday night before the final and left for the final leaving a carpet of yellow and blue balloons throughout the ground floor of Mums house for her to wade through whilst we were gone along with a giant 2D replica of the FA Cup covered in tin foil and garnished in yellow and blue ribbons.

Typically, Saints reached the cup final during a year when Wembley was being rebuilt. During the seven years it took to rebuild the English National Stadium, the cup finals were played in Cardiff, Wales, at the Millennium Stadium. Driving to Cardiff was an experience in itself. Motorway bridges were covered in good luck messages, flags and slogans from Saints fans unable to get a ticket for the final. Some people waited on the bridges to wave us by. As was customary, we had the obligatory scarf and flag hanging out of the car so our colours and allegiance could be identified. Fellow fans driving to the game would toot their horns and pump their fists and cheer as they went by us. Soon the goodwill messages thinned, and we entered Wales across the Severn bridge. We arrived in Cardiff's city centre early at about 9:00 a.m., some six hours before kick-off.

We enjoyed the day in Cardiff immensely (the same day that it had been reported that Curly had been sacked from Coronation Street). We were struck how friendly the locals were to us and seemed to be with Southampton for the day. We spent most of the morning in a coffee shop watching the city centre fill with a mass army of yellow and blue fans. It seemed we were outnumbering the Arsenal fans considerably and saw very few until inside the stadium. Dad was as visibly nervous as I had ever seen him at a match and he admitted as much. On leaving the coffee shop he realised that he had left his small miniature radio in the shop. I went back but it had been nicked. He was sad about that so I said I would get him another: seeing that we were in the city centre, we should replace it there and then. Most fans spend their cup final days in a pub, or in one of the especially erected fan zones that the organisers tend to make available for fans. Me and Dad on the other hand were spending the build up to the cup final in Argos, although he was very pleased that I could get him the same make and model that he had before.

We still had time for a pre-match pint, but every pub we saw was absolutely jam-packed with Saints fans spilling out the front doors like a wound. Eventually we found a pub, still quite close to the ground, that was not as nearly as full. On entry we found the pub not even half full with plenty of seating to perch on. We enjoyed a pre-match Fosters with some other fans, and then Dad went for a wee. When he came down his face was white.

"It's a bleeding poofs-pub!" he exclaimed.

I asked him what he was talking about.

"It's a gay bar, Russ! A woofter's palace! We can't bloody well stay here!"

Eventually Dad agreed to stay, with the other fans reasoning that "they wouldn't dare try anything with all us around" and that "you're okay if you don't leave your seat". In retrospect, you could not imagine a conversation quite so compellingly stupid I suppose. One Saints fan who got up to go to toilet actually straddled the wall making sure he remained pinned to it, walking crab like to the toilets, as if someone there who happened to be gay would suddenly grab him and take him from behind. I'd like to think that the rationale that persuaded Dad to stay was that we were highly unlikely to get in to any other pub at all with two hours to kick off, rather than any other reason. I do confess that whilst I was not complicit with these homophobic comments, I was not too keen to stick around either. When I went to the loo I realised how Dad knew it was a gay bar, as there was a notice on the toilet wall publishing 'safe' places for homosexuals to visit in Cardiff. It's all a bit sad that people have to live their lives like that, carefully picking and choosing which places they could go into without being ridiculed or hurt.

We stayed for another beer with Dad noticing some of the local frequenters to the bar. "Bloody hell, Russ! Look at that one!" Dad shouted pointing at a man in normal attire, but with a shaved head and in heavy makeup including long fake eyelashes. It was like he was pointing at some strange animal in a zoo. "He'd better not come near me!" I was glad to get free of the place and get Dad inside the stadium where he could settle down.

The Millennium Stadium was a magnificent venue. It was a bowl where the views were perfect, irrespective of where you were sat. Me and Dad got in the ground with about ninety minutes before kick-off. Dad was happy to go to his seat immediately and soak up the atmosphere. I agreed to get some lunch. After about twenty minutes I returned with a chicken pie for Dad and a hot dog and large fizzy drink for me. I put the drink down on the floor and gave Dad his pie. I also gave him my hot dog to hold on to whilst I sorted myself out a bit. Dad's nervousness got the better of him – he allowed my hot dog sausage to slip out of my hot dog and roll into the rows in front of us. That was my lunch gone. Dad immediately apologised and in doing so kicked my drink over.

"Sorry Russ," he shrugged, sitting down to eat his pie. I spent the remainder of the afternoon hungry and in a sticky pool of fizzy orange. There was no way I was going to queue up again for more food and drink and miss the build-up.

The noise in the build-up to the match was deafening – easily the noisiest I had ever experienced. The roof of the stadium had been closed – this would be the first, and only, FA Cup final to be played indoors. Close to kick off, Dad simply could not hear me as the roof trapped the noise within its confines. The Saints end was a sea of yellow and blue, equally as good, if not better, than the yellow that the Watford fans provided in the semi-final. Balloons bounced everywhere – I even helped some fans blow up some more balloons – not a good idea if you are an asthmatic like me wanting to shout your lungs off at a match.

For the final, Fernandes was removed from the starting line-up and replaced with Chris Baird. His job along with the team was to quell as much attacking instinct from the Arsenal side as is possible, in Baird's case help stop Robert Pirès from running riot as he did ten days before. But suppose that they could stop Robert Pirès for this game, what about stopping Freddie Ljungberg, Arsenals charismatic Swedish midfielder? What about stopping Thierry Henry? How on earth could they stop Denis Bergkamp, Holland's best player? Pirès, Ljungberg, Henry and Bergkamp were probably the best attacking force in the whole of Europe at the time, and in Henry and Bergkamp, Arsenal had two of the finest ever players to grace English football. Saints response was to inject a youngster into the team who had only played once for them before. It was at least a relief that Anti Niemi was fit again and back in the starting line-up.

Me and Dad were hopeful that in this match Saints would not be overrun and could get a foothold in the game to give us a chance. When we were at home we would sing along with the national anthem and the cup final hymn 'Abide With Me'. Today we had a chance to be part of the 75,000 singing it from inside the ground. It felt extraordinary.

With us both nervous and me still hungry and with sticky shoes, the game started.

After just eight passes in the match, in the first minute of the game, Thierry Henry immediately went clean through to goal. His shot was brilliantly saved by Niemi. Henry should have scored. He had wriggled away from our defender Claus Lundekvam to burst through on goal. Lundekvam, who got completely the wrong side of Henry, could only grab and tug hopelessly at Henry's shirt, desperately trying some form of rugby tackle. As far as cup final decisions go, I wonder if that is the most blatant, obvious penalty not to be awarded in recent times? Although Henry continued and shot, Lundekvam quite clearly fouled him in the area. I'm as biased as they come, but we had really got out of jail with that one. Me and Dad could not believe that either Henry had not scored, or that the penalty had not been given. And had the penalty been given, our defender must surely have been sent off for the challenge. Talk about dodging a bullet! We only needed to hang on for another 89 minutes!

Fortunately, Saints settled into the game quickly after that. Yellow and blue balloons bounced across the pitch as the game played on. Cries of 'Yellows! Yellows!' rang out from the Saints fans easily drowning out the trophy-softened fans of their opponents. But after seven minutes, Henry was set free again, his shot bouncing off the chest of the flailing Niemi. The ball fell to Bergkamp who skipped around Niemi and shot across the face of the goal. Young Baird raced back to clear the ball off the line. Shortly after Bergkamp raked a long pass to Henry who shot tamely at Niemi.

"It's going to be a long afternoon, Russ!" I remember Dad telling me.

In fairness, watching the game back on YouTube, Saints did counterpunch well, and were industrious, passing sharply, winning a couple of corners and getting a few teasing crosses in, but there was nothing clear cut. After twenty minutes James Beattie put the ball into the net, but was slightly offside (I'd've given it though!).

Saints had done well in the first half, but were undone by another goal from Robert Pirès. Henry received the ball on the edge of the box, and flicked it into the path to Bergkamp who pushed it on to Ljungberg in the penalty area, whose shot was blocked. The ball pinged about in the area and landed at Pirès' feet for him to score past Niemi from about seven yards out. Each of the four attacking superstars in Arsenal's team were all involved in the goal. A minute later, Pirès should have scored again, Henry again fizzing a ball across the box and Pirès, coming on to the ball, blasted over. Bergkamp then fired a ball into the six-yard box and again Baird had to clear off the line. Saints ended the half clinging on.

Saints made a promising start to the second half, but again couldn't fashion a clear-cut chance. It was Arsenal who went closest once more, Bergkamp forcing Niemi into another top-class save. Then Henry forced Niemi into similar save, both saves reaching down to Niemi's left. Shortly after, a kick up field by Niemi tore his calf, so dramatically his understudy Paul Jones had to come on to replace him. Jones was an experienced 'keeper who was kept just as busy as Niemi was.

Henry raced into the penalty and collapsed under a challenge. Me and Dad held our breath again. Again, no penalty, and Henry was booked for diving. The irony of that made Dad chuckle: if he'd gone down like that in the first minute of the match, he'd have certainly won a penalty.

You felt that whilst it remained 1-0 Saints still had a good chance. They were getting plenty enough of the ball, just not doing enough with it. I was horrified to learn that, after concentrating on the match so hard in the second half, there was only nine minutes left to equalise and send the game into extra time. Where the hell did the second half go? In the semi-final, it took an age for the final whistle to blow when we were winning, but here in the final I could only imagine that there was a mistake somewhere.

At the same moment of the match when Bobby Stokes scored the winning goal for Saints in 1976, Saints moment in 2003 had come. A long ball by the goalkeeper was headed on to Ormerod who chested the ball down and lashed a shot on goal. David Seaman, Arsenal's and England's aging pony-tailed goalkeeper instinctively parried the ball out for a corner. It was a chance from next to nothing and we had finally gone close. I thought that it was going in, the save from the goalkeeper just enough to send the ball over the bar without obviously changing the trajectory of the ball from my angle. Instead of crashing into the back of the net the ball kept going into the crowd.

Henry went close again near the end with Arsenal in total control, playing keep-ball, every pass to another Arsenal player greeted with cheers from the Arsenal fans, groans from the Southampton fans. The referee added a minimum of four injury time minutes to the match. Celebrations began at the Arsenal end. Me and Dad were totally and utterly gutted. Saints launched one last effort. In the fifth minute of injury time, with Arsenal fans whistling to the referee to end the game in a much better fashion than my attempt in the semi-final, Saints won a corner: it was now or never, the goalkeeper Jones coming up to join the attack. The ball was swung into the area and James Beattie met it full on with his head and thundered his header goalward. Both me and Dad leapt out of our seats to the roof to celebrate a goal, but Arsenal managed to scramble the ball off the line and with that our dream had died. The referee blew the final whistle and Arsenal had won.

Saints had huffed and puffed, and had gone toe-to-toe with Arsenal, but it was Arsenal who had that little bit of extra quality to make the difference. You felt, had Saints equalised that perhaps Arsenal would have gone up a gear to win the game. In the end Saints just didn't do enough in the game to win it. It was all very disappointing. It was an amazing day but a crushing result in the end.

It had been an adventure though, a journey in itself with Dad. With the cup run enveloped in the sadness of me leaving for New Zealand, we both desperately wanted to win this cup as a parting gift for each other. Sadly, it was not to be, and at the end of the match both of us would be sat back in our seats, our heads in our hands.

Leaving for Home

Monday, 5ᵗʰ of January 2004.

Saints beat Tottenham Hotspur 4-0 in the third round of the 2003 FA Cup. It was a thrilling and accomplished performance by a team having a great season. I didn't see the match. I was on holiday. At a wedding.

Ordinarily, going to a wedding on the day that your team is at home is an absolute no-no. Even if your invite has come from Dame Kylie Minogue herself, you cannot go – the pull of your team is too much and too great to handle. It is important to prioritise in such situations and football must come first.

However, I had an excuse. It was Kellie's brother David who was getting married, and he was getting married in Papamoa, New Zealand. Kellie's family, who were from Northern Ireland, escaped to New Zealand in the Sixties to avoid The Troubles. Kellie's Dad was sponsored to go over as a football referee, a vocation missing from the rugby-obsessed country. They returned, her parents inexplicably homesick in 1979 but Northern Ireland remained too dangerous, and so they moved to Winchester. Kellie and her side of the family had always held a desire to go back to New Zealand and David, whose nickname was 'Kiwi', had met a Kiwi was now going to marry the Kiwi and I was going to be Best Man.

I was outraged! I was a season ticket holder for God's sake! Did he not realise just how many games I would miss over that busy Christmas and New Year period? Three in fact, Tottenham Hotspur, Dirty Leeds and Liverpool, three of the most desirable games to go to all season. And when the draw was made for the FA Cup third round, I completely lost it when we were drawn at home to Tottenham Hotspur again. Did they not think to run this whacked out idea past me first? It wasn't as if I could walk up to the ticket office, and say "excuse me, I wonder if you could rearrange a couple of matches, because I am Best

Man overseas, you see?" Most people are honoured to be Best Man, I was offended.

One of the great attributes of my wife is that she understands football, and understands my obsession, well a bit anyway. But she has another great attribute, that of perspective. She put the wedding in context and explained that this was her brother, her family, and was frankly more important than football. After all, I had been given a great honour of being Best Man. Of course, that didn't wash at all and I thought her argument was a load of rubbish, so she used a further attribute in her diplomatic armoury, she pulled rank. We were going and I must be grateful for the honour. End of story.

The stay in New Zealand was life changing. By the time I was home, and before our fourth round match at home to Millwall, I told my Mum and Dad that I planned to emigrate to New Zealand by the end of the year. They took the news like a punch in the stomach. I destroyed them.

Ever since I have been with Kellie, because she was originally from New Zealand, Dad would occasionally ask whether I had any intention of moving to New Zealand. I'd always told him that I didn't think so, and I told him this because it was earnestly truthful. But things had changed. In 2000, I moved into a job in Slough for a start-up Internet company. They were quite happy to throw far more cash at me than I was worth. It was a rock-star job. You would work long hours Monday to Wednesday, throttle back on Thursday and work from home on Friday. We moved from Eastleigh to Hook, near Basingstoke, into a modern, albeit smaller, end of terrace. But the company squandered the 130 million pounds they had been given by venture capitalists and the company closed in 2002. It had been on the cards for months and I had applied for 130 jobs, none of which developed into an interview (I know it was exactly 130 as I set up a folder in my Inbox to keep a copy of them, and have them to this day as a reminder how tough it can be to get work). When the company announced their closure, I wasn't panicking. As luck would have it I had suddenly obtained three interviews and had them all back to back the previous week. During the actual meeting with staff to announce the company closure, this flimsy woman started to read from a pre-prepared press release. At this point I received a call on my mobile phone. This woman looked up and snootily asked me to turn my phone off whilst we were in a meeting. I told her to piss off and that it could be a job offer. I took the call and it was. It was for a job with NTL (now Virgin Media I think) who were based in my home village in Hook. Talk about landing on your feet: I took the requisite salary reduction but I could walk to work now so financially I could make it work.

The job was much more run of the mill and I missed the old days. Upper management seemed to hate everybody and would be offended if you simply walked in the door in the morning. I was good in my job, but in a bad environment and it wasn't long before I started to get depressed. Our home was small too and we needed more space as the children grew – Sarah was six and Shauna was four, and Shauna's bedroom was 6 feet by 9 feet (1.8 metres by 2.8 metres) – I have a cupboard bigger than that now. We would need to stay around Hook and housing was expensive there. I worked out to get further up the ladder there I would need to purchase a house that was for me, completely out of reach financially. I felt that I was failing as a father and a provider and was completely locked in. In truth, the Saints had never mattered less.

The invitation to the New Zealand wedding was a tonic. We arrived in New Zealand not in a holiday mode, but in a family mode, spending our days around Kellie's extended family. And for the month we were there, my eyes opened.

The houses were superior. They had space, front and back gardens, a driveway, double garages, a discrete laundry room, a lounge and a separate family room. Some houses had spas or pools. Most houses had decks. The houses were cheaper too, much cheaper in 2004. The pound was worth three New Zealand dollars. The weather was superior, the schools were superior, the environment was so much safer – Sarah and Shauna could play outside without their mum and dad worrying about where they were, what they were doing or who they were with. The reasons were endless. I had found a way out. Kellie never had any input to the decision, even though it has commonly been thought that because she is a Kiwi that she agitated for a move. That was never the case. I simply told her one day after we got back that we needed to move there as soon as possible and shortly after I told my Mum and Dad.

I sincerely believe that had I not moved from my job in Slough, I would not have gone to New Zealand. I would have generated savings for what I wanted out of life quickly. But those two years in the Internet start-up game were not based in reality and was always doomed to fail. In some respects it can be argued that I had taken an easy way out. To admit this would denigrate what my family has achieved since then but I can't argue that it was expeditious; it got me into a position in life much quicker than would have been the case had we remained in the UK.

Since the moment that I told them there has always been melancholy with Mum and Dad. I placed a proviso on the move in that I would not leave for New Zealand until I had a suitable job, which would serve only to give Mum and Dad an inkling of hope. Instead of asking me occasionally if I fancied leaving for New Zealand, Dad would tentatively ask if I'd found a job yet.

Kellie's Mum was pleased. She has always had an aloof personality where you couldn't really read how she was feeling, but it was a massive relief that she was so positive about the move. Kellie believes that her parents made a grave error leaving New Zealand and returning to Northern Ireland, and that with Kellie intending to return there, it stood to reason that such a mistake was being repaired to a certain degree. I suspect her dad, who passed away in 2001, would have had a cheery chuckle over the news, whilst sat comfortably in his armchair watching his team Rangers, smoking his pipe.

We would typically spend our Sundays with one of the girl's grandparents. During 2003, we made an effort to spend as many Sundays as was needed at my parents' home, with the blessing of Kellie's Mum. My Mum would make a fabulous roast dinner, and the kids still to this day say that when I cook a roast it reminds them of being at Nanny's.

Dad would sometimes simply ask me not to go. He qualified this by always saying that he believed that we were doing the right thing, and that he was purely being selfish. Sometimes he even asked me not to answer. He would lecture me about not spending money on a house in New Zealand until I was absolutely convinced about the move. This, he'd argue, give me the flexibility to return if it didn't work out. Mum would still pump Sarah and Shauna full of sweets and biscuits, but she would also pour over pictures of the kids and lament at some of the fun days, suggesting that there wouldn't be many more days like that.

In October, I had a breakthrough on the job front. I received a phone call at 3:00 a.m. one morning from the job agent saying I was in the frame for a post. The problem was I needed to attend an interview in New Zealand. I asked if I could do it over the phone from England, but this idea was flatly rejected basically because they wanted to know that I was serious – it was commonplace early in the 2000's that Brits would speculate over a move, get a job and then decide to stay. So I happily booked a two week stay in New Zealand with our friends there who we had got to know well the previous year. We had made some wonderful people in New Zealand, Brian and Dianne (Kiwis) and Nick and Yvonne (Welsh and English). Nick and Yvonne happily put me up and even let me borrow a car for the stay.

On day one in New Zealand I went to the interview in this dingy building in Auckland. Hilariously, I turned up for this interview, but the guy interviewing me had decided to work from home that day. I couldn't believe it, I'd just come all the way around the world for a phone interview! Fortunately, I was joined by a real person in the interview, a gentleman called Mike – who looked exactly like Father Ted, and I mean exactly like Father Ted. Suffice to say I knew I had secured the job then and there and it was just a case of filling my time for the remaining week and a half.

(Incidentally, this 'dingy building' happened to be opposite to a building owned by Neil Finn, lead singer with Crowded House. His building was used for their rehearsals when they re-formed – you could wander outside and have a bit of lunch listening to one of the world's best bands in the last thirty years rehearsing. How cool was that?)

Our friends lived in Papamoa, near Tauranga, about a two and half hour drive south of Auckland. It was a fantastic spot but I realised I needed to live nearer to Auckland where the work was. I decided to tour Auckland from north to south, and pick a spot for us to live. Looking back on this, this was an amazing responsibility – if I dare get this wrong, then I could make the rest of my family miserable, and that was only if they were able to settle in the first place. But I genuinely didn't feel this pressure at all and found the task hugely enjoyable.

Auckland is a big place. More than 1.4 million people live there and accounts for nearly one person in every three in the country. Auckland is basically split into two with water bisecting north and south, with only the Auckland Harbour Bridge joining the two. I didn't like the north, known as the North Shore – it reminded me of England, cars parked on kerbs, houses on top of houses, a bit dirty and very busy. I was damned if I was going to turn up in New Zealand and live the same life I lived in England. Dammit, I was going to have a garage, a garden and a driveway, and there wasn't much of this lifestyle going on in the North Shore!

Immediately south of the bridge is the Central Business District (CBD) or city centre, where I was going to start work. South of that were a number of suburbs that again didn't take my fancy one bit. I hadn't realised, but I'd travelled through the rough parts of Auckland. And like many big cities in the world, there are some seriously tough places here.

Eventually, I ended up in a small place called Drury, a bit fed up. I couldn't find anything remotely suitable at all. We had clearly been spoiled on our trip last year in Papamoa, and perhaps my expectations were simply too high. To cap it all the heavens opened on one of the fiercest rain storms I had ever seen. I certainly wasn't able to drive – you couldn't see in front of your face.

When the rain cleared I saw a sign for 'Pukekohe'. I remember Nick and Yvonne telling me what a nice place this was, so I gave my search one final go. It was this town or nothing. It looked really nice and spacious and looked similar to Papamoa. I liked it. I stopped off in the main town street and went in to a shop selling kids clothes and picked up some cool colourful clothes for Sarah and Shauna. I explained to the shop assistant my situation and basically said to her, "Look, I'm fed up driving around looking for a good town to live in with a good school. Is this town alright?"

She shrugged and said yes it was. So that was that. I put one of the biggest decisions in my life down to the feedback of a tiny lady whom I had never met, in a children's clothes shop. I had found a job and a place to live.

Back in England I missed Saints home game with Manchester City. I had arranged to fly out on the Sunday, the day after the Manchester City match, but the travel agent informed me by letter that my departure would now be the day before, on the day of the game. I was apoplectic and had a stern conversation with the travel agent over the phone. But for some reason the flights could not be reorganised any other way and I had to miss this game. I am sure Kellie saw this as a test of character for the move. But in fairness, I did go, and in doing so missed the match. It didn't matter, Saints had a nightmare and lost 2-0. They then drew with Bolton Wanderers away 0-0, so happily missed two of Saints worst games of the season.

Whilst I was away Kellie sold the house and organised a fantastically short process to exchange and move out. The international removers turned up within a week of my return and swept through the house with a giant roll of brown paper and wrapped everything, shoved it in a container and sent it out by boat. Had Sarah or Shauna had the inclination to remain still for a period of time I have no doubt they would have been wrapped too. We stayed with Kellie's Mum for our remaining five weeks in England, with our tickets booked for the first week of January.

The last games prior to my departure of course had special meaning. I had bought a season ticket but would only use half of it. Chris would sit with Dad for the second half of the season after I had gone. We beat Manchester United 1-0 at St Mary's thanks to a bullet header from James Beattie with two minutes to go. Manchester United had Ryan Giggs, Ruud Van Nistelrooy and Ronaldo in their team that day. Ronaldo was rubbish! We beat Charlton Athletic 3-2, and just before Christmas we had a crunch derby match against Portsmouth.

Southampton versus Portsmouth matches are highly charged, angry encounters from a fans perspective. Portsmouth supporters, living in the shadow of their south coast rivals for fifty years had built an inferiority complex and hatred toward Southampton fans, or 'Scummers'. Meantime Saints fans had built an apathy for Portsmouth as they were normally in a lower league to Southampton, and had generated a huge dislike for a foul Portsmouth following ('Skates'), renowned as some of the worst behaved supporters around. Because this derby didn't happen all that regularly, the stakes were raised even higher.

Clearly the worst derby (or best derby depending on your outlook) is Celtic versus Rangers, with a heady mix of football rivalry combusting with religious tension. Such religious tension doesn't exist (thankfully) south of the border, but I would argue that Southampton versus Portsmouth is the fiercest rivalry in the English game, easily eclipsing derbies in Manchester, Liverpool or London, for sheer hate. The 1984 match was a great win for the Saints but an abject advertisement for football: no match against Portsmouth ever showered itself in glory.

As a Saints supporter, you can't just turn up in Portsmouth in your gleaming Premier League red and white shirt: either you or the shirt might not make it out. When I used to travel into Portsmouth, I'd make sure there were no matchday programmes visible on the back seat, and ensure that any clue in my clothing to my allegiance was carefully covered up. There was one occasion that I was stupid enough to wear a Saints shirt in Portsmouth: that was the day that me and Kellie went to Navy Days at the docks on a May Bank Holiday Monday. Navy Days is where the Navy put on an open day so you can see all the boats and ships around the water and dry docks there. Since there would be so many people going from all over the South of England, I foolishly felt I would be okay. On the way home on the train, the train stopped at Fratton station. Waiting at the station were scores of blue-shirted Portsmouth fans: there had apparently been a lower league match that day. I took off my shirt double quick and sat on it. It'd been a sunny day so now I was topless. The train was heaving and supporters were having to stand in the carriage, packed in like sardines, whilst me and Kellie were sat down. She was beside herself with worry. My topless not-quite-Adonis body attracted strange looks and it was inevitable I would get quizzed from drunk fans about not having a top on. I somehow blagged my way through it and was thrilled to get off the train without incident.

We had played Portsmouth in the League Cup at the start of December at St Mary's. Saints won easily 2-0 but the occasion for both me and Dad was a real downer. Football in the twenty-first century had transformed itself from the ugly hooligan troubles in the 1970's and 1980's. There were a number of contributory factors to this. Policing at grounds and measures put in place to lessen the chances of trouble, such as closing pubs and not serving alcohol, was a sensible move (I scratch my head in New Zealand now when, at a sporting event, you are limited to only being allowed to buy four beers per person! – how totally absurd and irresponsible is that?). The Bradford fire that killed 56 fans at a football match in 1985 followed by the Hillsborough disaster in 1989 that killed 96 shook the establishment to renovate the game and ensure all stadia were all-seater. Then there was the World Cup in Italy in 1990 where England reached the semi-finals and was the genesis of a new football culture more interested in watching football rather than destroying it. It also helped that Margaret Thatcher, who openly despised football and was trying to shoehorn a membership scheme for all football fans, was ousted as prime minister that same year. Finally, the advent of the Premier League in 1992 poured in more money, more exposure and more comfort in the experience of watching a game of football. No longer were the hooligan breed welcome to matches. Instead, women, children, school groups, scout groups and children's football teams were welcome and were safe.

But this match against Portsmouth sent me and Dad hurtling back to the bad old days of the 1980's. We normally had an easy fifteen minute stroll from the car park to the ground. After five minutes we were met by a hoard of police, lined up, some with batons and helmets, some with police dogs. Police on horses were in attendance too. This was usual for London in the 1980's but not Southampton in the 2000's. We were shoved into a precession of supporters down a line of police acting as a wall between Saints fans and Portsmouth fans. Cans and bottles came pelting down over us from the Portsmouth contingent. We were pleased to get into the ground but angry all the same.

It just so happened that our former player, manager and director, Ted Bates, had just died at the ripe old age of 85. He had been at the club in some capacity since 1937, more than sixty continuous years' service. It is normal at such occasions for a minute's silence to be observed before the match. In my experience, these were almost always impeccably observed by both home and away supporters alike. But not tonight. Immediately the Portsmouth fans – a vast majority not a minority – tore into the minute's silence with cheering and foul chanting, which in turn set off a crescendo of boos and counter-chants from the majority of the crowd. It was just awful. You could legitimately argue that perhaps the powers-that-be in the football club should have deferred the minute's silence to any other home game rather than Portsmouth, as this outcome could certainly have been predicted. Nonetheless, Portsmouth Football Club were shown a courtesy that night that their fans duly shat on. We were pleased to win the match that night, but even more pleased to get home safe.

Our league match before Christmas was won too, 3-0 this time. I remember Marians Pahars scored one of his last goals for Saints that night. I was glad to get the games won, but I hadn't enjoyed them. Being pitted against Portsmouth is a match that lacks the class that the Premier League deserves. It was like the Queen being forced to dine at McDonalds.

But that win had sent us fourth in the league with only Manchester United, Arsenal and Chelsea above us. And it came a week after we had sauntered up to Anfield and beaten Liverpool 2-1. It meant that this Christmas wasn't going to be so melancholy after all.

My last game was against Newcastle United in the FA Cup third round on the 3rd of January 2004. Our last FA Cup match had been the final against Arsenal. Because I was on the move, the need to win that cup final was strongest of all. Me and Dad saw it as last chance to see our team win something together, and we were both devastated that Saints lost that final because there was the strong risk that it wouldn't happen again. So there was symmetry with this Newcastle match, but it meant that both me and Dad were sad at the beginning of the match. Shauna and Sarah came along for the first time, kitted out in red and white. We always beat Newcastle it seemed, Newcastle hadn't won in Southampton since 1971 – the year I was born. But irritating symmetry was to prevail and Newcastle stuffed us 3-0. Once the game was over Dad looked very, very sad. We hung around for a few minutes after the match; the score was of course incidental, I was saying goodbye and it was very, very sad to walk out of the ground that evening.

With Will Young at the top of the charts with 'Leave Right Now' we said goodbye to Mum and Dad on the 4th of January, left the UK on the 5th of January, and arrived in our new life on the 7th of January, 2004.

According to the Internet, New Zealand is in the Pacific Ocean about 1,200 miles (2,800 kilometres) east of Australia. It has two main islands, a north and a south island and has a total population of about 4.5 million, of which 1.4 million live in Auckland. If you buy Chicken McNuggets from McDonalds you normally get two shapes of McNuggets, an oval shape similar to the South Island, and an odd shape that is rounded at the base, flat on top with a bit sticking out the top left corner. This is shaped like the North Island. Auckland is at the base of the bit sticking up. Wellington, the capital, is at the bottom of the North Island.

Undoubtedly, New Zealand has been a great move. The people are nicer, and there are less of them. The weather is better and brighter (although this summer has been a shocker) – good weather starts in

October and can go through to May, and winter is really only June, July and August. It doesn't get as hot as England does at the peak of summer, but twenty-six degrees Centigrade will do very nicely thank you very much. We rarely see frosts in winter and we saw snow once, although it never laid (and that was apparently a once in a one-hundred-year event). When the kids went outside you didn't have to worry about what they were up to, what they were taking or who they were getting abducted by.

Holiday destinations are no longer Majorca, Ibiza, Corfu or Cyprus. Instead the destinations are Fiji, Rarotonga or the Gold Coast. Rather than visiting Paris, Dublin or Amsterdam, city destinations are Melbourne, Brisbane and Sydney.

Food is far, far superior – fresher and tastier, although I miss a good Chinese beef curry and boiled rice. There are even UK specialist shops to keep you topped up with Wispa bars, Bombay Bad Boy Pot Noodles and Monster Munch. But you can't get Fosters on tap, only from a can (you can't get it in Australia either now). I wouldn't know, but based on my limited consumption of local beer, I reckon New Zealand beer may actually be piss.

The locals have this obsession with cheese. Cheese has to be on or in everything. Tins of beans have cheese in it, sausages have cheese inside them (no, I am not making this up), even mince meat pies have cheese in them (you can almost hear Peter Kay shouting out in consternation at this point, "Cheese!? In a pie!?"). For someone like me who thinks cheese is the devil's earwax, it can be a nightmare at times. You can ask a waitress in a restaurant or café for a meal without cheese and they look at you like a scared animal. You can almost see them thinking – no cheese? Did he say, *no cheese?* What should I do? Typically, I end up with a meal with extra cheese on it. Pumpkins are another odd local eating habit in New Zealand. I always thought that pumpkins were only good for Halloween, but New Zealanders actually eat it, and lots of it. In every restaurant across the country, the 'soup of the day' is always pumpkin soup (which is absolutely rank), seven days a week, 365 days a year. I think it might be a law or something.

Work has been plentiful (touching wood as I type this) and with such a smaller pool of people, your reputation precedes you which is great if you are doing a good job. Mike, the guy who interviewed me for my first job in New Zealand, has sought to employ me multiple times since, so being in demand feels good. Work starts earlier, around 7:00 a.m. or 8:00 a.m. but you may well be home by 5:00 p.m. enjoying a beer in the last hour or two of sunshine for the day.

It's not all paradise. There is a dark side to New Zealand as there is with every country. Stuff is generally more expensive: England in 2017 is definitely a cheaper place to live. That said, there's plenty of poverty, racism, xenophobia and inequality kicking around, and worse. Attitudes in the country are such that police are always vilified, whilst perpetrators of crime are supported with sympathy and the victims of crime completely ignored. New Zealand are also in the bottom five countries in the western world for child abuse. It's a generalisation and an opinion I know, but the average Kiwi gentleman doesn't handle their drink very well at all. One or two little brown bottles of beer and that's the end of them basically. Stone age values, family violence and too much to drink is a grim mix indeed.

The biggest issue that affects me in New Zealand is that whilst almost every adult has a car, no bugger can drive properly. Honestly, driving in New Zealand is carnage. Again, generalising, but the New Zealander is an altogether a nicer fellow than the average Brit. Sit them in a car, particularly in the driving seat and they take on the mentality and anger that reminds you of the Jack Torrence character in The Shining (here's Johnny … in his Toyota Hi Lux). We were aware prior to our arrival that the United Kingdom consulate issued an advisory for any Britons intending to travel to New Zealand to be vigilant when on the roads because of the poor quality of driving; I don't know if that advisory still exists for travellers, I couldn't find it on the Internet. I didn't quite understand how stunningly arrogant and ignorant they are in a vehicle. The problems are endless: drivers have no awareness whatsoever, and drive their automatic cars as you would drive a dodgem at a fairground. The more kids you can pack in the back of the car the faster you ought to go, and the closer you ought to drive to the car in front. Ambulances might be blaring their sirens and flashing their lights, but the Kiwi driver in front won't move out the way, and probably isn't aware that they are even there. Drivers don't slow down around horses – in fact they speed up. For some bizarre brain-fade reason, beaches are classed as roads and so going to some beaches is like spending a day on a main road. New Zealand drivers have this fascinating ability to be completely unable to stay in their lane, or even make a token gesture to keep left. Just recently, the government raised the age of driving from fifteen (yes, 15!) to sixteen. Can you imagine anything possibly more stupid than allowing a dumb adolescent kid at the age of fifteen with their underdeveloped frontal lobe with legal access to a car? With so many unnecessary deaths every day in New Zealand – particularly so on public holidays, in true Kiwi style they point the blame at the 'foreigner'. For the record, foreigners with a license from another country, account for less than 4% of percent of all drivers involved in crashes.

My first car in New Zealand was a Ford Falcon (big Mondeo). It was formerly owned by an All Blacks New Zealand rugby player or official. I know this because before each Rugby World Cup the squad and officials are presented with a new car by Ford, with a small All Blacks emblem on the side of the car behind the front wheel, and the registration plate starts 'AB'. My car was from the 1999 Rugby World Cup and had the emblem and the registration plate. On the motorway one day a car crashed into the back of mine and caused whiplash to both me and Kellie. The driver of the car admitted to the police officer that he thought I might have been an All Blacks' player and wanted to pull alongside my car to see which one I was. According to the police officer the guy couldn't believe that he smashed into an All Blacks' car but was relieved when he found it was being driven by a 'scrawny pom'.

With my kids growing up in New Zealand the one nagging doubt I had about them living here was them learning to drive. I wasn't concerned about the girl's ability to drive at all – they are responsible and good drivers (and I made sure they were taught in a driving school, not on a paddock on the farm doing doughnuts), my concern was with other New Zealand drivers in the vicinity of them. Parents pass down the 'art' of driving down to their kids based on their own incompetence. It's almost a rite of passage and the culturally accepted way of teaching kids to drive: you rarely see a driving school here. Seriously, it keeps you up at night. And there aren't many weeks that go by until there is another sad story of a youngster killing themselves or others in vehicles that were cars until they entered the vehicle whereupon it become a missile.

I've seen drivers try to open bottles of beer whilst driving, blow up balloons whilst driving, even play the guitar whilst driving. At night, driving with your lights on appears to be optional. Roundabouts seem to be completely beyond the average New Zealander to negotiate. Indicators only seem to be on when drivers are attempting to drive straight. Don't even bother to let a fellow driver out of a junction: they'll just look at you in abject horror and not move as if they've arrived at a roundabout. One thing I do look forward to when I go back to England, other than the football and the beef curries, is the chance to drive. When you are used to the standard of driving I am used to here, driving in England is a genuinely delightful experience. Years ago, I had the opportunity to work a few stints in Italy, in Latina, outside of Rome one week in every six. I was told by my colleagues there that the road between Rome and Naples was one of the most dangerous stretches of road in the world. Having done that trip, I can honestly say that the trip from my home north into the Auckland CBD on the main SH1 Motorway is definitely without doubt worse. Cyclists are not much better: the average placid Kiwi gets on their bike and suddenly goes feral in their skinny fluorescent lycra, bursting through red lights, moving out to the middle of the lane without warning, moving on to pavements disrupting pedestrians. You may read this and think I might be overdoing it, exaggerating the facts a wee bit, but if you are an ex-pat in New Zealand, you are nodding your head in complete agreement right now, and thinking the same thing as me, total nutters.

The first six months were a whirlwind and a bit of a blur in hindsight. But they were exciting, fun and successful. The kids seemed to settle in the country within minutes, and picked up the New Zealand accent ('ixint') almost as quickly. I didn't really pick up much of the accent, and Kellie, riddled by an English accent because her stay there was so long, has been desperate to re-acquire her accent. Fourteen years later she is still trying. People who clock our accents assume we are both English both to my delight and Kellie's frustration. The Kiwi accent is much harsher than the Australian accent and harder to imitate, half way between an Aussie and South African accent. Most Kiwi females have a lisp, as do many blokes too, and the pronunciation of the letter 's' can be really grating listening to it on local television or radio. A report into Saints beating Southend 6-0 to go on sixty-six points for the season would sound like a constant hiss if a Kiwi was reporting on it. An 'egg' is an 'igg', 'yes' is 'yis', and they like the word 'awesome' ('orsim') and 'intense' ('intints'), especially when camping. When they mean 'no' they say, 'ah yeah, nah', and when they mean yes, they say 'look, nah yeah'. It may be English but it still takes some getting used to. A cool box for a picnic is called a 'chilly bin' (I thought it was some pre-cooked curry or chilli con carne). A fight is called a biff, and someone who gets beaten up gets a bashing. Sweets and chocolates are lollies, and ice lollies are icicles. Flip flops, standard issue attire for the Kiwi person, are called jandals. In Australia, they are called thongs. Imagine my surprise on my first visit to Australia when in a hotel room, the hotel pamphlet read 'thongs are not to be worn in the hotel'. I wondered how they would police this rule unless people were just going around in only their thong? Uncouth Aussies!

I went straight into work determined to make a positive name for myself, which I duly did. Kellie, the resident Kiwi though, found it toughest to settle. Our existing friends in New Zealand for the first few months would gravitate to me in the first instance and would ask if I was okay, was I settling in well and how was I coping without watching Saints. It simply didn't occur to anyone to ask Kellie how she was coping, how she was doing. In retrospect, it seems obvious to me that the toughest sell for New Zealand would have been Kellie as she would obviously had the highest expectations. But Kellie is not one to dwell on things and set about sorting it all out. She decided to forge a career as a midwife and her study gave her the anchoring she needed in her home country. In 2007 she graduated with flying colours. The South of Auckland has since been populated with hundreds and hundreds of children that my wife brought into the world. South Auckland is lucky to have such an accomplished professional as Kellie and I am equally lucky to have her.

We moved into our splendid house in Pukekohe in June 2004. Pukekohe is about forty minutes' drive south of the centre of Auckland. In true Kiwi style the house we bought wasn't even up for sale. The Real Estate agent asked the house owner – who she knew – whether he fancied selling and he said, "Look, nah, yeah!" which was great. I'm glad he did. We've been there ever since.

We made friends quickly, many more friends than we had in England. Typically for ex-pats, many people in our friendship circle were from the UK too, but although it is normal to gravitate to your 'own people' we had plenty of Kiwi and Australian mates too. It's a naturally friendly place. One day I went to the local hardware store to buy a small outdoor shed. It wouldn't fit in my car so I wheeled the flatpack shed back to the shop and asked the guy on customer service if the shed could be delivered. He handed me his car keys. He had a big van, a Ute, and was perfectly happy for this stranger who he had never met, to drive off in his property. It was an attitude that takes a bit of time to get used to.

Most of the ex-pats we have met have a story to tell, as to why they came to New Zealand. I have my suspicions that some of them are in witness protection. I suppose to some extent, because someone has taken the adventurous step of moving to a completely different country to live their life, your average ex-pat is a bit broken in some way. There has to be a trigger somewhere that makes someone say I've had enough. It's also inevitable in some ways that the tearing of one branch of the family tree from another branch leaves scars and a jagged edge that can never truly heal. And that is certainly the way I feel I suppose.

Despite the successes we have achieved here, by moving to New Zealand, I feel as though I had failed my parents and I had failed my father utterly. As a boy, he would take me to matches, and watched every match I played in as a boy or as an adult. There wasn't a week that went by without Dad coming home from work with a football programme for me: his mates at work who were following their teams each weekend would always bring Dad back a matchday programme for him to give to me. Not just Saints matches, but also matches from

Liverpool, Ipswich Town, Manchester United, Coventry City, Sunderland and Queens Park Rangers. If he went to the shop he would always come home with packets of football stickers to stick in my many albums. He kitted me out in each of Saints' strips in the Seventies and Eighties, from the old fashioned stripes (with the ironed hole in the back) to the fancy number from the Kevin Keegan years, a red shirt with a broad white stripe down it. He was completely and utterly proud of me and my idea of thanks was to pack up and walk out on his life. Mum was beside herself with heartache too. For her though not only was I walking away but I was taking her two youngest grandchildren with me too. I can't imagine Mum and Dad could ever be the same again, and bet that the pain cut deep. So much so that I am sure that there is plenty of quiet resentment pointed my way.

At the time of my move, my attitude was different. I was fiercely focussed on making sure everything was just right for *my* family. All other considerations – including the Saints – were absolutely secondary to me. I was sure that no matter how disappointed they were at the outcome, they would adjust appropriately and, frankly, get over it. For the first few months we furiously built ourselves a new, fantastic life. To give you an idea, within nine days of arriving I had started work, Kellie had found us a home and the kids were enrolled in school ready for the start of the school year in February. By June we had bought and moved into a new house – which had a garage and a driveway, something we had craved.

Many years later I can look back on the move with a little more pragmatism. Was it the right thing to do? For my family yes, absolutely – no question. But was it the right thing to do? At what cost? Emigrating has been mentally tough for me at times, but for Mum and Dad it has been a devastating experience – something I have to take responsibility for.

Ten years ago, if I were asked by anyone thinking of emigrating what advice I would give them, I would have said if you don't buy a ticket, you won't win the raffle. You might have a go and it not work out, but at least you had a go. It is exactly the kind of thing I tell my children all the time. Ten years later, I don't think I would give the same advice. I still maintain that if you don't buy a ticket, you certainly won't win the raffle, but I would qualify that by saying that, before you take a ticket, have a think about your relationship with your wider family. You need that bit of disconnect between yourself and your parents when you emigrate – an unspoken endorsement for you to go live your life. I'm certainly not saying the love needs to be less, but it needs to be more grounded. I envy Kellie, the relationship she has with her mum gives her the ability to have no regrets at all, whereas I have always been weighed down with the baggage forged by my relationship with my parents.

Initially migration is like an adventure, and it felt that way for us, and I absolutely don't regret it. But through the years there are signposts, reminders as to what you left behind. It makes you stop and think, I miss that. It could be family celebrating marriage, kids growing up, people succeeding in their careers, people getting older, or health beginning to fade. You have to have to a slush fund – money to dash back for weddings, funerals and illnesses. You also have an obligation to go back every couple of years, even though England wouldn't be in the top fifty places you would want to holiday, when you have a little bit of savings to splash.

For me, the most persistent reminder is of course the Saints, every single week. I've never felt homesick that I can remember, but there is one glaring exception. Three o'clock on a Saturday afternoon hurts bad. There is no football here, nothing happening on a Saturday afternoon in New Zealand. No matches to wind yourself up for, no Gillette Soccer Saturday to follow what was happening to other teams on the ticker at the bottom of the screen, no Radio Solent with commentary on the game, no tickets for the game, no frisson of excitement, no Dad to hang out with. It's the only time of the week I feel lost, as if there is something obvious missing. I hate Saturday afternoons.

For the upcoming cup final, I need to dip in that notional slush fund. After all, that's what it is there for, isn't it? I keep on at Dan and Sama, at Hannah and Charlie, and Hayley – organise your weddings on the same day so I can keep the trip costs down. Fingers crossed nobody kicks the bucket in the next few months, because I might be a bit bollocksed for money then. I've had stern words with Mum, I've told here don't you dare think about keeling over and conking out for the time being, just wait until I can replenish some savings first.

Black and Blue

The worst thing about New Zealand is of course Rugby. It's such a crap sport. When I was at school, the only kids who played Rugby were the ones that were not good enough to play football. Unfortunately, I went to a secondary school where rugby was compulsory. At the age of eleven I was already in the first years' school rugby team as a winger and I hated it. It was such a miserable experience devoid of any kind of joy or inspiration that most sports give to a child. I just stood there freezing my arse off by the touchline, at around 10:00 a.m. on a frosty winter morning, with absolutely no clue about what to do or where to go, wondering at what point were my legs were going to get broken. In a match, a kid on our team burst through toward the try line. For no other reason than to stay warm I ran with him. He was pole-axed by a crunching tackle near the try line that absolutely flattened this poor guy. Before he was tackled he threw the ball toward me. I caught it, trotted over the try line, placed the ball down and won the match for my school team. Afterwards the PE teacher was beside himself with praise, how well I did, how brilliant the try was. I thought to myself that 'brilliant' was Kevin Keegan scoring an overhead kick against Manchester United – not wandering over a line and plonking a misshapen ball on the frosty ground. There was certainly not the same thrill as hitting the back of the net with a goal. Incidentally the kid who was tackled had to wear a neck brace and this wired contraption to keep his head still for the rest of the school term. Dad came in to save the day again, to write a note to tell my PE teacher that Russell will not be playing rugby anymore because of my promising football career. Sure, I got more than my fair share of bullying from the PE teacher after that but, boy, was I grateful to Dad and relieved that I didn't have to be involved in that rubbish anymore.

I tried to get into the rugby a bit when I arrived in New Zealand. We went to a match or two, but saying it wasn't for me was a bit like saying the Queen prefers Take That over thrash metal. I would watch as, in front of me, large sweaty men would hold up other large, sweaty men by their thighs, as a squat, fat, sweaty bloke, bandaged on his head and thighs, throws the ball from the touchline into the line out. One guy catches the ball and everyone then jumps on him. How brilliant is that? Not particularly, to my mind. Then eventually, the ball squirts out to the one player in the team who can kick the ball who then proceeds to boot the ball as far into the crowd as is possible, to the cheers of the crowd and cries of 'well played'! There is no suddenness to proceedings. There is no incident beyond the predicted passage of play. It is so stop/start with more 'stop' than 'start'. The strongest team always wins; there are very rarely any surprise results. The view at the match in person is inferior to the view of the match at home. The laws of the game are so intricate and precise the players don't know them all. It is a sport that can cherry-pick from other sports at a certain age; that is to say, it is not a sport like football or cricket that has to be formed on talent and practise at a very young age. You can't just pick up football or cricket at the age of sixteen having never played it before. You certainly can with rugby. Despite my best efforts, the sport leaves me cold. Even the rugby competition here, the 'Super Rugby' tournament, doesn't impress me. It's a competition made up of teams that are not even the national club teams – the teams that have support, sentiment and club history. Instead they use shiny 'franchise' teams that are an amalgam of some of the club teams in a particular region. Dad used to think this idea was hilarious.

"Imagine if they did that in football, Russ?" he told me. "If there was a franchise team in the south, covering Southampton and Portsmouth, they'd have to call the team South-mouth." It'd never catch on.

I walk my dog around some rugby pitches at the end of our road. One day, a coach was taking his first training session with some young kids. As I walked by with the dogs I heard him say to the kids that rugby is the best, most exciting game that they would ever play. What an awful, mean, dreadful thing to say! I wanted to stop, go over to the guy, shake him and tell him not to feed such callous lies to the impressionable youths before him, and I'd tell the kids to flee, to run for their lives, at least across town to the local football pitches. For god's sake, a game of musical chairs would offer more personal gratification than a game of rugby. Of course, the coach was far bigger than me so I just kept walking.

New Zealand sport means the national rugby team, the All Blacks, national rugby teams and hardly anything else, very much like England with football. Now I know how people in England feel, who are not into football. It's so frustrating and boring listening to the constant non-news! There is cricket in the summer, which is great when India, Australia or England pop over for a tour, rugby league, basketball and football, with New Zealand having just a single professional team in the equivalent Australian Leagues. The Kiwis are good at netball too. Beyond that you have to really scratch around. Like rugby and netball, New Zealand loves to excel in sports that no one else in the world plays so they can boast that they are the best (not at all like snooker or darts in England). And they love their triathlons.

The New Zealander prefers the national team of all their sports to have a nickname or brand because the typical New Zealander feels an in-built insecurity to their country – the 'All Blacks' is the most obvious example. They have this amazingly pointless inferiority complex that impedes their ambition and their successes. When a rock star comes to New Zealand to play, at the press conference the eager journo will ask the exact same question again and again and again. "Do you like New Zealand?" I would love some guy to turn around one day and say "No idea, mate. I'm here for the money. I won't be coming again because it's too far away, and you don't have Fosters on tap!" David Beckham brought his LA Galaxy team to play here and he was inundated with questions about New Zealand – his normal trademark placid smile almost cracked under the strain that day. When Clive Woodward brought the British Lions to play the All Blacks in 2005 the nation almost went into meltdown when he kept referring to them as 'New Zealand' and not the 'All Blacks'. It was hilarious. New Zealand name all their national teams: the rugby union team are the 'All Blacks', the rugby league team are the 'Kiwis', the netball team are the 'Silver Ferns' and the football team are the 'All Whites'. The cricket team are the 'Black Caps' and the hockey team are the 'Black Sticks'. The basketball team are the 'Tall Blacks' whilst the wheelchair basketball team are the 'Wheel Blacks'. The New Zealand badminton team were called the 'Black 'Cocks', until they decided to reconsider the idea in 2005 (I can't think why). Now they are known as the 'New Zealand Badminton Team'.

The All Blacks are a damned team and I am glad I am not a supporter. I say this because it doesn't matter who is in charge of the team, how many Rugby World Cups they win, however many number of top players they have, how many teams they thrash – as far as the New Zealand public is concerned whatever they do, however they play, it is never enough. If they win well, then the opposition was too poor and they lament that there are not enough teams able to give them a good game. If they win a close game, there are endless enquiries and repercussions that last weeks about how badly they played. If they lose then the nation goes into mourning (which is brilliant fun though!).

For me, winning is everything, performance is absolutely secondary (although of course one is often needed to deliver the other). If we win the cup final 1-0 with an own goal after the most boring game imaginable, I will be celebrating just as hard as if we win 7-3 after been down 3-0. I will treasure the moment in exactly the same way. It's so stupid to think of things in any other way – what's the point?

I saw one All Blacks fan being interviewed after watching the All Blacks win against Australia, in Australia, a couple of years back. They won by more than twenty points (apparently that's a lot, like winning a football match 7-2). He was cross and frustrated, disgusted at the apparent poor performance. That small, single interview is exactly the problem the All Blacks have. They are easily the best team in the world, but it is still not enough: when they won the Rugby World Cup in 2011 in New Zealand people grumbled that it didn't count because they had home advantage. I don't imagine there were many England fans in 1966 writing off their World Cup triumph just because it was on home soil. I've never quite got my head round it.

In England, Kellie – being a New Zealander – was a big All Blacks fan, and would get up early to watch them play in the Tri-Nations on a Saturday morning. Fast forward to a life in New Zealand, she has completely distanced herself from being an All Blacks fan. I took her to a game once – after half-time as the All Blacks raced back on to the pitch, and this bloke behind me, decked in black woolly hat, black scarf and black All Blacks coat shouted grumpily, "About bloody time!" – I was always used to clapping and cheering when my team come out to play.

I find the behaviours of New Zealand supporters at sporting events peculiar. At the cup final in 2003, for instance, me and Dad got to the game early, all dressed up in the team's colours of yellow and blue, soaked up the electric atmosphere, cheered our team on until our throats were sore. Transpose that on to a major All Blacks test match, the New Zealand fans turn up to the game in their supporter's gear, soak up the atmosphere and when the game begins, immediately go off for a beer, hot chips and a squid ring, coming back half way through the first-half asking other fans what the score is. For the cup final this year I won't be leaving my seat for a moment.

Kiwis get bored at sporting events really easily (I'd be the same if I had to watch a rugby match too) and are often looking to organise a Mexican wave around the stadium. When Dad was over for a visit, I took him to a cricket one day international. The first Mexican wave was organised at over number three (out of 100 overs that day). Dad steadfastly remained seated each time the wave came around us. As everyone stood up and waved their arms in the air, Dad muttered "pricks!" under his breath (or worse), his arms stoically folded. As the second innings started and the cheap, poorly made beer was beginning to take hold of the locals, the wave became embellished with masses of plastic empty or full bottles of beer being thrown into the air. If you are lucky you might get a partially full bottle with the lid off to soak you as well as knock you on the head. On one occasion, amongst the hilarity of a wave and bottle attack, a full bottle came down on the hand of a young kid near the front holding a miniature bat (great for getting player signatures off the boundary). His knuckle came up like a tennis ball. Me and Dad agreed that we would not be surprised if he'd cracked a bone or worse. Very funny indeed.

With decades and decades of history with the All Blacks that consist of a precession of win after win after win, it has bred possibly the most vulgar type of supporter that I have had the misfortune to meet – and I would include teams that had a large hooligan contingent in that last statement. In England, Manchester United fans, off the back of constant success through the Nineties and Noughties, developed a chip on their shoulder the size of a King Edward, where they felt they were above and superior to other mere-mortal supporters. Well, I have to report that the chip on the New Zealand All Black fan is so large it can't fit on their shoulder as it would crush them to death. Like the sport itself they are an eternal bore.

Whilst the All Blacks are damned however well they play, the All Whites – the New Zealand national football team are equally lost but for different reasons. Football in New Zealand is gravely ill. The national team, stuck at the arse-end of the world exist in the Oceania confederation, which meant they get to play teams in the Pacific region to qualify for the World Cup, like New Caledonia, Fiji, Vanuatu and the Solomon Islands, hardly the most thrilling of fixtures. As you might imagine, there aren't many other teams wanting to come to New Zealand for a friendly match either. Although the football association themselves have meagre resources from which to develop players, typically they win out easily during World Cup qualifying and are paired with a team from South or North America to qualify for the World Cup. At the World Cup in Brazil in 2014, New Zealand were knocked out by Mexico, 8-3 in a two-legged play off. It could have been 18-3. For 2018, it looks like they will be playing Argentina in the play off. I may get to see Lionel Messi play, but New Zealand will get totally embarrassed and outclassed. The consequences of which will again mean that interest and momentum in the sport will wane, and kids playing the game (and there are far more kids playing football than rugby up to the age of fourteen) will disappear into other sports like rugby or to nothing. It's no surprise that the two occasions that New Zealand qualified for the World Cup in 1982 and 2010 were off the back of final qualifying play-offs against teams in Asia. In 2009, I took Shauna to see the All Whites beat Bahrain in the final play-off match to win through to the South African finals. It was a memorable night, far more atmospheric than the library-like atmosphere in rugby or cricket, and is widely regarded as one of the best nights of New Zealand sport in history. Unfortunately, these nights are once in a generation events, not events that happen twice or three times every year. Australia got fed up being in the Oceania Confederation and moved into the Asian Confederation. They regularly now play tough, meaningful matches that are played in front of full houses in big stadia, the consequence of which is that they have qualified for the last three World Cups and the quality of the game in Australia continues to improve with players like Alessandro Del Piero, David Villa, Robbie Fowler and Dwight Yorke spending a season or two playing there. By comparison, the All Whites always struggle to get ten-thousand supporters for matches against the likes of Fiji. This apparent lack of success bleeds down into the only professional team, Wellington Phoenix, who play in the Australian A-League, and the sad New Zealand national league made up of eight teams and amateur players with limited capability. The football association are also hamstrung by immense travel costs as all the other representative teams, under-23, -21, -20, -19 and -17 teams for both men and women always get a place in the respective FIFA finals because in those competitions Oceania has a place, a slot, all of its own. So they qualify for almost every single FIFA tournament going except the one that matters. I don't think there is another country on the planet that qualifies for so many football tournaments so regularly. If only there was ever someone decent to play.

In May 2003 I was at the biggest event in the English football calendar, amongst 75,000 other fans, at the FA Cup final, watching my team go toe-to-toe with some of the world's best players and against one of the most famous teams in the world. In 2006, I was at the New Zealand equivalent football event, the New Zealand Football Championship Grand Final, between Auckland City and Canterbury United. It was held at Auckland's Kiwitea Street ground which officially holds 3,250 people, although I expect in reality there were less than 1,000 people there that day. I went with Sarah and Shauna, with firm instructions from Kellie to make sure they did not get lost. The match was on TV just like in England, although the audience was probably hundreds rather than millions. Kellie watched it on TV though. During the second half I received a phone call from her. She told me to get out of the beer tent and look after the girls. It appears that the girls could be clearly seen on telly, in their bright red and white Saints shirts visible from the cameras, happily playing on the perimeter barrier behind the goal, doing somersaults and other gymnasticy-type things on the barrier. I could then be seen rushing out on national television to get the girls in hurry, and I received a follow up text that said, "That's better!"

It might surprise you to learn I have met many Saints fans here in New Zealand, and quite a few in my town. Not long after we had settled in New Zealand, Sarah came to talk to me about her new chum. I was always pleased when they announced that they had found a new friend. We were always worried about how the girls would deal to the move but to their immense credit they made it look easy. Sarah proclaimed to me that her new friend was a Saints fan, and so was her sisters and her Dad. I went on with the discussion, but found the idea a little far-fetched. Jovially I would say to the girls not to hang with boys in the playground, especially if they were Portsmouth fans. They would take the absurdity of what I said as fun and turn it round. "I met a new friend today, Daddy – but don't worry they don't like Portsmouth either!" they would tell me.

One night Sarah came home from her new friend's house. Her friend's Dad had given Sarah a lift home. I got to meet him and he was a Saints fan, Mick, from Romsey, and I had found a friend as well as Sarah. He's introduced me to three other Saints fans I can think of and has taken me on visits to Hamilton where every year or so about a hundred Saints fans or so meet up for a beer and to reminisce.

We've been to other sporting events together too, cricket or football. All the ex-pats wear their teams' colours. You will see dozens and dozens of different football shirts from all over Europe at New Zealand sporting events. And it doesn't take very long for likeminded people to gravitate to you. It's a peculiar thing, a person who wouldn't normally look twice at or think to talk to, is suddenly easy to talk to because the shirt that you are wearing illustrates an affinity and an interest you immediately share. It's certainly good to know that I'm not alone over here.

Alas, I found also that the customs system here is not what it should be though and have met a number of Portsmouth supporters in New Zealand. Until fairly recently, petrol stations tended to be manned: an attendant would come out to your car and fill the car up for you. The very first time I had to get petrol for my car at my local petrol station (in my Saints shirt), this tall curly-haired gentleman came out to greet me, singing "Scummer! Scummer!" at me. I couldn't believe it – I'd travelled all the way around the world and one of the first people I met came from Portsmouth. I made sure I observed what he did, just in case he tried to fill my car with diesel. I also had to plan which petrol station I could use, depending on the Saints result each week.

I went into a book shop once in a small holiday town north of Auckland. There to my surprise, was a gentleman in a white Portsmouth away shirt. After ensuring the children were safe with Kellie, I approached the man with caution. "Are you wearing that shirt for a bet?" I asked, using the stock standard opening statement in these situations, nothing too complicated that might confuse the poor fellow.

"What's the problem?" he answered indignantly looking up at me in my proud Saints attire, putting the book he was looking at down. "Have you never seen a Portsmouth fan before?"

"Well not one who could read!" I responded gleefully. Game. Set. Match!

One day in New Zealand in 2010, driving around with Dad some place in Auckland, he spotted this guy minding his own business walking along the footpath. Dad noticed the slightly faded worn blue shirt synonymous with the modern Portsmouth team.

"Pull over Russ!" he shouted excitedly.

"What for?" I hadn't noticed the guy.

"It's a dirty bloody Shite!" Dad said beside himself. I knew from many, many years of attending football with Dad what a dirty bloody shite was. So I pulled over, the man oblivious to what was about to happen. It so happened that neither of us were wearing a Saints shirt that day (it does happen occasionally). It was also at a time that Portsmouth had just entered administration again, in financial turmoil.

Dad rolled down his car window as the man neared.

"I hope you bastards go out of business! You're all a bunch of cheats and crooks!" he shouted from out of the window. The bloke was stunned, horrified at this elderly gentleman dishing out this volley of abuse to him! Cool as you like, Dad turned to me and said, "Drive on, Russ!" The man stood there motionless.

What Dad did could be construed as a little mean but I will come to his defence. To explain, Portsmouth won the FA Cup in 2008. They had beaten Manchester United along the way but otherwise had an easy draw of it. Even more fortuitously, the big teams had all knocked each other out on the other side of the draw and the small Championship team Cardiff City had reached the final to be their opponents. Cardiff were very unlucky and Portsmouth muddled to a 1-0 victory which ranks up there as one of the worst days of my life. However, the football club compiled a team of players that represented an average

Premier League team, and paid top dollar for them to sign on and then paid them handsomely. The problem was they were paying for players way beyond the financial means for the club. Eventually less than two years later, the club fell over owing more than 130 million pounds to creditors. Basically, he felt they had cheated their way into the Premier League with money they simply didn't have, and cheated their way to a trophy that was wholly undeserved. I accept that the Portsmouth fans themselves had been cheated too, but in football you have to take the rough with the smooth.

One thing that niggles me about the locals here in New Zealand is that when you are engaged in a conversation about football in England, I always get asked if I was a hooligan. Sometimes by the more ignorant, I am actually assumed to be a hooligan simply because I am English. Obviously the sensationalised news broadcasts has framed a certain point of view on this side of the world. True, watching the football in the Eighties was harsh at times as I have described, but Dad always tried to keep us firmly away from trouble and certainly never ever get involved with it. There are scenes from The Dell, and at Highbury in the FA Cup semi-final in 1984, plus other matches that will live with me forever and give me the chills thinking about it. The unsettling dull roar of hooligans in the distance charging closer like the mobbed horde that they were is not a memory I'll ever be able to shake off.

My Dad's friend Mr. King was a big Chelsea fan. Some Saturdays during the Eighties when Saints were not playing at home, we'd travel up to London to watch Chelsea play. Me, Dad and Mr. King used to stand at the famous Shed End of the ground, named so because it looked like a terrace inside a giant shed. The Shed End would be where you would find some of the most staunch and vocal support and where I would improve my swearing lexicon, adding words such as 'ponce' or 'melt' into my derogatory words memory bank folder. In hindsight you could argue that if, during the Eighties, there was such an epidemic of hooliganism within football, why on earth was Dad taking me to a game in Chelsea? They had one of the most notorious hooligan elements in the country, and whose away support had been banned from The Dell in 1984 following some of the worst and shocking scenes of organised fighting inside and outside a ground ever, in front of our own eyes. The thought process from Dad and Mr. King was that fighting wasn't something hooligans did at home games, it was always something that was instigated by the away contingent. And with Chelsea's reputation, no away contingent is going to try and intimidate Chelsea fans.

Mind you, I witnessed some rough goings on and I don't mean the language. In one game, deep in winter one fan struck her girlfriend around the face because she complained to him that her feet were cold. Nobody batted an eyelid; there was a game going on, after all. Even before the match, the surroundings were so different, police on horseback for instance.

We'd spend our pre-match in one of the now long-gone pie and mash shops near to the Stamford Bridge ground. To the uninitiated, a pie and mash shop sold ... pie and mash, in a bowl with a ladle of 'green liquor' on top. When I asked what that was, Mr. King told me that green liquor was a soup with chopped eel in it. Bugger that, I thought. It's the only establishment I can ever remember where the shop owner bullied the customers. "Big game today everyone, so eat up quick and piss off!" she shouted at the punters eating away at their tables. When I asked for no green liquor she told me, "Shut up – it's good for you nipper!" and loaded a dollop on my plate. She was like a crone or a witch from a fantasy movie with long uncut fingernails that had started to curl, so there was no way I was arguing with her. Dad came to the rescue again though – he swapped mine for his that was free of green goo. One time Dad thought the old lady was going to spill his bowl when she brought it over to him, so he got up and held his hands up to help. The woman belted Dad with her stick.

One game however changed Dad's mind about watching Chelsea matches. In 1988, Chelsea were playing Middlesbrough in a play-off match that would decide which team would get into the top division – Division One in those days, about four years before the inception of the Premier League. That day, we couldn't get into the Shed End – it was full, and we didn't have tickets. Most matches in the Eighties were so poorly attended by today's standards you could just pay at the turnstile. The only stand we could find that was not full to watch the match was the away end. This was risky because Mr. King was Chelsea through-and-through and this was a big game. We could inadvertently cause a bit of bother here. Mr. King promised to behave, and against Dad's better judgement we went in.

Whilst the three Chelsea ends were full to the brim, the Middlesbrough end had plenty of space. We pitched up along the terrace behind one of the barriers that were distributed across the terrace. We stayed quiet and minded our own business. Suddenly a police officer dragged me by the collar and dragged me down to the front of the terrace, the caged fencing now standing right in front of me. He was so rough with me he had ripped my cheap jacket.

"Leave him alone!" Dad said to the officer.

"Kids down the front!" demanded the police officer. I was sixteen then, hardly a child.

"Piss off!" shouted Dad back at him. "Russ, get back here with me." I went back and stood by Dad.

"Don't you move!" the officer shouted at me. "If you move I'll have you slung out." I walked back down to the front.

"Don't speak to him like that!" Dad responded angrily. "He's not being a bother." I walked back up to Dad.

"He needs to stay safe – that means down the front," argued the officer, gesticulating with his finger as to exactly where the front was. I walked back down to the front.

"That's right brother. He does, and that means he stays with me. Now bugger off." I walked back up to Dad. Another police officer came over and they both walked away. I returned to Dad seriously impressed about how he dealt with the police, and not quite sure how we weren't thrown out. The police officer was an idiot, no doubt about that, but that was the way policing was in the Eighties: one scumbag meant you were all treated like scum and no exceptions. We were used to it by 1988.

Chelsea needed to win 2-0, as they had lost the first leg of the final. After ten minutes Chelsea scored and Dad had to hold Mr. King down – he was about to explode but any celebration could have caused a riot. Chelsea couldn't add another goal and lost the tie overall. The Middlesbrough fans celebrated hard, many fans coming over and hugging us although we really couldn't care less about their team. Hilariously, Mr. King was getting bear-hugged the most.

"We've done it! We're promoted!" screamed one Middlesbrough fan happily to him.

In complete despair, with a face like thunder, Mr. King could only look sad then pretending to go along to the celebrations. The Middlesbrough fan then hugged and kissed him. I don't think I could have contained myself the way Mr. King did that day.

Meanwhile, hundreds and hundreds of Chelsea fans had broken down the perimeter fencing and were charging over the pitch towards the Middlesbrough fans. They were furious with the result and aimed to take out their fury on the Middlesbrough supporters. Bottles, coins and rubbish rained over on us. We were pelted. Some Middlesbrough fans climbed their own perimeter fencing causing fences to collapse. People were falling over themselves as Chelsea fans engaged with the kids at the front. How I am glad Dad stood up to the police that day otherwise I would have been amongst all that fighting.

We made an attempt to leave, moving up the terrace however we could. However, the police would not open the gates – the rule keeping away fans in the ground after the final whistle was being strictly enforced. We were fortunate, a steward beckoned us over and he let us slip out a side gate, whereupon we made a run for it as sporadic fights broke out outside the ground. We basically ran for our lives. The newspapers dubbed the match 'The Battle For Stamford Bridge' and the police came in for a lot of criticism for their handling of the event. We never went back to Chelsea again as neutrals, although I've been back in much better times, as a legitimate supporter watching Saints there.

I've watched a number of games without Dad, and I've never had any inclination to get involved in any such behaviour. I will admit one count of appalling indiscretion however. When I was twelve, in a match with Dad at The Dell, we played out a dull match against Stoke City. The game was played after a fall of snow. Most of the snow had been cleared before kick-off, but there was still a white dusting across the pitch and the teams were using an orange ball so it could be clearly seen. At a corner to Saints, I collected some remaining snow off the terrace and made a snowball that I managed to hit the Stoke City defender George Berry with on the back (he of the Eighties afro, if anyone recalls). Stewards immediately set about looking for the culprit. They never found out it was me, but Dad knew and that was far worse. I got a deserved clip round the ear for that one and was made to regret it completely. (I often thought when standing at that the same spot on the terrace in my adulthood, what an excellent shot it was to hit the defender from my position.)

Since then I've only been interested in watching my team. Anyway, hooligan problems had all but gone from the early Nineties thankfully, with only Portsmouth's classless fans to remind Saints support of a darker shade of football.

Saints in NZ

Saints were fourth in the Premier League when I left English soil. Eighteen months later they had been relegated into the Championship, after twenty-eight consecutive years in the top division. The team that got to the final in 2003 was slowly broken up, players such as James Beattie had left for pastures new, the manager Gordon Strachan had left the club too and had been replaced by first Paul Sturrock, who lasted only six months followed by Steve Wigley, a former coach promoted as a manager for the first time. Statistically, Wigley would go down as Saints' worst ever manager, with one win in this fourteen games in charge of the team. Although I'd argue that his successor, a certain Harry Redknapp must run him mighty close. Don't get Dad started on Harry Redknapp – as far as he is concerned Redknapp is public enemy number one.

At this time the club was like a soap opera. Redknapp had been manager at Portsmouth, and had engineered their dubious rise into the Premier League. He resigned in November 2004 after a falling out within the club and a few weeks, on the 8th of December 2004, popped up to replace Wigley. His task over more than half the season was to win seven matches out of twenty-one. Not a lot to ask you might think – after all he had a bit of pedigree with his experience at Portsmouth and at West Ham United before that. He brought in lots of new players, almost all of them adding zero value to the ineffectual players that were already in the club, and the team continued to struggle. The quality of football was feeble.

On the last day of the 2005 season, we still had a chance to stay up and sat outside the bottom three. All we needed to do was win our final game at home and we would be safe, irrespective of results elsewhere. We had been here on a number of occasions before and having your destiny in your own hands is mightily important. The problem was we had only won six matches all season so it wasn't something that the team could accomplish naturally, and we were playing Manchester United. And, in fairness, this time round there was no standout player like Le Tissier to make some magic. I settled down to watch the Manchester United match on TV at around 3:00 a.m. on a Monday morning.

We started the game well enough and went ahead, but Manchester United turned it round inevitably to win 2-1 and send Saints spiralling out of the league, flat last out of the twenty teams in it. In fact, as I remember, it was less a 'spiral' more a whimper or meek surrender by average players earning too much money. The players visibly just gave up, sauntering around the pitch without a care in the world, and not much capacity or talent to play football either. I was furious. I could not believe what had happened to the club. Supposedly Redknapp was a capable manager, but not at Southampton. Once the going got a little tough again the following season in the Championship, off he skipped again, damage done, back to Portsmouth. Portsmouth fans gleefully proclaimed, 'mission accomplished'.

After watching the match in despair, I realised I had to go to work. How I suffered that day. I went in to work, found a desk hidden away and stayed away from any human interaction as much I could. I was asked more than once if I was okay, but I said I didn't want to talk about it. I suspect they must have thought I had suffered a family bereavement. In some respects, I had. It was one of the longest work days of my life and I daresay not one of my most productive. When I got home, I found a large spare box that was used to transport some of our stuff from England, and packed up every shirt, football programme, flag, picture, ornament and Subbuteo team I could find related to Saints, and bunged it in the box. I felt like a jilted partner, angry, confused, wanting answers. My fury extended to my computer, all pictures, bookmarks of web sites, computer games involving the Saints were archived (note that I did not delete them, just in case).

As far as I was concerned we were done. Like a deep long-term relationship, one of the parties had done the unforgivable. There was no going back. It was over.

Out of the Premier League for a UK-based Saints supporter was crushing enough. For me, there was an extra blow. Sky TV in New Zealand only carried coverage of the Premier League. There was no coverage of the Football League Championship below it. Until Saints got back in the Premier League, or by some slim chance Sky TV found some sort of slot not covered by rugby, rugby, rugby, and decided to drain any spare cash they had in coverage of a subsidiary competition across the other side of the world for a sport precious few people here understood, then my access to Saints was gone.

I did have however ... have a plan. My broadband coverage was reasonable, and some web sites had started to stream coverage that was on television, on to the Internet. By today's standards that is illegal, but in 2005 there was definitely a grey area of 'interpretation' for a platform to watch TV that was in those days in its inception. So I took advantage of that perceived ambiguity of the law, presumed it to be legal, and found a way to meet one of the loves of my life again.

Nowadays there are plenty of legal platforms to watch your team in any league. You just access the web page, subscribe, press Play and enjoy the game. Back in 2005 it was a different experience altogether. What you had to do was go to a web page that listed all the football matches that were on live TV anywhere in the world that week. Once you found your team, you would be given a list of TV channels from a number of countries that are covering the match live. Depending on the channel you chose to watch the match on, you would have to go to another web site to download a program that you could watch the match through. This additional web site would often hold a number of dubious adverts that would be placed all around the web page but also on the web page just where you were meant to click 'Download'. The trick was to close the advert by finding the [X] button around the edge of the advert. Often, however, the [X] button was fake, and there would be a minuscule, almost hidden alternative [X] button somewhere else on the web page, randomly placed. Once you could find the real [X] button to close the right advert, then you could finally download the program. Once downloaded, you needed to open the program, pick the correct TV channel, based on the listings on the original web site that you visited, and hope the game would be on.

That wasn't the end of it though. The commentary was often not in English, and usually in an excitable Asian dialect, although that was the least of the problems. Sometimes, the sporting event on before Saints were on might overrun, so the first few minutes may be missed. Sometimes you would miss the first half hour of the match. Sometimes they didn't play the match at all. And sometimes the quality of picture was so wretched that you had to find another source for the match, which meant going to the first web site, finding another channel, finding another program, going to the next web site, negotiating past the intrusive adverts again, downloading the next program, and loading it. Fingers crossed that the new feed for the match would be better than the first. I shudder to think how many Ukrainian wives I have inadvertently expressed an interest in marrying during these lean footballing years, by missing the tiny [X] button.

It didn't do any good. I think Saints won only one of about sixteen live matches shown between 2005 and 2008. One such loss was against Watford away 3-2 early in the 2008 season. The first Saints goal to make it 1-1 was scored by their Polish international Grzegorz Rasiak. However, as I watched it, Rasiak was about to shoot when the screen froze for about three minutes. I had to do the web page / channel / program / web site / Ukrainian housewife dodge / download / play thing all over again, and didn't know he'd even equalised until the start of the second half. Saints' second goal to make it 2-1 was scored by a young Nathan Dyer, a small, speedy winger. In the build up to the goal before Dyer received the ball to shoot, my computer displayed an error and the program closed. It wouldn't reopen so I had to do the web page / channel / program / web site / Lithuanian bride avoidance / download / play thing once again. By the time I had it successfully up and running again, Watford had already equalised to make it 2-2. But now though the system was willing to behave and show the match in reasonable quality. Which was a shame, because Watford scored the winning goal in the last minute.

(Fun fact. Since Saints were relegated in 2005 until the start of the 2017 season, Saints had sold on or released 161 players. Out of all the many, many talented players who have left Southampton, how many players went on to win the Premier League? The answer is just one, but who? Gareth Bale for Tottenham Hotspur? No. Theo Walcott and Alex Oxlade-Chamberlain at Arsenal? Nope! Adam Lallana and the other 398 ex-Saints players that moved on to Liverpool? No. The only player is Nathan Dyer for Leicester City in the 2016 season. Something to impress your friends at parties I think.)

Saints were not on TV every week, so most of the time I had to make do with text updates. Dad agreed to keep me well informed about matches as they were happening. He argued though, wouldn't his text's wake me up? The fact of the matter is that Saturday nights, Sunday mornings are a difficult sleep when the Saturday afternoon matches are playing in England. If I know that Saints are playing then I can't get my brain to settle down. What team will the manager play? Will Marians Pahars be fit to play? What position might we be in if we win? The brain simply doesn't stop. I might well doze off or fall asleep but will bolt awake during the match. That's how it was in 2005, and that is how it is today. So I told Dad that texting me was not a problem and was preferred. However, he refused to give me bad news as it might ruin my Sunday. This made this process flawed.

The best example of this was Saints versus Dirty Leeds in the 2006 season.

Text number one from Dad. "1-0". That's a good start.

Text number two from Dad. "Bloody scored again Russ! 2". This was going well.

Text number three from Dad. "3-0 pen". A penalty? Fantastic!

That was all the texts I got. Brilliant – it's always gratifying to beat the Dirty Leeds, and 3-0 was a great score line.

It wasn't until Sunday evening when I had a moment to wallow on the BBC web site to relive this fine victory when I found out Dirty Leeds had actually beaten us 4-3.

This is what it had come to. Watching Saints through a tiny window on the screen in amongst 'Please Wait' messages at almost every throw in. Or receiving half a score from Dad. In the 2007 season though, it looked as though Saints were coming out of the darkness and back into the light. Thanks to a handsome win against Southend United on the final day of the season, Saints had finished a creditable (compared to previous years) sixth. This meant that they had qualified for the play-offs for promotion to the Premier League.

Out came the big box of Saints stuff. Out came the latest Saints away shirt – a homage to the yellow 1976 shirt. Out came the big union flag with Saints' crest in the centre, which got tied to Sarah's netball post (she was forbidden to play in case her netball dirtied my flag). Out came the ornaments and framed pictures. Out came the Subbuteo teams. The Saints web sites and computer games were neatly restored on my computer. The Saints were back, welcomed back into my house in open arms and all misdemeanours were forgiven and forgotten.

In the Championship, the play-offs are contested by the teams finishing third, fourth, fifth and sixth in two semi-final matches played over two legs. The overall winner in both semi-finals get a trip to the newly rebuilt and reopened Wembley Stadium in a match to decide who gets promoted. This year, in 2017, the promoted winner will increase their income by about 200 million pounds simply by winning this final match. In 2007 it was worth about 40 million, much lower but still eye-watering nonetheless. Saints would play Derby County in their play-off semi-final, with the first leg at St Mary's.

With the live feed streaming neatly on my computer, all Latvian Lovelies For Sale banners quelled, optimum resolution found with an hour still to go before the match was due to start, my house was open to all the many and varied Saints fans from around the town of Pukekohe and the surrounding suburbs. As it was, both of them came round and we enjoyed a nice take away curry and a Fosters before kick-off.

Saints started well and scored a whole goal to lead 1-0. I was stunned – I'd forgotten what a Saints goal looked like. We all duly woke Kellie up, and the girls. Normally when I watch football overnight I have developed this quiet, whispery cheer, a bit like letting air out of a balloon. I even learnt to clap using the join of my wrist and hands, which I found makes no noise at all, but does make me look highly dubious, like an excited homosexual. However, whilst I can keep the volume down to dull whisper for the majority of the game, as was demonstrated when Derby equalised soon after, I just cannot keep it going for ninety minutes. Eventually something happens that knocks each of the girls out of their slumber.

"WHAT'S THE BLOODY MATTER WITH YOU? YOU BLOODY PRICK!" was my loud advice to Pele during the second half of the Derby County match which again woke up the house this night, as he quite obviously grabbed at a Derby player's shirt in the penalty area. (Before we go any further, this Pele was Pedro Miguel Cardoso Monteiro, a Portuguese player from Cape Verde, and certainly not the legendary Brazilian. At the time the real Pelé – note the accent on the second 'e' – was 66, and in all likelihood, would have been better acquisition than this Portuguese version. At least he would not have had a brain fart like that and stuck his hand out like that.)

The penalty was scored and Saints lost the match 2-1. In the second leg in Derby, Saints needed a miracle to turn it around. Especially when they went 1-0 down early on, 3-1 down on aggregate.

I was at work for this match. In those days, I worked for a very small company as an operations manager, in a small office, part of a shared office block. It wasn't unusual for me to be on my own as I was for this match. Unfortunately, the work equipment blocked access to the web site and Estonian Bitches advertising so I couldn't watch the match, so through the magic of the Internet, tuned in to Radio Solent to listen to the match.

Saints equalised in the tie, when the Derby goalkeeper came out of his area. Unable to use his hands the 'keeper headed the ball straight to one of our strikers who swept the ball home from about thirty yards. In the second half, Saints scored again, 2-1 on the night, 3-3 on aggregate. Goodness knows what the other tenants in the other offices thought at that point. Maybe they thought the delirious screams coming from my office were from YouTube. Derby County scored again via a freaky own goal to push them ahead again in the tie and restore me to my slumped position on my chair, head in hands. But in the last minute of normal time I was out of my seat as if I had been ejected from the passenger seat of James Bond's Aston Martin. As Saints poured forward in desperate search of an equalising goal, the ball squirmed away from a Derby defender in the penalty box, into the path of Grzegorz Rasiak. Rasiak dug the ball out from under his feet and smashed the ball into the net. The final score was 3-2 to Saints, 4-4 on aggregate, and extra time was required.

There were no further goals in extra time and so the match went to Penalties: a penalty shoot out to decide who gets to the play-off final at Wembley and a chance to return to the Premier League. In subsequent years, the rules for penalties would change, and the team who, after extra time, had scored the most goals away from home, would win the tie. Typical again for Southampton, had this rule been in place in 2007, Saints would have already won it.

But in 2007 penalties it was. I bet Dad was pacing up and down his lounge at this point: that's what I was doing at work. No work was being done at all now. Life had stopped. Nothing mattered except these next ten penalty kicks. For people who aren't fans of football, and whose interest in the game flitters in and out, penalty kicks is an ideal fix. You can tune in to the nail-biting last few kicks in the match, pick a team to follow, and get a taster of what it feels like for a football fan every single week for ninety minutes. That sudden surge of delight or despair if your team wins or loses is the kind of electric charge that us fans feel *all the time*. Penalty kicks offers onlookers a peek into the soul of a football fan.

Saints would take the first penalty. This was good. Sixty percent of all penalty shoot outs are won by the team going first. However, Saints' first penalty was dreadful and was saved easily. Derby scored all their kicks and won the shoot-out easily. If any onlooker could have peered into my soul that morning at work they would have seen it as being totally pissed off.

Failure to get promoted in our second year in the Championship was catastrophic. Money was spent with a view to getting back into the Premier League. With that objective missed Saints inevitably started to have financial problems, and it was no surprise to anyone that they started to slide down the Championship table over the next couple of seasons.

At the start of the 2009 season, we appointed our eighth manager since we had been in the Championship (in three seasons). Later that season we would get a ninth. The club owners declared that the club would be focusing on giving youth a chance, which had honourable intent, except the youth team players were the only ones left at the club. Gallantly these kids soldiered on in a hard, uncompromising league. The team played good, compelling football but were weak and naïve. The season was a struggle.

As the season came near to its close, two things happened. Firstly, me, Kellie and the kids were travelling back to England in late April for a holiday. Mum and Dad had been out to us twice, in 2004 and 2006, so it was our turn. I would be back to witness Saints' last two matches at home, against Crystal Palace and Burnley. I couldn't wait.

On the 2nd of April 2009, the other thing happened. Saints went bust. Their parent company was placed into administration, and Mr. Mark Fry from business rescue company Begbies Traynor was appointed to save the club and attempt to pay out its creditors. As well as the very real possibility of the club going out of existence, they were effectively relegated from the Championship into the third tier of English football – League One. Clubs who enter into administration are docked ten points in the league. If they are relegated even without the points deduction, then the points deduction is deferred until the next season. From trying to stay in the Championship, the target now was to ensure that the points deduction happened this season – not next, whilst relegation was now inevitable despite appeals from the administrator.

As we were readying ourselves for our first trek back to England, the next home match was against Charlton Athletic. Pleas went out to fans to come to the match and support their team. In a rush of blood to the head I thought I would do my bit and bought a ticket for the match on the club web site, even though I knew I wouldn't be in England for another couple of weeks. It was a dumb thing to do in retrospect but I felt a long way away (because I was), and a bit helpless; I wanted to support the club in any way I could.

Saints went into administration owing five million pounds, slightly less than the 130 million pounds that Portsmouth owed when they fell into administration in 2010. I still could not get my head around how all the money was squandered given the talent that was sold. That year I created a spreadsheet (don't judge me) and listed all the players sold by Saints to other clubs since 2005 – the year they were relegated.

In those four seasons (2006, 2007, 2008 and 2009) I worked out that Saints got rid of 84 players, that's an average of twenty-one players gone per season – practically an entire squad leaving every year. This says a lot about the stability of the club and the decision making process behind the scenes. Of those 84, 78 players left for pastures new, whilst six players retired. Of the 78 players that moved on, 55 went for nothing – for free – inclusive of sixteen players loaned out to other clubs. That left 23 players who commanded a fee payable to the club, that's about one in four players who were actually 'sold' for money.

However, those 23 players sold for cash brought in, according to reports, brought more than 58 million pounds to the club (to compare it to today's market, maybe multiply all these figures by three). Of those 23, there were a number of noteworthy multi-million pound deals.

Gareth Bale (he now of Real Madrid and dubious hairdo) was sold for ten million pounds to Tottenham Hotspur in 2007, although only about five million ended up being paid: the instalment plan agreed did not fit with the club's immediate cash flow crisis so the clubs agreed a revised deal that gave Saints a bit of cash flow and also a goalkeeper who never played in the first team (effectively this reserve goalkeeper cost us a cool five million – Tottenham sure saw us coming!). Theo Walcott was sold at sixteen years old to Arsenal for twelve million pounds in 2006. Peter Crouch was sold to Liverpool (who else?) in 2005 for more than eight million pounds. Kenwyn Jones went to Sunderland for six million. The other nineteen players shared fees of 22 million pounds. Yet somehow the club still fell over. I'm sure that like me, every Saints supporter was feeling very sorry for themselves and were concerned as to what would happen next.

We arrived in England to have a great holiday. Going back to St Mary's for the first time in five years should have felt like a thrilling experience, but the mood there was somewhat sombre. I left the country when Saints were fourth in the Premier League. Now they were about to exit through the trap door to League One. Cleverly, Dad managed to get the same seats that we sat in when we were season ticket holders. On arrival to my old seat I noticed an ex-player, Matthew Oakley, shaking a bucket, and accepting coins into it. The club had organised a number of ex-players to mix with the fans and collect money for the club to help keep it afloat. With the amounts of money that were swimming around the top echelons of football, this felt like a sick joke that it could come to this. Dad was visibly upset. It was the first time me and Dad had gone to a Saints match together in five and a half years, yet my first visit back was hurting bad, and the match hadn't even started yet.

I decided to take a walk around the concourse and just try to take in this first visit back a bit more. I also considered getting Dad a Chicken Balti pie and tossing it on the floor in front of me for trying to starve me at the cup final six years earlier. I was able to walk around the concourse and come out adjacent to the tunnel where the players would come out. I spotted the administrator, Mr. Fry, talking with supporters. I thought that was very big and honest of him to do that. Fans were asking questions of him and he was doing his best to respond. I marched straight over and asked him the one question that had been on my mind since the 2nd of April. I asked him if he thought he could find a buyer for the club. His response shocked me. He admitted to me that the administrative team were hoping to find a buyer for the football club, at the present time it was more in hope than expectation. Wow. I wasn't expecting that at all. We were Southampton Football Club, the famous FA Cup winners of 1976, the home of some of the most talented footballers in English football history. How could there not be a number of rich potential owners not banging down the front door at St Mary's?

I thanked him for his blunt honestly, and I meant it. A lot of rhetoric had appeared in the press. It helped to know the real story on the inside when navigating through the speculation that would appear in the press in the coming days.

Saints won the match against Crystal Palace 1-0 and played well. But the result mattered little. It mattered more that I was there. I was at the final game of the season too, against Burnley who were chasing promotion. Again, Saints' youngsters played really well, dominated the match, but conceded two goals out of nothing and ended up drawing 2-2. That result meant Saints were relegated irrespective of the points deduction and therefore next season Saints would start on minus ten points. I don't ever remember a match when Dad was so quiet. He always had something to say at a game, even if it was a "shut yer trap" to some nob head who was irritating him. I suppose it was because the circumstances were just so melancholy. After all, it would likely be my last game for a few years too. Depending how things would go off the field during the summer, it might even be the last Saints game we both ever went to.

The England trip was exhausting. It was our first trip back and we had missed a trick or two. Talking to other ex-pats who return to England for a holiday, the key is to let people gravitate to you; don't spend your days travelling out to visit friends and family. Visiting friends and family was pretty much all we did. For the next time we knew better: people would come to us. If they didn't like it, that would be tough. If people didn't want to visit, then they didn't want to see us and therefore didn't get to see us. It distributed the responsibility on to each of them rather than having it all on us.

Happily, in July 2009, long after we had arrived back in New Zealand, Mr. Fry managed to negotiate an utterly fantastic deal for the football club. The club was sold to Markus Liebherr, former owner of the construction machinery company Liebherr (next time you see a crane, you'll more than likely see the 'Liebherr' logo on the arm of the crane. It'll make you go, "ah, that's who Liebherr are!"). He was part of an extremely wealthy dynasty from Switzerland. Both he, and the club's new executive chairman, Nicola Cortese, put a plan in place to move the club forward and have them back in the Premier League within five years. It was an ambitious plan, but it became clear in the following few months that the new owners meant business and although stuck in

League One with a ten-point starting penalty, they were already planning for a life back at the top table of English football.

The first match of the new season was at home to Millwall. Boy was I excited about this match! It would be on the television in England, at around 11:30 p.m. on a Saturday night, just about the best time you can hope for here in New Zealand. I opened my doors to all comers, including local Saints fans and their families.

I got a selection of curries from our local Indian restaurant. Often, in backwaters like mine here, a quiet night usually means early closing, and unfortunately when I rang for the curries, the owner said he was closed. He then asked if it was me on the phone, and on realising that it was me, he suddenly said that he would re-open his place for me – even before he knew about my big order. That's what it is like sometimes in New Zealand; it's so much easier to make friends with people and I had been a fair customer there. Sometimes for folk here, nothing's too much trouble. I arrived to pick up the curries and saw all the lights were out in the restaurant but the owner was standing outside the restaurant, in his dressing gown, with two big bags of delicious curries that went down well with the supporters in the house.

The live feed was set up well in advance, with English commentary too which was unusual, and the feed was relatively stable. To cap off an exciting night, as we watched the match preamble with the cameras panning around the crowd, we suddenly saw Dad there sharing a laugh and a joke at the match. I texted him to ask if I could have his autograph and that he looked really fat on widescreen TV. "Piss off" was his reply.

The match was a bit of an anti-climax, a 1-1 draw. But much like the last games of the previous season, the result from this match was a wee bit secondary to the fact that the match was on at all. It was a real celebration that the club survived. I was buzzing that night, especially after seeing Dad there, and everybody had a good time. As the first half progressed, the quality of the live feed began to degrade although wasn't an issue. We could see the players, and could see the action, but when a player made a long pass, the pixelated white ball would blend in with the lush pale green August pitch and simply disappear. It was like playing Spot The Ball but in real time, trying to anticipate where the ball ended up. It was particularly funny at corners as the corner taker would swing his foot at the ball that would then disappear in front of our eyes, reappearing in the penalty box, bobbling about or being headed away by a defender.

The 2010 season was a good season and even though we had started with a ten-point penalty we nearly made the play-offs. Good, young, hungry players were purchased and a winning mentality was brought to the club. From a club that made bad decision after bad decision, all of a sudden the big decisions on and off the field tended to be progressive, correct courses of action. In talking with Dad, he would tell me that fans were enjoying going to home matches at St Mary's but also visiting away grounds, often new and different places to visit. The club started to smile again.

The pinnacle of the season was a trip to Wembley that year for the team. Saints had got to the final of the Johnstone's Paint Trophy. Not a major trophy, the 'JPT' as it was known, is a knockout competition played between teams in the bottom two league tiers, League One and League Two. The two finalists get a day out at Wembley which, for some clubs, could be a once in a generation experience. This year was the first year Saints participated in the competition, and they won it, thumping Carlisle United 4-1 in the final.

Dad went with Chris and others in the family. Obtaining tickets for this final wasn't difficult and Saints took an incredible 55,000 fans to the game. Carlisle received a big 20,000 plus ticket allocation too, and with an average attendance between 5,000 and 6,000 fans, many Saints fans took advantage of this once the Saints allocation ran out, and purchased tickets at the Carlisle end. Even though the 55,000 is an unofficial total given many snuck in on a Carlisle ticket, I think I am right in saying that this is the biggest support for one team at a final at the new Wembley, except for when the pampered London clubs borrow Wembley for European matches.

That night I had a good solid picture from the Internet, and more good company to watch the game with. The kids made a grandstand in front of the computer screen in the lounge by pulling the sofa in front of the screen, putting dining chairs behind the sofa, and then putting tall breakfast stools behind the chairs. It was a good night, a nice result, and an extremely odd feeling that Saints had actually won a trophy of sorts, albeit a small-scale trophy. I wished I was there though, alongside Dad. He texted me to say he was sat "up in the bleeding gods" which I suppose meant he was in the top tier somewhere. He had a magnificent day.

The seeds of recovery were well and truly set. Saints may well have been in League One, but they were nurturing and acquiring Premier League quality. In defence Saints purchased José Fonte from Crystal Palace and it said a lot about the ambition of the club that Fonte was prepared to drop from the Championship to League One to join Saints. That doesn't happen very often.

In midfield Saints had the young excellent Morgan Schneiderlin, a tough but elegant midfield general who had been brought over from France as a youngster before the club imploded into administration.

Then there was Adam Lallana, a beautifully balanced footballer who seemed to be able to always find space on the pitch even though there was none. Like Schneiderlin, Lallana had been at the club since he was a youth and would enjoy great success with the Saints in contrast to the previous few years.

In attack Saints purchased Ricky Lambert from Bristol Rovers for one million pounds. Despite the undignified amounts of money sloshing around football, it was amazing to think this was the first one million pound plus deal between two clubs outside the top two divisions for more than a decade. Again, Saints meant business that season, and so did Lambert, smashing in thirty-one goals, more than anyone in all four divisions.

It seemed only a matter of time before Saints would rise again. It was a great time to be a fan and it was a thrilling ride.

To make up for the lack of Saints in New Zealand, I've been to many big sports events in New Zealand and Australia and ex-pat Poms always wear their team's shirt as a badge of honour. When you wear the shirt, it acts as a beacon, some kind of fluorescent light attracting moth-like fans who gravitate to you and talk with you as if you've been a mate for years. You may not even know their name, but you recognise them at the next big event and get talking again. When I go on holiday in Fiji, the Gold Coast, Melbourne or within New Zealand, an array of Saints shirts are taken with me. And it has its benefits.

In the Gold Coast for example, wearing the white 2011 version with red sash, I was wondering the streets going to pick up a take away for the family, when I was stopped at this pub and asked to come in. The owner was a Saints fan and hadn't come across another 'Scummer' as the Portsmouth fans would say, in a long time. He saw me ambling past and ordered me in for a free drink. As mentioned, Aussies don't do Fosters anymore, but nonetheless a beer tastes better when you haven't paid for it. Then, as bizarre fate and outrageous fortune would have it, I was then introduced by the owner, to an ex-Southampton player, Robbie Slater, an Australian international who had had success with Saints and before that Blackburn Rovers. Slater was part of the Australian Fox Sports network covering the Australian A-League football and was there with Simon Hill, the English born commentator who is the main sports anchor for football there. There was a match on tomorrow that they were due to cover, the Gold Coast United versus Wellington Phoenix match.

Me, Kellie and the kids went along to the match the next night and enjoyed the only New Zealand professional team, Wellington, beat the Gold Coast, at the Skilled Park arena. The stadium holds 27,000 but there was only about 6,000 there that night. We sat in with the Wellington supporters who had 400-500 fans there – very impressive seeing as that Wellington is in another country. To put it in perspective, the distance between Australia and New Zealand is about the same between England and Russia. The Wellington team also have the dubious honour of the longest away trip in football history. They have to travel 3,300 miles (5,300 kilometres) to play an away match in Perth. They hold this record jointly with Perth who coincidentally, have to travel the precise same distance to get to Wellington.

I've watched Wellington Phoenix a couple of times, either when we've been in Australia or when they play a home game in Auckland (it's an Antipodean thing in sport to play one of your home games not at home, but somewhere else, to generate additional interest or revenue. It would be like Saints giving up a home match at St Mary's and playing it in Sunderland instead). The quality of football is about the same as the lower reaches of the Championship – not fantastic, but certainly competitive. I follow their fortunes and am pleased when they win because the media here love to beat up football. The trusty New Zealand inferiority complex rises to the fore to knock down football whenever it can. When Wellington lose, they get airtime on the news – when they win they don't, it's that simple. There is a realisation here that because more kids play football than rugby, one day it could become a bigger sport and obtain a bigger market share here. We can't have that, now can we?

That was certainly the case in 1981 when the ramshackle New Zealand football team, those All Whites, were making progress in qualifying for their first ever World Cup. It coincided with the South African Springbok rugby tour of 1981 to play the All Blacks. Of course at the time, South Africa were banned from all sport because of their Apartheid laws. New Zealand however, yearning for good opposition for the All Blacks sanctioned the tour. The country became split between watching quality rugby against a decent, different team, versus the whole ethical nature of it. More than 1,500 people in New Zealand were charged by police in over 200 demonstrations – a bit like one Chelsea away match in the Eighties. With the All Whites doing rather well, people suddenly gravitated to their cause and dramatically qualified for the 1982 World Cup. The New Zealand Football Association even borrowed BBC's Barry Davies to come over to New Zealand and cover the home matches.

I happily accepted another free beer from Mr. Slater and Mr. Hill on that balmy warm night in the Gold Coast, fine gentlemen both, but then made my apologies and staggered off to pick up my take away and get back before Kellie murdered me.

At the end of 2010 Mum and Dad came to visit us in New Zealand for the third time. We were able to listen to some of the matches together against Exeter City, and Dagenham and Redbridge (they're one team not two). We'd won both scoring seven goals in the process. Next up was Oldham Athletic away which we won 6-0. What a match! What a performance – we all had a very fine day that day.

For the second time, I took Dad over to Australia with me to watch England play Australia in the Ashes at the incredible Melbourne Cricket Ground (capacity 105,000). We'd gone in 2006 and watched England get absolutely stuffed in three days. This time round we couldn't quite believe what we were seeing! On Boxing Day 2010, on the first day we arrived at this mammoth coliseum to witness Australia get bowled out by England for a measly 98 runs. It was hilarious. Dad wanted a beer but the wickets were falling so fast that I didn't have an opportunity or a break in play to get him one. "Let 'em have a few bloody runs so nipper can get me a bleeding beer!" he shouted to the approval of the England fans around us. I'd got tickets to sit in with the Barmy Army, and by lunch time on Day One it was already a party atmosphere. Around us were inflatable kangaroos with England shirts on, people dressed as the Royal Family (I got to meet the Queen). Some fans collected as many empty plastic beer cups as they could and formed it into a giant snake that wound its way across the crowd. Dad enjoyed singing the alternative version of Waltzing Matilda – the version where Matilda has intimate relations with the Barmy Army, and also God Save *Your* Queen. The Australian stewarding was particularly intolerant with every bouncing beach ball confiscated and burst, but it kind of added to the joy of the occasion, watching an overweight Aussie in a luminous bib chase after a beach ball which the crowd were skilfully keeping out of his reach. The party atmosphere didn't stop a Portsmouth fan sing out to me whilst I was having a wee however, shouting "Scummer! Scummer!", but overall, what a day!

By the end of the day, England were totally dominant, 157 for no wicket. On the tram going back into the centre of Melbourne, people spotted me and Dad in our Saints shirts and told us we had been filmed for quite a while on the big screen at the ground. We hadn't noticed but apparently we had made quite an impression, bickering with each other over something – maybe it was Dad gasping for a pint. After the match, we went over to Chinatown for a meal and had the privilege of sitting adjacent to Geoffrey Boycott and the late Tony Grieg. It was a long day. With the time difference we had been up nearly twenty hours. When we got back to the hotel the lift was out of order and we had to walk up twelve flights of stairs. Dad didn't care, he marched up the stairs without a problem. We both seemed to be knackered as each other at the top and I'm half his age!

On Day Two we visited the Don Bradman museum inside the concourse of the MCG. On the field England ended up 444-5, with Jonathan Trott not out 141. On Day three England had the game practically won, after a first innings score of 513, and Australia ending Day Three 169-6. It was on this day that the television coverage picked up our gormless faces with every four and six hit our way. The Australians in the crowd started to get a little bit larey with us gentle Poms and as the day went on, with more drink and the realisation of defeat upon them, more and more were being ejected by the stewarding.

Near the boundary, the England fans were singing about Mitchell Johnson, Australia's erratic fast bowler. "He bowls to the left! He bowls to the right! Mitchell Johnson your bowling is shite!" As the fans sung, they would raise their arms in the air and move them to the left or to the right, in time with the song. Hilariously, Kevin Pietersen, one of England's top batsmen fielding in the deep, was joining in, stretching his arms left and right in unison with the Barmy Army. No wonder the Australians couldn't bear the humiliation.

It was a great trip which got even better when we realised that Saints had won at home to Huddersfield Town 4-1. There was one blemish to our trip. On the way back to the hotel this young boozed up Aussie came up to us was angling for a fight. In these situations, the best approach is to ignore them totally, and they tend to get bored and wander off. He started on me first, then started on Dad. He then pushed him and knocked his hat off. All of a sudden red mist descended and I went after him. This is something that I never done either before or since. I got right in his face and told him to pick on someone his own age, asked him angrily if he thought it clever to pick on an old man, and I wondered if he was a coward. All this interspersed with lashings of expletives. Eventually we saw him trot off and was then picked up by the police.

Dad was shocked.

"It's alright, Dad." I tried to reassure him. "It's just one of those things. He's gone now."

"I just can't get over it Russ, I'm appalled." He said.

"Listen, we've had a great time, don't let someone like that pond life spoil it. It's not worth it." My cogent argument wasn't making him feel any better.

"It's not him Russ, it's you that I am shocked about," he said.

"I'm sorry Dad, I wasn't going to allow him to get away with intimidating you," I argued.

"No, no, no. It's not that. I couldn't believe your language! You were using the 'F' word and all sorts! Bloody hell Russ, I've never heard you swear like that! I'm going to have to tell your Mum about this." I was dumbstruck. I was somewhere around my mid-thirties and Mum would have to be told about my bad language. I thought he was kidding around but he was dead serious, and when we got back to New Zealand Mother was duly informed and looks were had.

Soon after they returned to England, Saints had a TV match away to Peterborough United. Once again, I had invited my Saints chums to come over. The dodgy live feed was working well, and we watched as Saints take a 4-3 lead in yet another exciting match. Disastrously however, the guy who had decided to make the game available on the Internet changed the channel and all of a sudden we were watching the build up to Barcelona versus Real Sociedad! Worse was to follow as Peterborough equalised in the last minute of the match.

As the season was drawing to a close, it was clear that Brighton and Hove Albion would be promoted as champions, and they would be promoted with either Huddersfield Town or Southampton. Saints had started to labour but a big win against Milton Keynes Dons 3-2, after being 2-0 with just twenty-five minutes to go, was a pivotal moment in Saints fortunes. With five games to go, Saints had a crunch match at Brighton. I've had to watch or listen to many, many matches in the early hours of Sunday morning and endured some pretty gruelling experiences. This night I practically lifted the roof off my house and woke the entire street with only Radio Solent for company.

Brighton led at half-time 1-0, thanks to a poorly weighted back pass that was gratefully received and dispatched. We hadn't played well, but Brighton were a good team unbeaten at home for more than a year. Saints improved in the second half, Ricky Lambert hit the bar, but we couldn't get the break through. I was beside myself, hearing every minute, seeing it my mind and kicking every ball. We had to get something from this game – lose this and we were in big trouble. With six minutes to go we poked in a deserved equaliser. I was delighted, and I think perfectly within my rights to wake up the house with the kerfuffle that I caused when we scored.

As the game moved into the penultimate minute José Fonte looped a header over the goalkeeper and into the net. It was pandemonium at the ground, as Fonte and his team mates raced away towards the Saints fans to celebrate the goal (in those days, Brighton's ground had a running track around it so the fans were a long way away from the pitch). There was pandemonium in my house too as the suddenness and the importance of the goal lifted me into the air, thrilled to bits that we'd won it. I celebrated as if I was at the ground in full volume, no whispering or muttering, instead a full-on doozy of a noise explosion that saw me race out into the garden leaping around like an experimental Seventies artistic dance. I saw lights come on in the houses around me. I snuck back into the house quickly. It was not quite four in the morning.

Inevitably, Saints won all their remaining games and were promoted to the Championship for the 2012 season.

In February 2006, I acquired two tickets to go and see Alan Ball present an after-dinner speech in Pukekohe. It's common for the superstars of yesteryear to make a decent living from the after-dinner circuit, but it was odd because firstly, hardly any ex-footballers come to New Zealand to do that kind of thing, and secondly it was odd that he had organised a night in small Pukekohe. As it was he had always harboured a desire to visit New Zealand, and he'd agreed to do a night in Pukekohe as the major horse racing stables were nearby in Karaka, south of Auckland. Ball was a passionate race horse fan.

I went with Saints chum Mick from Romsey. There were about 100 people there and we listened to him speaking about his life, about how his football manager father was tough, about being Blackpool's youngest ever player at seventeen years old, about the World Cup in 1966 and his pivotal role in winning the cup for England, about his career with Everton and Arsenal, and of course his time as a player then a manager with the Saints.

After the speaky bit was done, we all settled for a nice dinner (notice how his after-dinner speaking was done before dinner?). A gentleman came up to me and Mick and told us that Alan would like us to join him at his table. Out of all the people that were there, we were the only ones in football shirts: we assumed that this was the correct approach for the night, to wear your club colours, but as we found out when we arrived we'd ballsed that up, everyone was just in smart casual wear. So it is fair to say that we stood out like a sore thumb. But it had worked out brilliantly, Ball found this amusing, and so we had been summoned to join him.

Fortunately, I made a better job of conversation with Mr. Ball than I had with Mr. Le Tissier. During an in-depth conversation about the famous controversial extra time goal in the World Cup final in 1966 – the one where Geoff Hurst's shot bounced down off the bar and landed near the goal line, to make it England 3, West Germany 2 – Bally was telling us how German scientists worked out that the ball didn't cross the line and that it wasn't a goal. I disagreed with him and told the great Alan Ball he was wrong.

"Why's that Russell?" he asked.

"Because the referee gave the goal, therefore it was a goal" I replied. He thought that response was brilliant.

It turned out to be an incredible night, memorable for so many reasons. When you watch football, you see a player with talent who is part of a team whose job it is to entertain and win matches. We judge players on this completely, on how good and effective they are at their job, and develop a love or a loathing for them, with no idea about who they really are. I'd judged Ball as a great player and an excellent servant to Southampton Football Club as a player, and the best manager we had had since Lawrie McMenemy. I'd also read his excellent autobiography 'Playing Extra Time', but whilst I knew all about him, I had no idea who he was. I felt that night I got a sense of who he was and it was an utter privilege to meet him and effectively, spend an entire evening with him. He was an incredible person, the likes of which I don't think I've ever met. His personality was infectious and was a captivating character, an obvious leader, who oozed positivity. I think we spent the night hanging over his every word and he certainly left a lasting impression on me. He'd had to deal with both his wife and daughter both being diagnosed with life-threatening illnesses at the same time, and the eventual loss of his wife, not two years prior. He was a genuinely amazing man. Sadly, Alan himself passed away of a heart attack a year after his visit to New Zealand.

He told us some incredible stories. For example, when he went to Manchester City suddenly, it didn't become widely known that the board at Southampton didn't get on with Ball or some of his ways of managing and were happy to allow him to leave. The club allowed the perception of 'Ball moving to a bigger club for more money' to take hold in the court of public opinion, when in fact he didn't want to leave. The club disliked his approach of bonding the team together, for example allowing them to play cards on the team coach and on occasion joining in. The club's short-sightedness is jarring given Ball's meteoric success in his eighteen months at the club, and the club's subsequent regression back down the league thereafter.

At Manchester City, Ball admitted he struggled as manager. In one game, he wanted to take off a poorly performing player at half-time. The chairman got wind of his decision and came down to meet Ball and told him he couldn't do that. "Do you know how many shirts that player sells?" was the chairman's rationale, and Ball was forced to keep this player on the field. As bizarre as this sounds, it is not a stretch to believe that such a chairman, more interested in money, would do such a thing. Except, at the time, Manchester City's chairman was a former professional player. During team talks and dressing down of players, he would be met with resistance to comply with his instructions. Players would tell him that he couldn't speak to them like that, or you can't tell me what to do, or do you know how much I earn a week? Ball admitted that he was the only person in the dressing room who was not a multi-millionaire.

Having worked with Matt Le Tissier so closely, and brought the best of him as manager, the tales about him were equally absorbing, how he got the team just to keep giving him the ball, making Le Tissier the fulcrum of the team. It sounds obvious really doesn't it, give the most talented the most responsibility and they tend to blossom. It's such a shame that so many managers weren't brave enough to do that. Ball believed it scandalous the way Le Tissier was treated at international level, and debunked all of the supposed negative elements of his game, about him being lazy or unambitious about wanting to leave such a small team. I knew I was right about Le Tissier, but it was great to hear exactly the same from someone who actually knew about the game and worked with him.

Another great story was about the legendary Johan Cruyff, the Seventies Dutch maestro, one of the very, very best players that ever played the game. Cruyff and Ball were friends, and both Ball's team and Cruyff's team (Barcelona, no less) happened to be staying at the same hotel during pre-season tours. They met for a beer and Cruyff asked Ball how his team were going. Ball lamented that he was short of an attacking midfielder. The following morning after the Barcelona team had checked out of the hotel, Ball came down to the hotel reception to find an attacking midfielder waiting for him, left behind by Cruyff. The player, Ronnie Ekelund, from Denmark, was a superb acquisition for the Saints, although a back injury effectively ended his time at Saints after just one year.

Ball was looked after by Sam Malcolmson, a New Zealand international defender and who played against Scotland in the World Cup in 1982. He also was a gentlemen and tremendous company.

When I heard the news that Ball had died, I was really affected. It's silly really, but I had only got to meet him for one evening, but he had that kind of effect on you. We all seemed to have a terrific night, and for me and Mick it was a night never to forget. We had a chuckle over the incident when I was a boy asking for his autograph. We stayed late, after most of the other attendees had gone home. I learnt a great deal that night and I was very sad to learn of his death.

One of the things we lost forever was the FA Cup final day ritual of me and Dad watching the game together. For the first cup final in 2004, I waited up until 2:00 a.m. on Sunday morning to watch Manchester United ease past Millwall. For obvious reasons, watching the cup final alone, in the dark, with the volume down, doesn't even begin to compare to the ritualistic private party me and Dad used to have. I didn't bother after that and would put the match on record and watch it in the morning before I could know the score. The next year, the final between Arsenal and Manchester United went to penalties and the transmission of the match ended before the penalties started, so I missed those and had to look up the winner on the Internet. In fact, over the years the quality of coverage of the FA Cup is pathetic. Unlike the Premier League coverage, the FA Cup coverage was run by the American ESPN channel with poorer quality pictures and sound, and inferior analysis and commentary. The main pundit was Tommy Smyth ('Tommy Smyth with a 'Y'' as he was always introduced as), a naturalised Irishman whose tone and opinion I found irritating. Whilst watching the FA Cup final nowadays is a relatively miserable experience, imagine me watching the FA Cup final in 2008 when Portsmouth won it. I made myself sit through it, a genuinely horrible experience. Watching an entire series of Jeremy Kyle would have been more palatable.

In 2017, being a Saints fan in New Zealand has its distinct advantages. For example, Saints fans in England can watch Saints on the TV live only when they are scheduled to be on, on a Saturday lunch time, Saturday evening or a Sunday. When the games are played at the usual time of 3:00 p.m. on a Saturday afternoon, then it is UK law that the match cannot be shown live. As you can imagine Sky Sports in the UK will always be seeking to show Liverpool, Arsenal, Manchester United and Chelsea ahead of the Saints. Here, there are no such restrictions in New Zealand, and every Premier League match, every week, is played live on separate channels on satellite television or the Internet. This means I can follow Saints home and away every single week, and from 2017, in every competition, in HD, not through fuzzy, pixelated dodgy feeds from someone's bedroom. This year has been tough for me because since Saints have been in the Europa League whose matches are on a Thursday night UK/Friday morning NZ. This means their Premier League matches for the following weekend get moved to the Sunday, normally 2:00 p.m. UK, 1:00 a.m. or 3:00 a.m. Monday morning NZ – positively the worst time for me needing to go to work that morning. But I have no complaints: it's great for me, I get to see more of the Saints than I could do in England, but watching it on TV is nothing compared to being there, which is why the Wembley trip has to be done.

Getting the time of the match right can be tricky. The Saints' next match as I am finishing this body of bunkum, is at home against AFC Bournemouth at St Mary's. Kick-off is on Saturday at 5:30 p.m. in

England, moved from 3:00 p.m. because of the UK television coverage needs. But for me it will be Sunday at 4:30 a.m. because of the time difference. If the game had been played two weeks earlier, I could have been watching the match on a Sunday at 6:30 a.m. which would have been a lot better, but in England the clocks have gone forward one hour, and here in New Zealand the clocks have just gone back one hour on the Saturday night, Sunday morning. I'll need my smartphone to work out when I need to get up.

Postscript. The match was 0-0. Saints were bloody rubbish.

Saturday

Here's a handy hint and tip for you when travelling through the United States. Don't answer back to airport security; they are thugs and will slaughter you.

The flights were uneventful. A couple of days before I flew out, I'd picked out an Economy seat near the back of the aeroplane with a free seat next to me. I fancied that the seat could remain unsold and I was right. I managed to sleep about ten hours across twenty-two hours of flight time, which I thought was pretty good.

I confess I have a bit of an anxiety problem when there is a free seat next to me at a match, a concert, in the doctors waiting room, or in this case on a plane. I always imagine a giant, really big, enormous, person sitting next to me, with any space I plan to enjoy swallowed up by them. I'm not talking about a big or overweight person – I'm talking about truly enormous people. This anxiety exists because it happened to me once. Me and Kellie booked tickets in 2000 to see The Lion King Musical at the Lyceum Theatre in the West End of London. It was a big deal to us, Sarah and Shauna were both very young so a night out, let alone a night out in London, was a rare night indeed. We'd been looking forward to it immensely so took our seats quite early. As people poured in around us, the seat next me seemed to be impervious to an arse being sat on it. Seats were being taken everywhere except this seat next to me on my left. The show was about to start. In the West End if you haven't taken your place by the start of the show, then too bad – you are locked out until the interval. The show started and the seat was left empty.

At the start of the Lion King show, what happens is that all the cast, dressed in flamboyant costumes that imitate animals come on to the stage from every entrance, from the sides and behind you. Me and Kellie were in the middle tier so there were no 'animals' around us but we could see the spectacular start to the show below. I then spotted what I thought was an elephant coming up the stairs slowly. I thought that the costume was a bit rubbish but it then dawned on me this was a member of the audience struggling up the stairs. She would attempt one or two steps, then pause to regain her breath, with a flourish of drama just so people around her knew she was suffering. I frantically looked around for another empty seat. It appeared that the seat on my left was the only seat left in the whole theatre. As she neared our row, without any help or interest from other audience members, I hoped she would huff and puff on to the rows behind us. Our interest in what is now one of the longest running theatre productions had disappeared, our focus remained on this woman.

She reached our row and gasped at Kellie to move so she could get by. We stood to allow her by, just. I was so pissed off – I had to sit next to Jabba The Hutt for the night. What I hadn't realised was that the seats in The Lyceum had arm rests so Jabba couldn't get into her seat. She made such a fuss as she grunted and sweated and squeezed one arse cheek into the seat. The other arse cheek she perched on me. Kellie asked me if I was okay. I wasn't, I was getting properly squashed and couldn't see the stage. I tapped her on the shoulder.

"Excuse me, you are sitting on me," was my to-the-point statement to her.

"I'm a lawyer," she grunted to me, like the female version of Mr. Creosote from Monty Python. "I can't do anything about it," she said.

So I watched half of the Lion King with a sweaty, smelly fat woman sat on my lap, seeing very little and hearing less, as her gasps and grunting were all too audible. In the interval I asked if I could be set free for a bit and went to complain. I was told I wasn't being very nice, which I thought was outrageous. I told them I couldn't see or hear and was being sat on! The management refused to do anything. When I returned, Jabba had gone, and with a stroke of good fortune, either because she left, or couldn't handle the stairs a second time, she never came back. It was a horrible, horrible experience, one that I refuse to go through again.

It almost happened again at a Top Gear Live concert in New Zealand. Again, there was only one seat next to me free, and another enormous bloke came puffing over to the seat. This time he looked at the seat, looked at her ticket, then growled that he was in the wrong row.

"YEESSSSS!!!" I jumped up, punching the air, much to his confusion.

The first game of each season when I was a season ticket holder was always a nervy experience, not so much because I wondered what team

Saints would put out and how we would compete, but because I wondered if the person next to me would be super-big. Imagine being squeezed by flesh for an entire season? I couldn't face it and was the kind of thing to leave me awake at night. Dad would always be grumpy with me about it, "What's the bloody matter with you?" he'd complain. But it was always a relief to see a much slimmer person take the seat next to me. I would even ask them if they were sitting there for the season, just to confirm.

"Thank God for that!" I'd exclaim when they said they were (something that would come off a bit wrong if it was a lady sat there).

Imagine my nerves waiting for the aircraft to complete boarding in Auckland with a seat free next to me, when the biggest rugby-playing fella you have ever seen, whose arms were bigger than my torso, shuffled up the Economy aisle towards my row. I didn't think I could stand at least twelve hours pressed up against the side of the aircraft. To my relief he walked on by.

I had left Auckland on the Friday night, and arrived in Los Angeles about nine hours back in time, on the Friday afternoon of the same day (it's best not to think on that, it will mess with your grey matter). LA is renowned as a difficult airport to negotiate in transit and I had been concerned about going through security because of the extensive queues and the unnecessary hoops that security put passengers though. There were known stories about how slow and inefficient airport security is at Los Angeles, and that it can be a mission to get back to your flight in time. All I had to do though was to get through the punchy Los Angeles security, and wait to get back on the plane. I nearly didn't manage it.

The process is that you disembark the aircraft, walk round to customs, then once cleared, queue through security and return to the gate through the shops at the terminal. Often, ground staff for specific flights come through the queues with signs for their flights to get their passengers through to the front, so even if there were unreasonable delays, if ground staff were to come and get me then this should be a task I should easily negotiate.

I had only been through Los Angeles once before and that was a bit of a debacle too. You'll probably recall that when you go through customs they have these organised queue barriers made up of vertical plinths and seat belts that attach to adjoining plinths to ferry the volumes of people through the process. Me and Kellie had arrived in customs to be greeted by a number of distracted airport staff members in crimson blazers. They gestured for us to go through an enormous set of queue barriers, around 100 metres long. We marched up and down, up and down – as you do – being careful not to go under the barriers (you couldn't sneak under the barriers as you would get barked at by the undisciplined staff), until we soon found that the staff had failed to configure the queue barriers correctly. Whilst we could get in there was no opening to get out and attend a customs booth at the other end. We ended up, like in a maze, back at the start. We tried to tell someone but the airport staff wouldn't have it. Eventually a staff member ushered us into a different set of configured queue barriers and to our relief we eventually found a customs official.

This time on my own was worse. I was fortunate that the flight arrived early and gave us all who were transiting to London Heathrow a longer chance to get through. There were about ten to fifteen claret blazered staff waiting to direct us, except no one knew exactly where we should go. I just followed other people on my flight who, en masse, had gone completely in the wrong direction. I had to use a kiosk to validate my US ETSA visa, but it had no option for me being in transit, so I was redirected to a booth, who redirected me back to a kiosk. They told me to say I was in the US for 'pleasure'. Ironically, the last question on the kiosk was to confirm that I was telling the truth, which I wasn't, but only because I was told to. I saw one airport staff member jostle a passenger and shouting at them "Find the correct line! Find the correct line!" The passenger looked bemused and asked very politely if he could be told which line to join. The staff member said he had no idea but just kept saying "get in line!"

In contrast to the confusion, what was nice here was that there were four different people who came up to me in my proudly adorned Saints shirt (2016 Adidas version, not the pyjama top of 2017) wishing me all the best. All professed to be Saints fans, obviously travelling from the UK to Los Angeles. One even had tickets for the final but had to give them up owing to his work commitments in the States. It has always been a nice feeling to talk football with a fellow Saints fan on the other side of the world. In Los Angeles security, I was the centre of attention for these people.

With customs successfully completed, next was security. Here you have to put your belongings on to a tray, along with your shoes, glasses and belt ensuring you emptied all your pockets. Your hand luggage bag has to go an another tray, and you push the trays into a queue that moves them through a conveyer for x-ray scanning.

I then had to join a queue of people waiting to go through a body x-ray machine. A nasty squat security woman appeared and started barking at us passengers and at first I took no notice. It was actually difficult to hear her because other security staff were hollering out other instructions. Then I realised she might be shrieking about me.

I asked her, "I'm sorry, I couldn't hear what you were saying. Is there a problem?"

She looked at me, eyes wide, as if I had insulted her mother.

"Is there a problem?" she said, hands on hips and head bopping from side to side. "Oh my god! Is there a problem???"

Evidentially, there was.

"Is that yours?" she demanded.

"I'm not sure what you are pointing at." I said. Her stubby little fingers could have been pointing at anything in the queue, but realisation was dawning on me that she was pointing at my small hand luggage bag.

She picked it up. "Well if no one is goin' to claim this bag maybe I should put it straight in the garbage!"

"That's my bag." I said.

"Well then put your goddam bag on a tray!" Someone had taken my bag off its tray and taken the tray. I'm not surprised; there were a stack of trays waiting to be used, but some clever staff member had placed them all out of reach of passengers.

"I'm sorry," I offered politely, albeit starting to feel agitated inside. "Someone's obviously taken the tray. Just pop it on a tray and it'll be fine."

This was a mistake.

"Sir? Can you hear me? Did you understand what I just said to you?"

I responded. "Can't you do it, you are right there? I'm in a queue here." Suddenly she exploded with rage.

"Sir. Get you f- bag and put it in a f- tray and put it in the goddam x-ray machine!"

That was nice. Suitably embarrassed and sore of the injustice of it all, I went back, asked for a tray then placed my bag in it and popped it back on the x-ray machine. Thinking this was over, she started to goad me.

"Just remember sir you are an Economy class passenger!"

A bloke in front of me turned around and sympathetically suggested I just ignore it.

"You are an e-con-em-y class citizen, sir!" she ranted, her face the colour of a beetroot and her arms hanging like a marionette. It took all my powers of restraint, but focussing on the prize of Saints at Wembley I stayed deathly quiet and soon enough my Los Angeles security hell ended.

I arrived in London, at first wide eyed and excited, and then eyes shut tightly and choking on the smoky, dirty, English air. This was my first visit to England post-Brexit, and I had thought that there might be some UKIP Gestapo-like officers in uniforms demanding to see my papers and looking to see if my skin pigmentation was slightly off white or whether I had any kind of hint of accent that could expose me as slightly 'foreign' that could consign me to immediate expulsion from the country. To my relief I found England to be just about the same as when I was here last, with nobody in sight, just a machine to welcome me into the country.

I jumped on a tube and headed straight for our hotel at Wembley Park. I had booked a hotel for Dan and me to ease his concerns over travel disruptions on the day of the game, and to save me travelling down to Hampshire then back up to London the next day. The train services to London were erratic, and I had read that services from Woking were turning into a bus service for Sunday. Southern Rail had decided that fans had to wait outside Southampton Central and Eastleigh stations, and their entry on to the platform would be regulated. One wag at the match (as in someone with wit, not a wife or girlfriend of a footballer) had a flag with the slogan 'Gabbiadini strikes more than Southern Rail'. It just about summed up the situation as some fans took a 6:00 a.m. train just to be sure to get to the game on time which normally takes ninety minutes. It was standing room only from Southampton Central. There was also a Six Nations Rugby match on at Twickenham that day so staying over the night before was a great idea.

I got off the tube station at Wembley Park and started the walk to the hotel. Immediately from exiting the tube station I could see the mammoth stadium and its arch reaching out over the sky.

I had made it!

With all the build-up and excitement generated for this adventure, all of a sudden I suddenly found I was actually here, and I had to pinch myself; I couldn't believe it! Every twenty or thirty paces I took closer to the stadium I had to stop and take a photo of the stadium with a gigantic screen on the side wall advertising the match, with Saints' emblem splashed across the side of Wembley. People were wandering around, going about their business, taking no notice of this mammoth coliseum behind them. We're they mad? Did they think it was just a big office block? In amongst them was me seemingly the only one transfixed on the sight ahead of me. I couldn't take my eyes off the place, and I reckon had I lived there, I don't think I would ever consider it as mundane as the populous there seemed to, I would have stared at it every day and dreamed about Saints winning the cup.

I knew the hotel was near the stadium as some of the rooms offered stadium views but I had no idea it was only about 50 metres from the stadium! Peering out to my left out of the hotel room window was the giant arch.

I then caught up with Debbie and Dan by phone; Dan was on his way. I'd also caught up with my emails. My Daily Echo article made it in.

The Daily Echo article appeared on page five on the Saturday. The title of the article depended on whether you were reading the paper or the web site. The paper asked, "Is This the Most Dedicated Saints Fan?" as the title, whilst the web site version went with the snappy "New Zealand-based Saints fan Russell Budden is making an 11,000-mile trip to Wembley". The article appeared in the Daily Echo, Hampshire Chronicle and other syndicated web sites across Europe in various different versions.

It was a good article, except it appeared that Debbie had been quite chatty with the reporter. She had already told me that she had spoken with the reporter but she hadn't let on that she had issued him with an extensive version of my entire life story, with almost every detail lavished with the accuracy of an average Daily Mail article. Almost all the information she gave was wrong, including saying my age was sixty-six. When I read the article I almost fell off my chair when I saw that Debbie had told the reporter the price of the touted ticket. "Mr. Budden got a 'good deal' on flights, but had to fork out 486 pounds for a ticket". I wasn't thrilled about that.

There is no getting away from it, it is a vulgar amount to watch a football match. It's not a price that I wanted to pay, but it was a price that I had to pay if I wanted to go to the match. My attempts to be discrete about this part of the adventure was suddenly in print for all to see.

My paranoid mind then started to work overtime. After all, the ticket I purchased was most likely not permitted to be transferred for money, irrespective that 'everybody does it'. What if Club Wembley saw this article, corroborated my name to the transferred ticket and were able to cancel my ticket? What if Club Wembley then cancelled the Club Wembley membership of the ticket owner? Would that mean that Dan couldn't go either? What if the Club Wembley ticket owner saw the article in one of its many forms and rescinded his transfer? I had prided myself in leaving no stone unturned in this adventure, and suddenly there was an imponderable caused by my blabbing sister.

Otherwise the article was good, and the reporter had corrected my age to my relief. I was pleased that Kellie got a mention about her saying that "it might never happen again in my lifetime" and her positivity about it all – "She's helped push me into this but there are limits to her patience! I decorated the house (as I do with big occasions) with flags and banners – she wasn't thrilled about that." I was also thrilled that there was a reference to Dad – "My Dad brought me up on the Saints, so being a genuine Saints fan for such a long time, this simply had to be done."

At the end of the article I killed it with a perfect response to the reporter's dopey question about whether it was worth it – "I'm like any other fan - desperate to see us get our hands on a trophy. I just live a bit further away."

The article can be read at:

http://www.dailyecho.co.uk/news/15117076.Is_this_the_world_s_most_dedicated_Saints_fan_/

What was even better than the article however, was the comments on the web site. Like most web sites these days, each reader can leave a comment about the article. Thirty-three people did! They were hilarious – from the sublime to the ridiculous, from the rational to the irrational. They included Portsmouth trolls attempting to gazump the pre-match celebrations, people who don't even follow football, fans with wit, fans with no sense of humour whatsoever, Saints fans taking issue with the assertion that I am dedicated (there seems to be a prevailing attitude on the Internet that Saints fans should all be co-located near the stadium, and if you travel or live away from the city, in UK or abroad, you should be castigated for your blasphemy).

Here are some of my favourites. (By the way, I've brought in these comments almost verbatim, but there are words that I have removed because they are really sweary that might offend my Mum, or basic grammatical or punctuation errors that offends me. Some of the more horrendous spelling errors have been kept in to re-enforce the paucity of IQ in the commenter. For the aged community reading this, lol means laugh out loud, COYR means Come On You Reds, COYS is Come On You Saints, SO14 is a Southampton post code, Moderator Deleted means that somebody in charge of the web site has removed a comment owing to its offensive nature, OMG means oh my god! and Mum I am sorry for the implied effing and jeffing that follows).

Comment: If his first game was the '79 league cup final can someone keep him away from Wembley on Sunday? Do they need bad omens on good ones lol. Safe travels mate and enjoy your day.
Reply: <Moderator deleted>

Comment: Earning money online is very easy in these days. Google now paying 500USD to 800USD per day depends on you how much you work. I have received 14,834USD in one month by working from home online. Everybody can join this job and make extra income from home.

Comment: What a complete plonker travelling all that way to watch such a poor team. Better idea-helping out a charity.
Reply: You've got CONFUSED – you would be a plonker going to see POMPEY.
Reply: Do you think that it is possible that a few Saints fans did a bit of Winding Up on the Pompey newspaper when Pompey headed for Wembley?
Reply: Helping out a charity, that from a Skate who's more likely to help himself to charity funds, jog on pal!

Comment: Good on yer!! It is fantastic being in the final of the EFL CUP. Saints Fans can savour the wins at each stage – beating Arse-nil and Liverpool home and away and now the whole Wembley experience!!
The lead up to the Final – the travel to the game – the pre-match pubs and all the banter and chanting with all the other Saints fans – that is what the manager and team have done for our supporters with their GOALS and the football producing the WINS.
There is no fear – 15 days is a long time to prepare and by now the staff will have looked at all the threats that ManUre have – especially Zlatan – and we will be ready to go on and WIN SILVERWARE.
THIS IS OUR BEST OPPORTUNITY IN DECADES and we all hope to be back at Wembley again and again in the next 10 years!!
WE ARE NUMBER ONE IN THE SOUTH.
WE ARE SOUTHAMPTON. COYR+WS
Reply: You should really get that caps lock fixed.

Comment: How did he score a ticket?
Reply: Money.

Comment: Yawn yawn yawn.
Reply: If you are that tired at this time in the morning, I suggest you wear boxing gloves in bed.
Reply: Leather ones ????
Reply: I am glad that you asked as, having read many of your posts, it would appear that you have a similar habit – one that football referees are often accused of.
Reply: Just regulation boxing gloves.
Reply: HOW VERY DARE YOU????? I am not blind and anyway I am a latex man.

Comment: My cousin is flying in from Australia to go to the match!

Comment: World's biggest idiot.

Comment: <Moderator Deleted>

Comment: How can he be Saints "most dedicated fan" when he f-'d off to New Zealand and is only coming back for one match. Surely a more dedicated fan is one that goes to every home and away game season after season?
Reply: A most dedicated fan is surely one who refuses to move away from the Southampton area, especially one who has been offered a much better paid job, because s/he wanted to go to every match.
Reply: I'm getting fed up with this false notion that some supporters are better than others.
You are either a Saints fan or you aren't. It doesn't matter whether you live in Southampton, or on the Moon, whether you go to every game, or have never been to any, whether you watch on telly, or listen to the radio, whether you know every player's name, or just the name of the club, if you love the board, or hate it, whether you are affluent enough to have a season ticket, or you aren't, or whether you scrimp and save to buy one, or you chose to spend your money on more important things, or if life has simply decreed that you are unable to attend.
If you want Saints to win, and succeed, and get better, and it gives you a buzz when they do, then you are a true Saints fan and a supporter and are as one with all the rest.
Reply: Here, here. In the 80s I rarely missed a home match and went to most away. 1990s moving away and getting married reduced my game time. 2000s moved to York so mostly Northern away's and occasional home's. My son, York born and bred, is a very passionate very loyal Saints fan. He spent his childhood getting the rise taken out of him for supporting a lower league supposedly no-hope team.
We all have our supporting journey and we all have our reasons for supporting in the way we do. I have never ever lost the passion I instantly got after attending my first game in 1975. All that matters, as [another commenter] so rightly says, is that you support your club for your own very good reason.
Reply: I agree.

Comment: I am coming from Dorset – makes me no less dedicated – and I attended many homes games this season...... Just saying!!!!

205

Reply: You should have said you live near Christchurch then we would have all thought you came all the way from New Zealand as well.

Comment: Nice one mate. I'm traveling back from the Middle East. F- all you miserable twats that just can't stand to see other people enjoying life. COYS :-)

Comment: Have a safe trip and I hope you have a GREAT trip home :-)

Comment: Earning money online is very easy in these days. Google now paying 500USD to 800USD per day depends on you how much you work. I have received 14,834USD in one month by working from home online. Everybody can join this job and make extra income from home by just follow the instructions on this page.

Comment: Good on him enjoy it. Wish I could make it back from Australia.

Comment: Well done that man! And well done you, [other commenter]. I know you won't blow your own trumpet but, if I remember correctly, you'll be there having come over from Japan. (I'll text you when I'm on my way) but, YES, as [other commenter] says, 'You are either a Saints fan or you aren't.' And all of us are. We're all in this as one, all marching together, coming from every corner of the world and from SO14. It's going to be a whole lot of fun.
Reply: OMG ... stop it!

Comment: The lot of ya need to grow up. Going on about a lowsy [sic] game of football. pathetic. Do something with your lives. Saints are shitesters and always will be. Marching and all that nonsense. Sound like a [sic] idiotic kid. Get a life!!!!!!!
Reply: IZ IT COZ U A SKATE?
Reply: As a Skate, is it difficult typing with six fingers?

Comments: Good on you Russell. Glad to have you there representing the NZ Saints Fans ... meet up on your return with the victory. All the best.

Comment: So many people moan about having no money, but they pay high prices for football tickets. The players are paid thousands... living the high life and Saints fans funding their lifestyle. Never got this... cannot stand football. So much trouble. You don't see massive trouble in other sports, look at cricket, look at rugby... ONLY FOOTBALL!!!

For the record, none of the comments caused me any offense whatsoever, just sore ribs from laughing. Mum and Sama seemed unhappy about some the comments, but everyone else in the Budden Mafia got great value out of it. I cannot fathom what possesses some people to spend, I assume, so much time trawling such inconsequential material such as this, then to respond with some of the banal comments they make. I would expect that some of the commenters would not be able to fathom what possessed me to do what I did.

Dan arrived at around 3:00 p.m. We spent the afternoon having a little look around the area and the hotel. The hotel was dominated with fans there for the final, but we seemed to be the only Saints fans around.

Manchester United fans have a deserved reputation about not actually being from Manchester. This is not an urban myth at all. When me and Dad went to games against United (which Saints typically would win) our walk to The Dell or St Mary's took us past the away team coaches. When United came to play there were always a lot of coaches, but neither Dad nor I could ever find a coach that came from Manchester. We would see coaches from Banbury, Devizes, Tamworth and Folkestone. We would see placards and flags hanging inside the back windows of coaches such as 'Irish Reds', 'London United' or 'Welsh Red Devils'. There would be coaches from overseas too, typically Norway, Belgium and the Netherlands. Dad would always make an extravagant fuss of it all by deliberately checking every coach and lauding up the fact that the coach was from Stockton-Upon-Tees or Newcastle-Under-Lyme – anywhere except Manchester.

In the hotel, there were fans who had travelled from Malaysia, Dubai and Hong Kong, kitted out in the shirt, tracksuit top, tracksuit bottoms, official Red Devils cap, official Manchester United hand luggage bag, and official Manchester United passport cover. I found this inexplicable! Why on earth would these people who lived so far away from Old Trafford spend all that money and expense just to watch them in yet another cup final?

Dan looked at me with an expression that demonstrated my lunacy and hypocrisy. Suddenly I was no longer a mad nomad traveller from the other side of the world, I was a Southampton boy again, born and bred. He had to point out that these people had only done the same thing as I did. I pointed out to him that I had come twice as far as them!

In a shock development, there were also people in the hotel who were from Manchester. I had heard some of them speak in their Oasis nasal Mancunian drawl ("yaarrat our kid?") whilst other people looked pale and gaunt. The sight of a cross section of lower working-class society milling around in such a middle-class hotel was jarring to the senses and I didn't approve (my football head was now completely dominating the rest of my thoughts and personality). Shouldn't the concierge ushered these people back into their hired stretched Hummer and sent them on to the Holiday Inn or to Nando's?

My football-based tribal prejudices were working overtime and were at DefCon Four overload, and were due to get me in a spot of bother.

Many of the United fans were milling around outside the front of the hotel (seriously degrading the hotel's normal reputation no doubt). The Manchester United coach pulled up alongside the hotel. Clearly the Manchester United team were staying at the hotel too. Dan and I agreed to treat this with the incredulity it deserved and whilst wide eyed United fans were treated to the sight of the most expensive player in the world, Paul Pogba, one of the world's best goalkeepers in David De Gea, and one of the world's most prolific goal scorers, Zlatan Ibrahimović, stepping off of the coach to the adulation of fans both young and old, we popped around the corner to TGI Friday's and a bit of dinner.

Tiredness and the last remnants of jet lag caught up with me just after dinner, saving me from any misplaced comment to a Manchester United fan. I'd thought up some crackers to wind up the opposition clientele. I planned to go up to a United fan, topless and ask them if they liked my grey Manchester United away kit and then exclaim in a mocked shocked voice, what do you mean you can't see the shirt? Look (pointing at my body-is-a-temple rounded pot belly) – can't you see it? It's right here!

In the end, I had to make do of standing in the window of our hotel room, Saints flag hanging behind me, dancing topless to the passers-by below who took absolutely no notice of me whatsoever, before crashing fast asleep on my bed. One more deep confused sleep until the day of the final.

Before dinner, we'd been to the hotel bar for an overpriced beer. Out of our window to my left was the stadium in all its glory. With this as our backdrop, we analysed the match ahead fully.

You cannot have a conversation about football without somebody saying something completely irrational. I had a noteworthy contribution as testament to this during our discussion. I said to Dan that Saints should win, because Manchester United win trophies year after year – if they lost this cup final, no United fan is going to be crestfallen, they are just going to pick themselves up and win something next year. I even suggested that United ought to let Southampton win. Now I am a lightweight when it comes to political views, but I do believe in capitalism over socialism. But here I was swinging madly from right to left in my views just because it was football. I find this happens a lot. When Saints are foremost in my mind, I suddenly become a socialist, bemoaning and whinnying about minor injustices and the general unfairness of it all. I'm the same with religion. I've not got a religious bone in my body (and with in-laws from Northern Ireland I've also developed a distaste for it), but come match time, suddenly I'm praying far more frequently than a Catholic Priest who's been caught in The Act. Who to, I have no idea, maybe Le God, but certainly not God, as I am sure there isn't one. (With everything that is so twisted in this world, if there was a God, I am sure he would at least have got a written warning from his superiors over creating the world so sloppily in just seven days. Maybe if he had been much less sloppy, took his time over creating the earth, say, over two or three weeks, and invented light first so he could actually see what he was doing, then I am sure the outcome would have been much better for everyone.) The prayers themselves are the same: either to stop a goal, score a goal, play better, or to hurry up time. My prayer of choice is "KEEP THEM OUT!" which gets blurted out many times during each and every match. This prayer was perfected over many years in The Nineties when relegation from the Premier League was a very real threat.

Me and Dan did invest some time trying to work out what it would take for Saints to win the match. I thought that a number of things need to be in place for Saints to succeed. I cited three key areas.

Firstly, Manchester United must not play to their top potential; if they do, Saints will lose. I thought this was unlikely, they had played three matches in the last ten days whilst Saints had not played any, and I fancied United to be below their best. Their form was good, certainly better than Saints, but out of all the 'big' teams in the country we surely had the best chance against United.

Secondly, the referee and his assistants must get the decisions right, or go the way of Saints – we can ill afford bad refereeing judgements or calamitous refereeing errors like a rash sending off. I would be perfectly happy if all the officials had dreadful games provided all the decisions go Southampton's way, but when you play the top teams, this never, ever, happens. It would certainly be more likely that United would get the benefit of bad decisions.

Finally, we also need Saints to play as well as they can, defend well, take our chances in front of goal (for a change), and be heroic around our own goal, even though our central defensive pairing would not have been in the first team prior to Christmas. This would mean a massive improvement was necessary from their recent games, although we had beaten an extremely poor Sunderland side away 4-0 to give us an ounce of confidence. Interestingly for me, the manager, Claude Puel, and adjusted the formation slightly for the Sunderland game, pushing Dušan Tadić behind our new striker Manolo Gabbiadini, providing him with a much better platform to influence the match, with his supporting forwards pushed slightly wider to stretch Sunderland going forward. And stretch them we did: this was a much more positive development, I thought.

All these requirements meant the probability of a Saints win was relatively low, but going in to the day, both Dan and I were enthusiastically positive and optimistic. There is a chance here, and we seemed to sense that something special was about to happen.

Dignity

Monday, 27th of February 2012.

During Mum and Dad's visit to New Zealand in 2010-2011, Dad and me were sitting on our newly built deck out in the back garden, in the shade of the parasol on another sunny, summer's day in January. He told me that he hadn't been feeling quite right and couldn't quite put his finger on what was going on. He placed his right hand on the table and he showed me how his little finger would move, jerk and spasm of its own accord, without Dad being able to control it. He also told me on occasions about he was forgetful, how me might go into the kitchen for something then immediately forget what he went into the kitchen for.

I told him to stop being a worrywart, and that he would just have to face up to being an old fart now. Things like that happen to seventy-eight year old people for no other reason than that they are old and knackered. Hell, even I wander into the kitchen for a snack and forget what I want when I get there.

Also though, when we were in Melbourne, I noticed that his left leg wouldn't travel while he walked. It would occasionally sort of drag and scuff the ground a little as if his mind had completely forgotten how to propel his left leg forward in a walking motion. Once back at Auckland International Airport Dad tumbled over. His left leg didn't follow through properly at the point where the pavement started to slope downwards. He missed his step and over he went. He wasn't particularly injured, just a little embarrassed. But he had gone down spectacularly and we all enjoyed it and I gave him some stick about it. In all honesty, we just laughed it off. We had three very long days in Melbourne and on the first day the time difference meant that we were up for twenty hours. Factor in the fact that Dad also marched up twelve flights of stairs to get to his room, then was it any wonder that Dad was tired and missed a step on return to Auckland? Dad never complained about it; he never made a fuss about it; he just laughed it all off.

Mum reported back to me that when they arrived back at London Heathrow, Dad did a very funny thing. Whilst standing, waiting for their luggage to turn up on the carousel, Dad, spotting one of Mum's cases, launched himself on to the conveyer belt, like a child might when freeing themselves from the watchful eye of their parent. He climbed on and rode the conveyer belt. Later, Dad admitted that he didn't know why he did that. We all put it down to the exhaustion of two elderly people undertaking a twenty-five hour flight in Economy Class.

Things went back to normal upon their return, with Sunday morning reserved for a good chat about the week gone by and of course the football. We weren't Skyping a lot then, most of the calls were done over the phone; I can't recall why because I know Mum had the capability to do it and later on that year we would use Skype regularly. The conversations were the same starting with an assessment to what time it was 'out there' in New Zealand which always took fifteen to twenty minutes, each and every week: the idea that it is basically twelve hours' difference give or take one hour because of Daylight Savings is a concept that has been beyond Mum, and Debbie and Tracey for that matter, for the last fourteen years. Mum would then provide a report on family, friends and issues of the day. Then the phone would be passed to Dad and we would assess the weekend's football and particularly how Saints were doing. It was the second half of 2011 season and although in the third tier of English Football still, League One, Saints were on the march to promotion to the second tier, the Championship. We would talk about other stuff too, like Dad getting a bit drunk up the pub and the consequences of that, but Saints were the priority of the day with Dad still going to matches with Chris or Ian, or sometimes with Kate or Hayley.

Sadly, on return from New Zealand, Dad's current dog, Ben – a beautiful black Labrador – needed to be put down. Of course, he was inconsolable for a while. Dad loved the dogs that he had. He'd freely admit that he preferred animals to humans. Even killing an insect was off limits. In New Zealand we argued about killing a White Tail Spider, New Zealand's only venomous spider (and the bite is right nasty too, I know – I've been bitten). Over the years he has always had a dog; Jason the black Labrador, JJ the golden Labrador, Dougal the Old English Sheepdog, and Bessie the deaf mongrel (who would sleep in the walk-in wardrobe and wear Mum's false teeth). Whenever Dad was in trouble with Mum at home, he'd summon the dog and say, "Come on, we're going up the pub."

Around April or May, occasionally Dad would not come to the phone. Mum would inform me that he was tired and had gone to bed, usually around seven o'clock. This I found odd. I knew the Saturday night/Sunday morning call was important to Dad. We still texted each other often but this was our only voice connection of the entire week. After the seminal match away to Brighton and Hove Albion which Saints won in the last minute causing me to wake the street, I couldn't wait to talk through the match with Dad. He didn't show up for that call, and turned up for the call less and less as the months ticked on.

By about August time, when Dad was on the call, the conversations would be difficult. It seemed that as you talked to him about something – normally the Saints – he would just go off at a tangent and talk about something else as if he hadn't been bothered to listen to what you had to say. Other times he would just cut in over you and talk about something else. I had already pieced together back in January that there was a problem here and by now everyone was certain of it. Dad kept falling over and Mum was very worried that he was going to seriously hurt himself unless he learnt to stop toppling over. Why was this happening?

Dad never, ever went to the doctors. But then again, Dad was rarely ever ill. For a seventy-eight year old, Dad was physically very fit. He had developed an odd dry cough that, when allied with Dad's peculiar behaviour was enough for Mum to coerce him into going to see his GP. Bizarrely Dad had been diagnosed by the GP of having some asthma-like symptoms and had been given an inhaler to take. He had also been referred to a specialist who had identified problems with his gait.

I was in an interesting position. Whereas Mum, and to a certain extent Debbie, was with Dad all of the time, they would see this degradation happen really very slowly. This meant that it was very easy for them not to notice a problem with Dad, or to think that Dad was simply being a bugger more and more. For example, Dad always used to lose his keys when he drove, and always either lost, or sat on and broke his glasses. The fact that he was beginning to lose more things or be more forgetful or lazier than he was, was not necessarily a cause for concern. But if I was speaking to him, say, twice a month rather than every week, I was certainly noticing a degradation in his personality. I felt he was going doolally. His texts remained actually still pretty normal and cogent, but they – like the calls – were much fewer than before, as if I had caused some profound offence and that he just didn't want to speak to his son. Perhaps the seismic hurt that I had caused him moving so far away had ruptured our relationship knowing that Mum and Dad's most recent trip to New Zealand was undoubtedly their last.

In September, Deb contacted me to say it would be a good idea to return for a visit. I arrived in October 2011 for two weeks and quickly realised things were not going to end well. In no uncertain terms I told Debbie and Mum to hope for the best but plan for the worst.

In some ways, it was a good visit. I got to spend good time with Dad and provide some respite for Mum. And of course, me and Dad got to go to the football together.

Saints had been promoted back to the second tier of English football. Their manager, Nigel Adkins and the new club owners had bought players who were already Premier League quality. Fonte continued to dominate in defence and Schneiderlin similarly marshalled the midfield. He was joined in the engine room of Saints' midfield by Richard Chaplow, one of Saints standout players for Saints throughout this season. Our striker Ricky Lambert showed that the step up from League One to the Championship was irrelevant to him and was scoring goals for fun. A big, strong centre forward, Lambert's game was so much more than holding the ball up front and scoring goals. He had magnificent touch and vision and would go on to be a true heir to Matt Le Tissier's Number seven shirt. This really was a Saints team to be genuinely proud of, playing top, top quality football albeit not in the top league. The jump to the Championship was made to look inconsequential by Saints who had taken the division by storm and were firmly top of the league. As luck would have it, Saints next game was against West Ham United, newly relegated from the Premier League and hot favourites for promotion. I could not wait to take Dad to the match.

We parked up in St Denys, near the train station, and walked the fifteen minute walk to the stadium adjacent to the River Itchen on Southampton water. It took us much more than fifteen minutes though. Dad continually staggered towards the water, as if there was some magnet drawing him to it. Sometimes he was oblivious to it, sometimes he knew it was happening. We chuckled through it. One supporter walked by and suggested that Dad had had too much to drink already.

"I wish I bloody had!" Dad chuckled back to him.

It was hard work but I ensured Dad didn't go into the drink. Kerbs and small steps were really difficult for him, his mind betraying him utterly, and at one point I had to catch this large old man in my arms as he tried to negotiate a single step. Dad didn't complain about it; he didn't make a fuss; he just laughed it off.

I got him into the ground and settled him down. I was exhausted and wondered how on earth had Mum even begun to cope with this. He was all over the place.

Chris was kind enough to let me have his ticket for this match. I noticed when Dad sat down that both Dad and Chris had got to know some of the supporters around them. Remarkably it appeared that Dad had not pissed them off at all. On the contrary, they were pleased to see him. I remember thinking how cool this was and how different things were in 2011 from the hooliganism and general malaise that existed back when me and Dad first went nearly thirty years prior.

The game was exciting and was in front of a record crowd. West Ham were a good team, but Saints were better and won the game by a single goal. It was brutal at times, West Ham's tactic was to kick the ball as far forward as possible and kick the Saints players even higher into the air. But Saints fought around it, played the better football and won out. It was a true statement of intent for the league. Me and Dad were delighted.

I turned to Dad and said to him, "Super win, that, Dad eh?"

"Did we win?" he asked, confused. "I thought we drew 1-1?"

"No Dad, we won. We won 1-0."

"Bloody Brilliant!" he said, cheering as if we scored a goal there and then. The disease that had taken his mobility, was quite obviously eating away at his mind and now had started to take his football away from him. I was heartbroken.

It did seem though that, if he put his mind to things and focused hard, he could beat down his illness. Getting to the game and during the match Dad was generally 'with it'. But as he started to tire under the midweek floodlights he couldn't seem to keep the levels of lucidity required.

On the following Saturday, me and Dan took Dad to Reading. We had a great time. It was a tough match but Saints ground out a 1-1 draw, equalising late in the game to make it feel like a win. It was one of the best away venues I have ever visited and you were treated like good customers rather than Eighties hooligans. Moving Dad into and out of the ground was slightly easier without the enticing River Itchen there to beckon Dad toward it, and despite a small tumble that caused him to lose half his Fosters (oh! The shame!), Dan was a big help.

During the match, Dad was at his best – or worst, depending on how you would look at it. He stood for the entire ninety minutes. On occasion against West Ham, he would wobble and topple over, hardly able to stand at all, but against Reading he stood from the first minute to the last minute, totally upright. Me and Dan would offer him to sit down for a bit but we were told to bugger off. If the entire Southampton away end was going stand, then bugger it, Dad was going to stand too – and he didn't wobble a bit. He heckled his way through the ninety minutes, watching the match intently and barking out Saints songs with the away fans. I was delighted (although during the match, losing was offending me, and being down to ten men due to a sending off wasn't helping). Then, cool as you like, Dad would turn to me and ask, "What's the score, Russ?" This damn disease seemed to offer him some leeway and some space to be happy when he most wanted it, and then ridicule him all over again. He was tired when we got him back to the car and no wonder. But we were happy.

I got to see one more match with Dad at St Mary's before I returned to New Zealand, the following Saturday against Middlesbrough – another top of the table clash. Saints were outstanding – their opponents didn't get a kick for the entire ninety minutes. The match was won at a canter 3-0 and the third goal was scored following twenty-six consecutive passes, one of my favourite ever goals. It had struck me before the game that this could be the last time we ever saw a home game together. I was glad we won so wonderfully, and I was glad this day that Dad held on to the score throughout the game and wasn't so confused as he was against West Ham.

Whilst I was back in England I was determined to get Dad some proper treatment and some proper help. He had seen a specialist, who could see how wobbly he was, but he was not due to go back to him until January. Dad was also waiting on results of his tests that were now overdue. It was very evident that his symptoms were escalating quickly and we felt he needed to be seen now. In talking to the specialist's secretary, they were in no mood to assist. They told me that 'no news was good news' and that if we were still concerned, perhaps we should visit his GP.

Okay, I thought, let's follow process. I called the GP for an appointment. They could only offer an appointment in five weeks' time. I was staggered: in New Zealand you can get an appointment same day or next day, and I had forgotten how backward Britain was in this regard. Mum shrugged at me as if to say, 'welcome to my world'. I wasn't settling for this: that day Dad had decided to vacuum and proceeded to hoover over the cables, cutting them up and nearly electrocuting himself. He kept getting in his mind that he needed to fix the back of the telly and would pull out all the plugs and cables into a tangled mess. I rang the GP again and would not settle until I got an emergency appointment next day. It appears that, in England, the need for an emergency appointment must to be met by the secretary with total indignation and resentment, as if you are fooling the system, rather than compassion and sympathy associated with someone who needs help quickly. Nonetheless we had an appointment with a doctor. Not *his* doctor of course – throughout Dad's illness Dad never actually managed to get an appointment with his own doctor – but *a* doctor. I took Dad myself.

Whilst sat in with Dad in with the GP, I could see immediately the problems that Mum and Debbie had continually faced. Dad was all over the place both physically and his mental focus was not there. But as soon as Dad stepped in to the GP's clinic's room, his disease would play with him some more, suddenly making Dad as sharp as a tack, just as he was, with an immediate massive improvement in his balance.

The GP asked Dad what the problem was; Dad replied that he'd been having a bit of trouble but generally there's nothing wrong. Confused, the GP looked at his notes and I tried to intercept the conversation and explain some of the clear problems we were having. The GP held her hand up to me as if to say 'stop'. She asked if there was anything wrong with me, and if there wasn't then she would continue to talk to, and assess Dad. She looked him over with all the typical checks that a GP would do, blood pressure, temperature, listen to his chest, look in his ear. She even got him to walk in a straight(ish) line.

This was unbelievably frustrating. I wanted her to communicate with the referred doctor to expedite his assessment, diagnosis and treatment. Despite the fact that I explained that the symptoms were getting worse, and quickly, she saw no need to do anything of the sort and said that Dad looked fine. She asked Dad if what I was saying was accurate. He said "Dunno". In the end, I begged and pleaded with the doctor to have the specialist look at Dad again. I told the doctor that everything she had told him would be forgotten as soon as he left. Eventually, the doctor relented and agreed to expedite his treatment with the specialist. This was without doubt one of the saddest moments of my life, having to plead with a doctor for basic help, having to talk about Dad's symptoms in front of him, some of them quite awful, when he had no recollection of them. I remember seeing Dad dip his head sadly, ashamed of himself but not really understanding why.

I also found out that the specialist had crafted a letter that had been received by the GP some three weeks before. We were told that we could get a copy of the letter from reception. Perhaps we were going to start to find out what was going on with Dad? I went to reception to get the letter but the letter was medically confidential and could only be requested by the person who it is about. So I asked Dad (who was standing next to me) to ask the receptionist except he couldn't remember what to ask for.

It was farcical. Dad stood next to me and across the counter was this secretary. I would say to Dad, "Can you ask the lady for your medical report from the specialist, Dad?"

At which point Dad said, "Er, yes – whatever he said!" pointing at me. The receptionist refused. The key to getting around this kind of Private Information Act is for whomever to agree for you to become 'Power Of Attorney' so you have the legal right to make decisions on their behalf and to receive their documentation. Power of Attorney is vitally important if your loved-ones have any form of dementia but we didn't have that for Dad.

But it didn't stop me trying. I informed the secretary at the front desk that I had Power Of Attorney for Dad at which point the receptionist said, "oh! In that case, here you are!" No checking, no documentation validation, nothing. She handed me the letter and sent one to me in the post for good measure.

As it happened, the letter written by the specialist was inconclusive. There was no diagnosis. Basically, the specialist was stumped and admitted in medical speak that he had no idea what was wrong with Dad.

I remember that the GP also prescribed something incidental to Dad, antidepressants I think. As we left the doctor's clinic to go next door to the chemist, Dad could barely walk, his symptoms back with an extravagant flourish.

As I was finding out, the system had no capacity to support Dad. He was someone who never needed a doctor, never needed medical help, suddenly needing medical help and support from a system simply not prepared to provide it. Dad didn't complain about the situation and never made a fuss about it; he just laughed it off.

One lunch time I decided to take Dad up the pub, the 'Rising Sun'. We walked to the pub – normally a ten minute walk – of course it took us longer. We entered the pub and I helped sit a wobbly Dad down at a table to the left of the entrance. At the bar, there were about six or seven men sat on stools, hunched over the bar enjoying their lunch time pint. A couple of guys turned their heads and said hello to Dad. Cheerily, Dad said hello back. I got Dad a beer, and a Fosters for me and sat down with him. He'd spill his pint a little bit, trying to channel every bit of strength into the tips of his fingers for grip. But otherwise, this was all very nice, thank you very much.

Dad caught my attention and pointed to one of the guys at the bar. He looked at me with a grin on his face. He explained to me that the guy at the bar in a cricket jumper went with Dad to the cricket at the Rose Bowl to see either Hampshire or England. They had been a number of times and had become friends. Sadly this gentlemen was not at all keen on a conversation with Dad today.

Dad was trying to get the attention of someone else at the bar, serving a bit of banter to the man. I don't remember what he said nor the man's name – let's assume it was 'Eric', it would have been something like 'hey Eric? How are you doing you old bastard!' The man hunched up his shoulders and dipped his head as if to hide from Dad.

These were people who drunk with Dad in the pub. These were people who were friends with Dad. These were people who had been out with Dad. Dad had shared his time and personality with these people but because Dad quite visibly had a problem – I mean there was absolutely no getting away from it, you could see there was a problem there – this was enough for him to be shunned. We stayed, had our lunch and I watched as the 'shunners' left the pub without a goodbye, or an 'all the best' or a 'cheerio' to Dad. Dad knew too. But he didn't complain, wouldn't make a fuss about it and just laughed it off.

On the way back from the pub Dad explained to me how frustrated he was with what was happening and how depressed he was. In his right mind, he could see the pressures he was putting on people around him; I can only imagine how miserable this was making him.

On another day, I took both Mum and Dad out. On the way out Mum asked Dad if he had the front door key. Dad confirmed that he did and off we went. When we got home Mum asked Dad for the key and Dad said, "I haven't bloody got it!" The front door was locked. The back door was locked. The patio doors around the back were locked. All the windows were shut tight, except one window upstairs in Mum and Dad's bedroom. We saw the funny side but Dad was beside himself with laughter. Mum sent me off across the road to another one of Dad's friends who had long since gone into hiding now Dad was poorly. The fella gave me a ladder for me to climb up and get into the house. Going up the ladder I think I was wobbling more than Dad, and getting in through the window was a problem too. The window was double glazed and the outer window opened on a horizontal pivot. So all I could do was open the window outward, climb into the open space in the top half of the window and very, very carefully balance myself over the frame of the glass making sure that I didn't lean on the glass itself. Eventually, and after a couple of squeaky moments, I managed to get in and unlock the front door.

It was good for Mum – she needed a laugh. Whilst my primary focus was on Dad, I couldn't help but notice how strong Mum had become, poised, alert and articulate, as if a switch had gone off in her head. One month after I emigrated to New Zealand, Mum had a stroke, most likely owing to the pain and pressures I had dumped on to her by waving goodbye to her. Mum and Dad decided not to tell me until they arrived in New Zealand to visit at the end of that year. I still remain very unhappy about this but Debbie filled me in on the details prior to their arrival at Christmas 2004. One of my friends said to me after meeting her whether she came out of an aircraft or a coffin. It was certainly unkind (but very funny all the same), but there was an element of truth to it. She was frail and weak and needed attention from doctors on a couple of occasions in New Zealand. Fast forward nearly seven years and suddenly Mum was having to lift Dad when he fell over, pick up meals that he dropped, clean up after him, bring him back to bed. The care necessary was endless. It was as if Mum was getting younger as Dad was getting much older.

Laughter was a good tonic too. Mum, Debbie and Tracey all enjoyed a good laugh with Dad. You can't have an illness like this and not see the funny side. Sometimes the hilarious side.

It was a good fortnight and all too quickly it was time to go. I'd met Dad's new dog Dougal. This new Dougal was a small, ugly shih-tzu puppy. Sadly, the timing of getting this puppy could not have been worse. Dad's problems started to flare up almost as soon as they got him and consequently with the level of care required for Dad there was no attention for the dog and certainly no time to teach it how to behave. He was good fun though. Dad found it now impossible to sit on a chair properly, he would stretch out his legs and his body and sit in a continually slouched position. Dougal would bite his ankles, run up one leg and down the other before Dad could react. This sent Dad off on one, "Get that bloody dog off of me!" he would roar, much to mine and Mum's amusement. Even better, whenever Dad took his inhaler, the dog would jump up on the chair and nick the inhaler out of his hand and run off with it in his mouth. I think the dog knew what we knew, that the asthma diagnosis was absolutely stupid. He's grown up to be just as ugly but a good dog nonetheless, and I understand his breathing is excellent owing to all the time he took Dad's inhalers.

The timing of little Dougal arriving meant that Dad sadly didn't warm to him. When he needed peace and quiet the puppy ensured he would never have it. It was as if his disease had conjured an external torment to complement his growing internal ones. Even saying goodbye to Mum and Dad was punctured by the dog's naughty self-taught behaviours.

Saying goodbye this time was of course desperately hard. I knew full well that I was unlikely to see him again. I hugged him goodbye and gripped my arms around him for as long as I possibly could, and walked away without looking back. Dad, on the other hand, was happy to say cheerio to me, because in his mind I didn't leave for New Zealand. In fact, he firmly believed I still hung around. He handed Mum a boiled sweet one day and asked her to pass it on to me. One day he was agitated and told Mum to tell me to stop buggering around from behind the bed. He would sometimes tell Mum that I would be home in a minute.

After I had left for New Zealand again, Dad only got to go to one more home match, against Peterborough United (won again 2-1). And then that was it. He couldn't go again, his body and mind failed him. There were just four weeks between the match against Reading where Dad stood for the entire match and the first home game that season that he missed, against Brighton And Hove Albion. He never got to see Saints play again.

At least now he was able to receive medical help. He still didn't have a diagnosis but come November he was finding walking very difficult. Debbie would diligently take Dad to all his appointments as Mum couldn't drive. He wasn't entitled to a disabled car sticker because medically there wasn't anything wrong with him, so Debbie would have to park at the hospital, far away from the clinic he was supposed to be at because there were always so few car parks, and Mum and Deb would have to carry him in for treatment.

It was horrendously difficult for Mum. As well as stumbling over, he would attempt to run away. He would also get up at 5:00 a.m. and get ready for work, even though he had retired twenty years earlier. He would wake Mum up demanding to know what she had done with his car keys, even though he hadn't driven for ten years and didn't own a car.

Finally, there was progress of sorts. He got his specialist follow up appointment. During a test, Dad was asked to draw the face of a clock which he drew perfectly, except the numbers were backward and a mirror image of what the picture was supposed to look like. As a result of this session, there was an initial vague statement of dementia in the documentation. We could have told the specialist that! At least he was given some drugs at last to combat the effects of the disease.

Debbie had been looking to find what benefits Mum would be entitled to, or to just give her some help to give her some respite. Even when Debbie could work out which benefits to actually apply for she'd find that they didn't qualify. Just before Christmas, the Mental Health Clinic did get involved, and communicated plans to care for Dad, and to support Mum. This included getting Dad off the distressing drugs he was on, and provide care for Dad. A commode was promised to be installed in the house and a chair lift and pillow lift. Mum would receive a 'social package' (hopefully a little more than a Facebook account) and would be enrolled into a 'carer's course' to support the incredible stress she was under. Mum was also promised a 'home help starting tomorrow'. They never saw the lady from the Mental Health Clinic again and none of the items devised on the plan ever materialised.

I have a video of Mum and Dad filmed through Skype on New Year's Eve 2011. It's only a very short clip and it is a little depressing to say the least. It shows Mum sitting on a chair on the right of the Skype window, Dad on the left, sat uncomfortably, very skinny, his face thin and gaunt, in a dressing gown, with a walking stick to lean on. He giggles through the video like a small child – this wasn't Dad at all, this was the face of the disease – how I hated that giggle. But I want to keep the video, I can't bring myself to remove it because it was the last time that I 'saw' him. I spoke with Dad but the conversation was incoherent. Sometimes he would role his eyes deep in thought, perhaps desperately thinking how he should answer. Often he would just say "Yeah!", even to an open question.

Sometime during the conversation, long after the video stopped filming, Mum went out into the kitchen, perhaps to rescue little Dougal from some kind of mischief, and left me with Dad on his own. Suddenly Dad rose out of his slouch and sat himself upright. He held on to his walking stick tightly and pulled himself to the edge of the seat and closer to the camera.

Whereas the man I had been speaking to was clearly an imposter, suddenly Dad was there and he spoke. "Hey Russ. I don't know what this is all about, but this thing's bloody got me. I can't get rid of it." I told him to hang on in there and keep fighting. "Yeah," he said. Then he paused for thought, looked up at me and said, "Russ, I'm scared."

His face then slackened, he regressed back into his chair, his slouch more pronounced. Mum returned and Dad started to giggle again. I will never forget this sudden, final moment of clarity from him, as if he had wriggled free of the clutches of the disease, just for a moment, before being captured and made a prisoner in his own mind again. Just a few days later, Dad went into hospital.

The doctors at the hospital, like the GP, would treat Dad as a normal patient; that is to say, they communicated and conversed with Dad in the first instance and not Mum or Debbie. Of course this is right, but there is a tipping point when a dementia sufferer can't hold in the information being presented, and family have to step in to support. It is comical to think about it, but whilst Dad was in the hospital, direction and agreement would be reached about Dad's care, with Dad, who would then duly forget all of it. Mum and Debbie would ask doctors as to what was going on, but no information was forthcoming. Following Dad's admission to the hospital, Mum and Debbie didn't receive any word or notification from any doctor for two weeks. Debbie sought out the original doctor she saw when Dad was admitted. The doctor said that Dad wasn't her patient, although when we received documentation in review of his care, we found that Dad was actually this doctor's patient.

According to Mum, I was there. Dad would often tell Mum that I was in the waiting room and she should come and get me. I wish I was. I was helpless over the other side of the world, receiving regular updates but completely unable to contribute. It was a brutal price to pay, New Zealand was my bed and I had to lie in it. I felt utterly, utterly useless.

At home Mum set about the task of cancelling subscriptions and agreements that Dad made. His dementia was such that he couldn't say 'no'. In the summer months he would get a call from companies selling fringe insurances like boiler insurance. Even though they already had such insurances, Dad would, confused, agree to purchase the insurance. I intercepted a call from such a company when I was over and explained the situation and that they should not call back. They called back the very next day and secured the sale from him. Mum attempted to cancel Dad's Sky subscription: they refused to cooperate as they needed to 'talk to the bill payer' and the account was in Dad's name. The insurances could not be cancelled for the same reason. Not only were the privacy laws hindering the communication of Dad's treatment, it also manifested itself in what was left of Mum's now lonely home life.

The lady from the Mental Health Clinic apparently visited Dad in hospital. Even if she had, Dad would have forgotten because Mum and Debbie never got to know about it. According to the documentation we have she did 'have a telephone conversation' and 'spoke to staff', and apparently attempted three times to contact Mum at home during the day (when Mum was always at the hospital), although for her to leave a message on the answer phone seemed to be beyond her. Crushingly, the report vindicates the level of support Mum and Dad received, citing a seven-week performance indicator between discussions for staff which, up to that point, had not been missed. Seven weeks later Dad was in a home.

At the end of Dad's stay in the hospital, Mum and Debbie were instructed to attend a 'Care Plan' meeting for Dad. This meeting was to be attended by a doctor, a ward nurse, occupational therapist, a social worker and a physiotherapist. Neither a doctor, ward nurse nor occupational therapist attended this meeting. The social worker who did attend left her job two days later. At this meeting Mum was told Dad needed to move into a home. The documentation states that the 'clinical staff found it to be a difficult balance to present such a bleak prospect to the family without dashing all hope.' Except there were no clinical staff members in attendance at that meeting to communicate such a bleak outlook. Up to this point Dad saw at least eight different doctors (including a 'junior' and ward doctor) according to the documentation received across December and January, all without a specific diagnosis.

Because the illness escalated so quickly, there was no continuity of care and the system could not keep up. Documentation kept about his care was wrong, for instance the GP documented a 'slow but steady loss of social skills and only later with problems with mobility' which absolutely did not happen to Dad: his mobility quite obviously went first, his personality went later, in a ten-month period not over the course of years.

The specialist that Dad was referred to initially prescribed Dad the wrong dosage of drug – ten times the correct amount in fact. It caused Dad's side effects to be absolutely horrendous, including frightening hallucinations, coinciding with much faster deterioration in his health. Mum and Debbie were told that he would be seen again in mid-January, but Dad was seen again by this doctor in New Year, who ordered the error-strewn prescription to be stopped. Except it had already been stopped by other doctors two weeks before and replaced with an alternate drug treatment, which in itself was planned to be stopped in an 'action plan' following the assessment from the Mental Health Clinic. But for some reason that wasn't actioned either, so was stopped by doctors in the hospital just after the *original* doctor stopped the *original* prescription! Still following?

Throughout all this, nobody ever listened to Mum or Debbie. Despite exhaustive efforts they simply could not get through to the clinicians, as if they were on mute or sounding off on a wavelength not understood by doctors or nurses.

Moving into the nursing home in Wickham was inevitable but brought its own challenges. Firstly, without a communicated diagnosis Debbie couldn't locate a nursing home prepared to take a dementia patient. Eventually it was discovered that some doctor had diagnosed Vascular Dementia and a home was found.

By the end of February, Saints were still top of the Championship and heading back to the Premier League. They had just won away at Watford 3-0, Ricky Lambert scoring all three goals. In the nursing home, Deb would sit with Dad and listen to all the matches, including the Watford match. But Dad was in a poor way, lying on his bed holding Debbie's hand. When Lambert scored, she squeezed his hand and told Dad that Ricky had scored. Dad squeezed her hand in return and tried to speak but couldn't. A single tear trickled down his face.

At about 5:00 a.m. on the 28th of February 2012, New Zealand time, Deb called me to get on a plane right away. By the time I had booked the tickets I received another call to say that he had passed away. It's odd that to me Dad died a day later than when he officially did. In England, he died on the 27th of February. For me it was the 28th.

For this trip my feet hardly touched the ground. There was so much to do – my first job was to sort out the obituary for the Daily Echo. Truth be told this trip was a blur.

We needed to sort out Dad's death certificate, so went to see the Registrar in Winchester. The lady there told us two really important things. Firstly, she was a little deaf, and secondly the council had recently introduced a new computer system called 'Tell Us Once'. It sounded brilliant: all the information we told them would go into this super-database and shared with all the other councils and local bodies so, for example, the council will know to stop charging Mum council tax.

Mum had diligently brought all the right paperwork, Debbie came along as group leader, and I just came along to support. Everything was going swimmingly until the system did not accept Dad's National Insurance number. The registrar suggested we had the number wrong, although we didn't as was evidenced by Mum's paperwork. So the registrar cancelled the application and we started again. Once more, Dad's National Insurance number was apparently invalid.

After about the third time we had provided the requisite information for the Tell Us Once system, Debbie's belly started to get a but chatty, making this loud gurgling sound. This, along with the registrar asking us to repeat the information because she couldn't hear, the fact that this was the Tell Us Once system, and the fact I was probably a bit jet lagged, I started to snigger.

Like the chuckles you used to have at school with your mates, at first the laughter had to be quiet so as not to disrupt the serious work that was being done here. This was not so easy when Debbie's gut was playing a version of Mozart's 41st symphony in C major. I was fast becoming fit to burst. There was nowhere else for the laughter to go. The thing to do here, I thought, was to keep my lips shut tight and not to make eye contact with Debbie.

So I immediately looked left and looked at Debbie right in the eyes. She had one hand on her tummy trying to muffle the cacophony of noise, and one hand over her mouth, her face beetroot red and fit to burst.

That was that. We both fell apart laughing.

"What?" asked the registrar trying to hear.

"I'm sorry about this," said Debbie, "I missed my lunch and am a bit hungry." Cue further gurgling from her midriff, as if there was somebody gargling in the room.

"What is the matter with you two?" Mum scolded. "This is no place to be skylarking around." But Deb and me were completely finished. We had totally lost all control, tears of laughter racing down our faces, and nothing, not even the confused, quizzical expression on the registrar's face, was going to stop us.

I don't actually remember if we did get the death certificates that day. I don't think we did because my next priority job was to ring up all of Dad's subscriptions and insurances and get them finally cancelled. Deb had stopped all the direct debits once each company refused to deal with anyone other than Dad, so of course Mum was starting to get aggressive mail and further bills from these companies. The insurance company were staggering, flatly telling me that they didn't believe that my father had passed away, and that he would have to call them to arrange to stop the service, or we would have to send an original copy of the death certificate to them. We couldn't send a death certificate to them because I don't think we had them. In the end it took Debbie some months to get these awful malevolent companies off Mum's back. Mum would receive these letters every day and not even open them, and simply passed them over to Debbie to deal with.

Despite the sad circumstances around this visit, there was still time for football. Saints were pushing hard for promotion although were being closely chased by West Ham United still and Reading. We went round to Debs and sat with Chris to watch Saints play at Dirty Leeds. Saints scored with a Ricky Lambert goal on fifteen minutes, but from then on we were battered. Dirty Leeds played way above themselves that night and Saints were off colour. It required a number of last ditch clearances and fantastic saves by our long serving goalkeeper Kelvin Davis to keep us in front. It was one of those remarkable nights when it didn't matter what Dirty Leeds threw at us, the ball wouldn't go in for them (in my memory these nights normally happen the other way with Saints unable to score and the other team nicking the win). It was a great result and a brilliant way to win a match, with your opponent's beside themselves with the injustice of it all. Dad would have chuckled and gone straight up the pub to crow about it.

I did get an opportunity to see Dad after his death. We got to visit the undertakers prior to the funeral and I was shuffled into a room with him settled neatly in his coffin. He looked a lot smaller than I remembered, as if his illness or his death had shrivelled him up a bit. He was wearing his trademark jeans and shirt, with his favourite 'That's It! I'm Telling Grandad' tee shirt from my girls.

As said, I don't believe in God or all that nonsense, but in this situation, you do question yourself a little bit. Rationally you think, well there is no point having a chat because he can't hear you. Then you think, but what if your wrong and there is some fandangly nether world where we go to for the best Fosters ever when we pop our clogs? What if there is some omnipresent life kicking about after death? Then I just got a bit confused because if Dad had become this floating omnipresent ghost-like thing, surely I didn't need to talk to him either because obviously he'd be able to read my thoughts and that would be enough? Having never been in this situation before, I didn't really know what to do or how to do it.

Anyway, I decided to have a little chat with him, just to cover off all the bases. I talked to him about my flight on Malaysian Airways (the seat belt light was on but I got up for a wee and got into trouble with the cabin crew). I brought Dad up to date with results, Watford and Leeds, and speculated that whilst we were still top of the league we were running out of a bit of steam as we neared the finish line. Then I apologised in case he was now all-seeing and all-knowing and if I was just repeating stuff that he had come to know. I asked him if he was comfortable, and remarked how big his nose was from my angle, sat down on a chair. I suggested that we might need to turn his head around at an angle in case we couldn't get the coffin lid on properly. Ultimately though this chat was about saying a final goodbye, a final farewell. I simply told him that I loved him, I thanked him for everything he did for me and my family, and I told him I was sorry.

The funeral was organised to coincide with the timing of my stay and I remember little about it, even where it was held, but I do remember it being hugely enjoyable. That sounds like a bonkers thing to say but it was a good day, a happy day, a genuine celebration of my old Dad.

The morning was an amazingly sunny and warm day for English March morning. Dad's favourite daffodils had already started to show in the front garden. There were flowers strewn across Mum's lounge – there was hardly anywhere to walk. It reminded me of the 2003 cup final when Mum's lounge was a carpet of yellow and blue balloons. Except today it was flowers decorated across the carpet. Each of Dad's grandchildren pitched in to get a massive bouquet spelling 'GRANDAD' which was placed adjacent to the coffin in the hearse. If they had used the alternative spelling of 'granddad' with three 'd's then there would not have been room for it.

The ceremony was nice. It was held in a modern place, which was utterly packed out with people wearing black. There was standing room only it seemed with Dad, with people even finding it difficult to get through the doors there was so many people there. That was great. Me and Dan were part of the six people on coffin-holding duty. As we were walking through with Dad on our shoulders a massive fat fly landed on the back of Dan's head, and decided that this was a nice place to rest up for a while. Dan didn't notice, but Debbie did. It looked like Dan had a hole in the back of his head.

I had my sunglasses on because of the unseasonal sun, but forgot to take them off and sat through the entire ceremony as if I was a bouncer rather than immediate family. Debbie asked me to write a eulogy but don't think it was used. At the end, off Dad went to the tune of 'Oh When the Saints Go Marching In'. Of course he did.

Then it was off to the 'Dog and Crook' pub for the wake. It was a good session, meeting loads of people who had come to see Dad and whom I had not seen for at least fifteen years. At about seven o'clock I was called over by Chris. He gave me his coat. I didn't understand what was going on. He told me that his and Dad's season tickets were in the coat pocket and I was to go off to the match that night with Dan. There was no time to argue, the taxi was waiting and paid for. I knew Saints had an important match at St Mary's that night against Ipswich Town. They needed a win to keep the pressure off them for promotion. However, I had realised that today was genuinely more important than the Saints and had no inclination to go. But it had all been planned and agreed as 'what Dad would have wanted', and we were swept into the taxi and off we went. The taxi driver, seemingly under instructions, had only forty-five minutes to get to the match before the game kicked off, and consequently drove like a grand prix driver / New Zealand driver in rush hour, pre-match heavy traffic. Near the ground, he even drove on the kerb, fans scurrying out of the way. He did his job though, and got us there in double-quick time, with five minutes to spare. We sat in Dad's and Chris's seats looking odd in our black suits and overcoats, and informed Dad's friends around him of the news. They took it sadly but then the teams came out and we all rose to clap and cheer our team on. It was a hard-fought game, with my thinking that Saints were just a little bit off their early season form proving right. Eventually Ricky Lambert scored to put us in a great position to win the game, but Ipswich Town fashioned an equaliser in the last few minutes and we had to settle for a 1-1 draw. It was not the way we wanted to end the night and it had seemed that Ipswich had not consulted the script appropriately. At the end of the season Saints were promoted back to the Premier League in second place behind Reading, who beat Saints in a calamitous home defeat on Good Friday at St Mary's. But Saints muddled through to the end of the season and held off West Ham United into third place. The final match was at home to Coventry City – Dan and Ian went to that game. Saints won 4-0 to secure promotion and Dan and Ian celebrated with thousands of other fans on the pitch at the end of the match. It would have made Dad very happy.

Dementia has no respect for how people are. It destroys people's dignity without compunction. It eroded my Dad's dignity too, but the systems and bureaucracy served to test Dad's and Mum's dignity as well. The systems, processes and procedures in place only managed to make it far, far worse, rather than to ease the difficulties. I'm sure Dad's story is not much different to many, many other families who have gone through similar pain. You spend the first part of your life being shipped to people to don't know as part of the evacuation in World War II. You grow up to meet a wife, build a home and work hard to form a career, and a family. You bring up your family as best you can and pass on everything you have learned in the hope that the little people you bring into the world turn out to be a little bit better than you. You retire and watch as your children work through the same process with your grandchildren, and you can be satisfied. That is until you find yourself in a hospital corridor, confused, put there to live out your days because – even though you can't help it – you're upsetting the other patients. Meantime your wife is coming to terms with the fact you will be gone one day, but is caught in present-day circumstances that entitles her to no benefits whatsoever, and whatever pension money is left has to be sunk into your remaining clinical care. That is not the way that things are meant to be.

Debbie started a process of complaint that took many months to resolve and took a number of reports and enquiries to be addressed by a number of organisations (the reports of which have assisted me with writing this section of the book). These institutions included Southampton, Hampshire, Isle of White and Portsmouth NHS, Hampshire Hospitals, Southern Health Community Mental Health Team and Stokewood Surgery near Eastleigh. Hampshire County Council failed into their required obligation to provide a report into their findings of their internal conduct. That was a shame because they really did excel with their incompetence: as well as sending the Mental Health Clinic lady to promise everything and deliver nothing, the County Council lost forms that Debbie completed, caused errors in processing others, kept demanding council tax payments months after Dad had passed away and were no longer payable. Mum also received highly confidential information for other patients. But of course the *pièce de résistance* was processing the Death Certificate, which at least gave us such a laugh I don't remember laughing so hard at any time since (can you imagine anything quite so macabre as the process of registering the death of your father being remembered for such an agreeable and funny experience? Let's agree to put it down to a cathartic release of emotion).

We found out from our own research that it is very unusual for Vascular Dementia to progress so rapidly, and the lack of continuity of care brought us to question the diagnosis. Vascular Dementia is where blood is progressively blocked from entering the brain causing mini strokes that causes a step-based decline in the patient. Normally these changes occur over a very long period, often as much as ten years, not ten months. Certainly, Lewy Bodies dementia seemed to fit much better with what was happening to Dad. Lewy Bodies is an aggressive form of dementia that normally goes undiagnosed because of its similarities to Alzheimer's and Parkinson's disease. The disease attacks the brain and other systems simultaneously and sufferers are particularly sensitive to the medications to combat it, often very negatively so, as what happened to Dad. Behaviours, physical fitness and mental cognitive abilities degrade simultaneously but at different speeds. Early diagnosis is critical to extend quality of life. The comedian Robin Williams was found to be suffering from Lewy Bodies and it was speculated that this was one of the reasons why he took his life. At the end of the day though, there were just so many stakeholders involved in Dad's care (I'm not sure you can call it 'care' though) that it is absolutely no surprise that there was no continuity of care or even valid, consistent expertise in his care to make such a difficult diagnosis.

We were lucky in a way that this all happened within a timeframe of about ten months. There are thousands of people who care for their loved ones in the same way Mum and Debbie did over the course of years with – in all probability – the same poor or inconsistent levels of care that Dad had received. The problems associated with long term care such as job vulnerability or care support, hardly applied to us because it all happened so quickly. We'd like to think that in the future, a GP advisor is not compelled to say in writing that "it can be difficult to get a speedy response from services where there are rapid changes in a patient's symptoms". Maybe for someone else in the future it could be something like "thankfully, services were able to respond to the rapid changes in the patient's dementia-related symptoms".

By the way, I don't think I have mentioned, my Dad's name is John.

This is Dad's eulogy that I wrote to help the vicar with his speech at the funeral. I don't remember it being used. It's a nice piece though – see what you think.

John was born in Southampton in September 1933, and grew up on Floating Bridge road, almost on the site of the Football Stadium. During the War, he was evacuated to numerous places, including Bournemouth, Farnborough and West Wellow. He enjoyed cycling, cricket and dancing, but football was his passion, and he was spotted by the Saints and played in goal for their Youth team.

When he was sixteen, he met Nan at a Youth Club in Woolston. John and Nancy were married in 1954. In 1957, their first daughter Debbie was born, and in 1960 Tracey came along. They always believed that their family was complete, but in 1971 a son added to their family – Russell.

John did his National Service in The Navy, and on completion joined The Police Force. He spent most of his professional years – 29 – at Fords in Eastleigh before retiring in the early Nineties. He lived in Colden Common since 1975.

John certainly had an opinion. But however staunch he was in some of his views, he was an extremely compassionate person. He had strong principles that were simple but intelligent, and these were passed on and practised by all of his children. John was an extremely reliable and completely trustworthy, and his words were always honest and true.

Yet, John would never cause a fuss. He would go out of his way not to be a bother or a burden. People may have an opinion of him as a loud character, and it is true his voice could carry. But in reality nothing could be further from the truth. He was always at his most effective with a quiet, reasoned word in your ear. He could be something of an enigma – he was tremendously intelligent and often extremely sharp and clever, but wasn't terribly academic. He had a seemingly endless thirst for general knowledge, but you would never see him on a quiz team (although he knew all the answers!).

Certainly many will remember John for his wit and character. He wasn't a joke-teller or a jester, but he had an uncanny knack of delivering acerbic slices of wit and wisdom with the precision of a Swiss watch. He also had the unenviable knack of almost always seeming to find him in the wrong place in the wrong time, usually with consequences as hilarious as they are legendary.

John was the consummate family man. With three children, seven grandchildren and two great-grandchildren, he certainly had plenty of practice. His family always made him very proud. As children they are, or were, all bundles of fun and energy. John played a major part in crafting, shaping and polishing every one of these treasures and all have been deeply devoted to him. In his last days, no one in his extended family needed to be asked, prompted or coerced to support him. They were all already there for him; irrespective of any trials and tribulations in their own lives, John came first and foremost.

Despite his extended family, there was always time for the Saints. When he joined Southampton as their Youth Team goalkeeper, each boy was minded by a professional, and his minder was the great Sir Alf Ramsey. He played with Southampton for a season or so and ever since, he has been a staunch, unwavering and loyal Saints supporter.

John loved animals and always had a dog. His dogs were always an intrinsic part of the family unit, and he loved them all completely. And he was an animal lover too, and would always flee a spider to safety, and would agonise if someone was unkind or cruel to an animal – even if you squashed a fly his typical response would be 'what had it ever done to you?'

He enjoyed going to pubs on an evening with his dog of the day. He always seemed to own a dog almost as charismatic as himself. Whether it was with Jason, Dougal, Bessie or Ben, both man and dog were terrific company. You were never far away from a memorable night of laughter or some crazy scrapes when John and his dog were around. Many people had a friend in John. He was a social man and made friends easily, although was never a sufferer of fools.

John enjoyed a fine retirement. He travelled around Britain with Nancy, and in later years enjoyed trips to New Zealand and Australia to stay with Russell.

A few months from returning from a third trip to New Zealand exactly one year ago, the life this sharp, fit man hit a snag.

As usual, he didn't want to be a bother. As usual, he would not cause a fuss. As usual he would make a good fist of it and smile doing it. As usual, he felt sure he would get fit again. He was an extremely proud man whose body, and then his mind, would betray him.

But wouldn't be a bother.
Wouldn't cause a fuss.
Made a great fist of it.
Smiled and laughed all the way through it.

John passed away peacefully on February 27th 2012.

The Family has received great warmth from all the condolences since his passing, from friends and relatives remind us all of the respect, worship and love that everyone has for him. He has been described as 'larger than life', a 'top man' and 'one of my best friends'.

In short, John Budden was a Good Man.
To his family, he is the Best of All Men.

2017

English Football League Cup Final 2017, Manchester United versus
Southampton. Wembley Stadium, London, Sunday, 26th of February.

As chance would have it, I have discovered a completely 100%
effective satisfaction guaranteed way of solving the feelings of jet lag.
Once you reach your destination, all you need to do is go to a nearby
cup final, where your team (who haven't won a trophy in forty-one
years) is playing. Your mind will be so pre-occupied about your team
and how well they are going to do, that there is simply no room to feel
the onset of the confused tiredness that jet lag brings.

I had woken at 2:00 a.m. and seriously contemplated setting off the
fire alarm which would have undoubtedly disrupted the vital sleep
patterns of Manchester United's megastars in the hotel. But at the
excitable thought of doing my bit for the team I promptly delivered an
enormously harmonious fart that stopped Dan's steady unconscious
breathing in his tracks. I wasn't sure if I had awoken him or killed him.
We both promptly fell back asleep (in our separate beds in case you
were wondering).

We were awake and ready for breakfast before 8:00 a.m. and felt
ready to take on Manchester United ourselves. I did the normal hotel
thing of having an extravagant cooked breakfast that I couldn't finish,
followed by a bowl of fruit and toast, which also I couldn't finish. Dan
was in and out of breakfast, his bowels playing tricks on his nerves. He
had a total of five poos between breakfast and the match and we
pondered just how it was even possible to accomplish that. Imagine if
you had the runs at the cup final, and needed to go badly with twenty
minutes to go? Would you go? I wouldn't – not a chance, I'd rather soil
myself good and proper rather than miss out on the memory of a
lifetime. Dan agreed; poo yourself and win the cup rather than save
your pants and miss the moment.

Two of the hordes of Manchester United fans staying in the hotel sat at the nearest table to us. Whilst Dan was navigating poo number two, one of the guys looked at my red and white Saints top and asked me, "Ay! Juthunk yullava cannelchump of wintay?"

"I'm sorry?" I said, shocked that I had stumbled on an actual Manchester United fan from Manchester. I suppose it was a bit like Sir Richard Attenborough setting eyes on an endangered species.

"Arsey, juthunk yullava cannelchump of wintay?" he said. I could not understand what he was saying. My brain was frantically trying to break down his thick Mancunian accent into something resembling English.

"I'm sorry, I didn't hear what you said." I am sure you have been in this position at one time and another and you realise there is a threshold of impatience that the questioner can reach. If you keep saying 'pardon' or 'what' you end up looking as though you are taking the piss. I was nearing this moment soon.

"W'arse-head was, juthunk yullava cannelchump of wintay?"

"Nope, sorry. Didn't get that at all. Try again, a bit slower?"

"Na, feggit!"

My brain was still translating and I think he wanted to know if I thought we had a cat in hell's chance of winning today. Had he stayed around after I figured this out I would have told him: yes, I bloody do.

Eventually we were out of the hotel and milling around. We stopped at a coffee shop and sat outside with substandard English attempts at coffee. Inside we saw Peter Rodrigues chatting jauntily with a colleague. Rodrigues, you'll recall, was Saints captain in 1976: the only captain we've ever had who has lifted a big trophy. I had understood that he'd been quite ill. He certainly looked up and at it today which pleased us.

I realised I was unlikely to see Sama on this visit. Dan told me that Sama now had a car and was driving with mixed results. I'd spoke with Sama over the phone and she was a bit down because of some of the scrapes she had been in. I told her to keep her chin up and go for it. If she thinks she's a bad driver, she should come over to New Zealand and see what a genuine bad driver is like.

We saw some people kicking a ball about in the shadows of the Wembley arches. A ball was miscontrolled by one guy and his ball bounced in my direction. I decided to pass my own football wisdom on this fella: I would get the ball under control, flick it up into the air with my trusty left foot and boot it back straight into the air and into his arms. Except this gentleman decided to run over and tackle me. Off balance, all I managed to do was kick the ball all the way down the street. I decided to avoid the ball games from then on.

If football really is my religion, then Wembley is my cathedral, my Mecca. As a kid, whilst Wembley was not the first ground I visited, it was the place I saw my first 'real match'. It was my citadel of dreams where each year I hoped and I hoped that Saints would return. With each season of failure, the focus would immediately turn to the next year. Dad and me would watch the cup final on the television, both thinking that next year, we could be there. With each cup match won, Wembley became closer and closer. With each poor season, Wembley looked further away. In 2000, Wembley was demolished and rebuilt at a cost of around one billion pounds, reopening in 2007. Dad had got to visit the 'new' Wembley in 2010 for the Johnstone's Paint Trophy final, but I had never been. Regular visitors to the stadium – fans of the big clubs – tire of its presence, bemoaning the cost of a burger, the views from the very back of the highest tier, the cost of a ticket and the congestion in trying to leave the ground by car. That wasn't going to be me. Whilst the twin towers of the famous old stadium had been replaced by a huge arch stretching across the sky line, it was still Wembley to me, where I had always dreamed Saints would eventually return. I was beside myself with excitement waiting to get in.

With the giant 90,000 seater stadium looming large around us, we decided around 11:00 a.m. to venture out to a pub. Such is the organisation these days, 'official pubs' are designated to each team, about seven each. The nearest Saints one was The Green Man, less than ten minutes' walk away.

We could hear the singing and chanting and noise from streets away. When we arrived, the pub, the car park and beer garden was awash with red and white striped Saints supporters, in the fullest of spirits. The pub owners had a military operation-like approach to serving punters quickly and keeping fans circulating around the bars, so it took us no time to move through the crowd and get served. To cap it all they were serving Fosters on tap, the Amber Nectar. Today was going well and the omens were aligning well in our favour.

We stood out in the beer garden and enjoyed and contributed to the singing and chanting. Flags of St George, adorned with Saints badges, 'Pride of the South' slogans and pictures of Matt Le Tissier were hung everywhere. This was certainly the Saints fans' base camp. Flares and rich red smoke bombs were being constantly fired off, with air horns frequently sounding out, maintaining an intense party atmosphere.

We'd been there less than an hour, when many of the fans were throwing their full plastic cups of beer (I'm assuming not Fosters – that would be a terrible waste) up into the air for everyone else to be rained on. Instead of being frowned upon, it seemed to be wholeheartedly agreeable and so more and more pints were tossed up. We also noticed one or two fans who had no chance of being allowed entry to the ground – they were so drunk they could hardly stand or talk. It was about 12:30, four hours from kick off.

We'd had our fix of Saints fans in a pub and quickly had quite enough of that, so made back for Wembley. At 2:00 p.m. we decided that the moment of truth had arrived. Were our tickets, costing 486 pounds each (900 dollars), as everybody now knew thanks to Debbie, real or were they fake?

When we arrived back at Wembley the number of fans had thickened considerably, mainly Saints fans at our end of the ground. Kids had their flags and hats and painted faces, clinging tightly to the hands of their mums or dads. They would be asking the same excitable questions to their parents as I did with dad, thirty-eight years earlier. Where do we go? What will be the score? Who will be playing? When will we get there? It was fast becoming a mass of red and white. Some fans were dressed up in fancy dress such as superheroes or cartoon characters. Silly hats were *du rigueur*. Small games of football were breaking out in spare spaces and the burger and coffee vans were doing a roaring trade. BBC TV were operating an outside broadcast unit and were milling around for interviews. By this time, Dan was fed up with me proclaiming to everyone that I had come all the way from New Zealand so I didn't promote myself any further. We followed the gentle surge of people up a concrete slope to the main elevated concourse that sits around the perimeter of the stadium, and made for the Bobby Moore statue by the entrance of Club Wembley.

We queued at the Club Wembley entrance, alongside the smart and the suave. Although we couldn't wear our team's colours, it didn't say anything about dressing up sophisticated. I had Dads old woolly jumper on with a pair of neutral blue Adidas trainers. The jumper was there for warmth as much as for sentimental reasons, and is frankly, the only jumper I own.

Once we had finished being scanned for guns and bombs about our person, we went inside and up an escalator where we reached the entrance. Here we needed to scan our tickets. My heart was racing.

Dan went first; he coolly reached his ticket into the mouth of the barcode scanner. The glass doors swished open immediately with an agreeable beep of the scanner. He was in! It must be a real ticket!

Me next. I shoved the ticket into the scanner.

Nothing happened.

Stay cool, I thought. Try again slowly. I did. Nothing happened.

I tried again. Nothing.

Now I should say at this point, that I have worked on projects with barcode scanning technologies, both the traditional striped barcodes and the square 2D barcodes. I understand how they work, how they scan and why they sometimes don't. For reasons most likely related to the team and the day, I had suddenly lost any and all knowledge of how a scanner works. I was like a little old lady or a man who had been in a coma for twenty years in my approach to getting in. I turned the paper over, turned it back, moved it on its side, tried to look into the mouth of the scanner, flattened the paper, all the while frantically pumping the ticket in and out, in and out, of the scanner. I found myself panicking. Dan had walked off.

Dan told me later how all the colour drained out of my face in fear of not getting in. Eventually, the glass doors almost begrudgingly opened and I dashed in before the doors had a chance to change their minds.

The tickets were real.

Club Wembley was an amazing experience for the uninitiated who is used to bland kiosks, inside bland concourses, part of bland stadia, run by bland teenagers, serving bland food. This place was sensational. It had bars, fine dining and live bands; even the burger bar was 'gourmet'. I thought Wagyu played for the Ivory Coast in the last World Cup – I had no idea that it was a posh steak. I'd bought myself four matchday programmes for friends back in New Zealand at a cost of forty pounds, although had I realised I could have had as many as I wanted for free in here.

We decided first and foremost to see our seats, just to make sure they were there. Along the concourse there were glass double doors that automatically opened for you to enter the stadium bowl. Either side of the doors were security people who greeted us cordially. I imagine they had seen it all before. Fans from Arsenal, Chelsea and Manchester United would, I expect, nonchalantly make their way to their seats about five minutes before kick-off, almost bored at the prospect of another big game cup final and a possible trophy. Fans of teams who rarely get to a final, like Southampton, turn up hours before kick-off, giddy with juvenile excitement, bouncing on the balls of their feet, not sure what to do with themselves, pinching themselves to make sure they are not dreaming. This was me and Dan this afternoon.

Walking through the doors into the bowl took the breath away. The view was magnificent. Red seats across three huge vertical tiers of terracing dominated the eye line in every direction, ready to accept the 90,000 supporters. The tier below us stretched about fifty rows along the side of the pitch, and seemingly twice that behind the goal. The tier above us rose until it was out of view. Across at the other end of the ground, we could see blue seats that spelt out the name 'Wembley' across the terrace, soon to be obscured by thousands of arses supporting Manchester United. The electronic advertising hoardings around the perimeter of the pitch ran the message 'Welcome to the EFL Cup Final 2017', the letters scooting around the ground. The pitch looked like the Wembley pitch of old, two distinct tones of green stripes drawn across the pitch in every direction. The players tunnel and royal box, where the winning captain would retrieve the trophy and hold it aloft to his adoring fans, sat to our left, with a bank of press seats with desk space directly above that at the top of the lower tier. The roof was huge, complex looking and deep – there was no risk of us getting wet today, nor it would seem would most of the fans if rain were to fall. There were two giant blue scoreboards, one just above my head and behind me, dazzling with blue and white messages of welcome, with the two teams' emblems adjacent to the score of '0-0', as if anyone inside the ground would need to remind themselves to correlate the score to a particular team. We were sat directly behind the goal in the middle Club Wembley tier, a television camera perched slightly to our left, with a crystal clear unobscured view of the action to come. The seats were padded for extra comfort, although I was only intending to use the edge of it that afternoon.

I received a call from Michael, my friend from when I played football as a kid (whose dad as football coach had put me straight when I was fourteen). He had selflessly tried to organise me a ticket and was sat with his sons in the tier above us. I manoeuvred myself across the near empty middle tier of Wembley Stadium, whilst he moved down to the front of the upper tier. We waved as we spotted each other as dots and edged as close as we could to each other. We then tried to engage in a chat. With Michael about forty metres higher up in the stands from me, shouting up across Wembley stadium wasn't that productive and in the end, we gave up with a thumbs up. We should have used our phones when I think about it now – I didn't think about that at the time.

Time disappeared quickly and the ground was fast filling up. With thirty minutes to kick off, the atmosphere at the Saints end was electric. Southampton Football Club generously placed a red and white Saints scarf on every seat, in both the lower and upper tiers, and the fans were spinning them round their heads whilst belting out 'Oh When The Saints Go Marching In'.

Next, an enormous 'Forever Saints' flag was unravelled in the lower tier over everybody's head, which then crawled slowly around the crowd. The flag paid homage to the late owner of the club Markus Liebherr, who purchased the club in 2010 when it was poised to go out of business. Two massive balloons adorned with the Southampton and

Manchester United badges hung from their underside floated on to the pitch to a thumping soundtrack coming through the speakers. Fireworks went off. Giant ribbons were placed across the pitch. Huge replica shirts were unravelled across the penalty areas. The teams were announced. All of a sudden everyone was seated and it was time for the teams to come out.

The Saints team was unchanged from the previous match with Sunderland – the first time this had happened this season. Forster was in goal, his hairstyle reminded me of a bushy Seventies European minge stuck on his head, from my position in the stands. Our defenders were Cédric, Maya Yoshida, Jack Stephens and Ryan Bertrand. In midfield was Steven Davis and Oriel Romeu. In front of them Nathan Redmond, Dušan Tadić and James Ward-Prowse. Our new striker, Manolo Gabbiadini was up front.

The Manchester United team had De Gea in goal, the most expensive player in the world in midfield in Paul Pogba, who had signed for Manchester United at the start of the season for 90 million pounds, and Zlatan Ibrahimović as the lone striker. England international Wayne Rooney was only a substitute.

At home, Kellie and Shauna were getting ready to watch the game at 5:30 a.m. Shauna texted her University friend who was from Manchester. "United or City?" she asked, probably in some fandangly text speak. "City" was her friend's reply to Shauna's relief. I could have told her that.

People who I knew in Pukekohe who were also Saints fans also got ready to watch the match. Niall and Ryan gave up their Liverpool allegiance for the morning to watch the game. When I got back to work I had also found out that some of the guys from work decided to watch the game too.

Mum tottered over to a neighbour at her Assisted Living place. She doesn't like anyone else staying there at her complex but when there is a lady staying nearby with a modicum of marbles left rattling round, and in particular who has a subscription to Sky Sports, then today this lady was Mum's BFF. Debbie, with a pile of ironing to do to support the team on, watched at home in their gorgeous little cottage. Kate, Ryan and Luke went to watch the match in a grown-up way, in a pub. Hayley watched the match with her boyfriend, also called Dan, alas though a Portsmouth fan so the nuances on how the game of Association Football is played at such a high professional level would have been completely beyond him.

Dan and I were incredibly pumped and nervous. The teams came out to the remarkable cheers of the fans. The national anthem was played. I normally get to sing this at England cricket matches in Australia or New Zealand. The words get adjusted for our colonies ('God Save *Your* Queen') so I had to remind myself that this wasn't necessary back in the homeland. Before kick-off I took one last video of the incredible scenes around me. I realised that today I was well fed unlike 2003, and was not sitting in a deep puddle of fizzy orange. This was good, another positive omen. But it reminded me that Dad wasn't here and that was really sad. Mind you, if he was here, who knows what kind of drink I would have to have stood in for the duration of the match.

A guy sat to my left. To my relief he was normal sized and not supersized. Another great omen. He was a Manchester United fan but a skinny United fan was much more palatable than a bulging Saints fan.

I received a bundle of messages on my phone just before the match started. Shauna represented the world's population of blondes perfectly with her text: "COOOMMMEEE OOOONNNN YYOOOU REEEEEDSS!!!!!!!!" Knowing Shauna as I do, I realised immediately that she had not suddenly changed allegiance to the red shirted Manchester United team, she was just being a bit dim; Saints were in white today, United in red.

The referee blew his whistle and the match was underway.

From the moment Dušan Tadić kicked off, Saints looked positive and not at all overawed or nervous. As early as the second minute Tadić managed to turn the United defence down the left and squeeze a cross that fired past everyone in the penalty area. Ward-Prowse collected the ball on the right-hand side and his cross needed to be scrambled away.

Paul Pogba had Manchester United's first chance and shot from outside the Saints penalty area. Forster beat it away strongly. In response, Redmond ran at the Manchester United defence, and fired a shot that was deflected for a corner. Another corner followed.

Saints seemed to find space behind United's midfield megastars effortlessly. All that was needed was that final pass to give us a real chance of a goal.

In the eleventh minute Saints had that chance. Redmond burst past the United defence down the left and fired in a low cross that, again, no Saints player could respond to, Cédric charged down the ball as United tried to clear, skipped into the box, and played the ball behind the defence with the outside of the boot, two yards from goal. Manolo Gabbiadini, sharp as a tack, nudged the ball into the goal.

Saints had scored!

Except it was disallowed for offside.

I then immediately received a text from Shauna that threw me into a rage: there was no gentle descent of the red mist, it came down like a bolt of lightning: "He wasn't offside," exclaimed her text. "Bertrand was! Commentators saying the goal should stand."

Debbie corroborated the news with her equally informative text: "The linesman's a dick!"

I made a point of telling this news to everyone around me and kicked my chair, paid homage to Dad with a range of expletives and a smattering of angry vents of "bollocks!" to nobody in particular.

At the time I didn't get to see how bad the decision was. I have seen it a number of times since, and the decision gets worse and worse with every view. The goal was disallowed for offside, except Gabbiadini who scored the goal was easily onside when he scored. Ryan Bertrand, who was at the far post was stood in an offside position but was not involved in the play. The laws of the modern game are crystal clear, Bertrand's position was irrelevant so the goal should have stood. The linesman, or should I say the assistant referee, or perhaps I should call him a dick as Debbie did, must have thought Bertrand scored the goal, hence why he raised the flag. But on replay I can't work out why on earth he could come to that conclusion: it was a basic, simple, easy decision. Meantime, the referee must have seen the players close to goal, but did not seek to clarify with the linesman who had scored. Had he done so, the goal would have stood, no question. Even now, writing this tome of nonsense, I am still incensed at it and cannot believe the incompetence of the decision.

As Matt Le Tissier said as a half-time pundit for Sky Sports: "It puts a whole new complexion on the game … if Southampton score the first goal this is a completely different game of football, and at this level that assistant has to get the decision right. How can he think that Bertrand's has tapped that in? This is a cup final, and you have to get those big decisions right". He's absolutely right.

In the eighteenth minute Oriel Romeu clumsily fouled United's Ander Herrera twenty-five yards from goal and earned a yellow card.

Up stepped the irascible Zlatan Ibrahimović to take the free kick.

Me and Dan were directly behind the goal. We could immediately see that Fraser Forster's wall of defenders was set up all wrong. The players were far too far to the right as we looked, exposing much of the goal, and there were only four players in the wall — we could see we needed another player. Forster edged to the left but the wall didn't. Steven Davis, one of Saint's shortest players set himself as an extra member of the wall but we could still see a gaping gap for one of the world's deadliest strikers to shoot at.

We both knew it was a goal before he had even taken the kick. The ball landed in the net, curling past Davis' head, an easy metre inside of the post at a salvageable height. Forster didn't get near it.

It was a goal against the run of play, but Saints were behind 1-0.

Although it should have at least been 1-1. It hurt.

Saints responded diligently, keeping their shape and continuing to probe at United. Tadić, Redmond and Ward-Prowse were all having excellent games. Yoshida was having perhaps his best match in a Saints shirt and Stephens did not look at all out of place despite his youth and inexperience. Ward-Prowse hit a bullet of a shot that De Gea saved with one hand stretching to his right, our left. I thought it was a goal – I simply didn't see De Gea through the mass of players. Saints continued to take the game to United. Redmond again found space to play a ball into Tadić whose shot was saved by De Gea, this time to his left. From another corner, the ball bounced invitingly in front of the United goalmouth: the ball bobbled off a United defender to Stephens whose hooked pass to Yoshida was clipped away at the last moment, right in front of goal.

Unbelievably, Manchester United then scored again. Saints' defence stood off of United's attackers and allowed Jesse Lingard to sweep the ball past Forster in the thirty-eighth minute. I was choked. How on earth are we two-down when we were by far the better team? How many teams come back in a final from two-down? How many teams come back from two-down against the defensive-minded José Mourinho's teams?

To my left sat four Manchester United fans. The guy next to me said, "Job done. Game over!" All four of them got up and left. I assume they had decided to watch the remainder of the game in one of the wine bars. Maybe they had gone home. I couldn't imagine being a fan like that.

I sent Kellie a text. "I'm not enjoying this now," I wrote.

It got worse. Jack Stephens charged forward. The ball got away from him a bit, and he lunged in hard at the United defender to get the ball back. His tackle was late and it looked from my position to be a bad foul. I felt sure this was going to be a red card. The United players surrounded the referee, doing their bit to influence him.

What I had not seen was, that Stephens had been fouled himself just before he made his rash challenge. This worked in his favour, and he only received a yellow card. What a relief! Jesse Lingard, the original Manchester United perpetrator also received a yellow card for the first offence, and Saints got the resultant free kick. Without the benefit of being that close to the action, I thought Stephens was a lucky, lucky boy.

The referee added two minutes of stoppage time at the end of the half. Redmond found space again, for one last sorté on the United goal. He pushed the ball out right to Ward-Prowse to power another low cross into the six-yard box. Gabbiadini again was too sharp for the United defence and poked the ball through De Gea's legs and into the net. Thankfully the linesman kept his overworked flag down this time and the goal stood. It was 2-1 and suddenly we had something to cheer and hope on. The first half ended and we could take a breath.

A half-time score of 2-1 was significantly better than 2-0. A goal right on half-time like that was a psychological boost for the fans and most likely the team too. It was a shame though that we weren't ahead at half-time. It would have certainly been more reflective of the first half had we been ahead and it might have given Manchester United pause for thought about changing their shirts at half-time again.

I spent all of half-time going through the mountain of text messages I had received during the first half. Kellie had said the scenes were amazing and that Saints were the better team. Shauna said she could hear me yelling and said that Manchester United were a bunch of little bitches who needed to grow some balls. My mobile phone provider kindly mentioned that I had used eighty percent of my monthly allowable text messages whilst roaming. That was impressive, I'd been in the country less than 36 hours and I'd used a month's worth of texts. By the time I had finished communicating with the outside world the players were back on the pitch.

Saints were immediately on the front foot in the second half. They seemed to have more energy, were first to the loose ball and just seemed to want it more. The noise from the Saints end went up a notch still.

Ward-Prowse earned a corner shortly after the restart. United struggled to clear it when it was fired in from Tadić. The ball fell to Yoshida who floated the ball back in for Redmond to blast a volley at De Gea who could barely stay on his feet. Another corner. More noise. The next corner arrived at Yoshida's feet again, this time on the by-line close to goal. He was clumsily challenged by the United defender; it wasn't penalty (although had I been refereeing the match on the pitch rather than in the stand, I would have given it), but it was a another corner. Even more noise. United were being run ragged. In came the next corner from Ward-Prowse, whipped into the box which Pogba headed out, but only to Davis who headed it back into the centre of the box where Manolo Gabbiadini was being held by the United defender Smalling.

Undeterred by the close attentions from Smalling, Gabbiadini swivelled sharply and wrapped his right foot round the ball. Me and

Dan were already up in the air in an explosion of jubilation before the ball had even crossed the line and the ball crashed the back of the net before De Gea had time to think about moving. We'd recovered from being 2-0 down. It was now 2-2.

The four Manchester United fans directly to my left had not returned, so I kind of ended up bouncing across the empty space, arms in the air like a lunatic. I expect I was roaring like a madman, red faced, eyes bulging ready to pop out. I managed to bounce back over into Dan's arms for a bit of an equalising goal embrace. He couldn't hear me, I couldn't hear him, the noise was monstrous. I had never, ever, experienced anything like it. Nor had I experienced cramp in both calves at the same time before. We took our seats again engulfed in a raucous celebration all around us. Saints charged forward immediately from the kick-off again as I desperately tried to rub each calf free of their knots. The game had turned on his head, and was heading in only one direction.

The United fans around us showed their distinct lack of class: one fella called me a tosser for celebrating the goal, and another tipped his beer over my jacket as he looked me in the eyes. At that time I didn't even care.

Meanwhile, Mum was asked by her neighbour to quieten down or she would have to leave. I imagined Kellie and Shauna camped in front of the telly, the dogs being completely ignored. I expect Debbie was ironing furiously, and ironing clothes she had already ironed in the first half.

United continued to wobble in defence. Redmond charged forward and had his heels clipped by Jesse Lingard, who had already been booked. Redmond stayed on his feet and charged on, but when the ball went out of play, the referee made his way over to him. His challenge was identical to the one he made on Stephens in the first half. He was surely going to be sent off. Inexplicably though, the referee didn't issue a red card. Instead Lingard got just a ticking off. I couldn't believe that we had been robbed of another decision.

Some good intricate passing from Saints found Ward-Prowse out on the right wing. He drilled the ball into the box hard to Gabbiadini who was able to negotiate the difficult ball and lay it off to Davis who put Cédric through beyond the United defence, on the edge of the penalty area. Cédric pushed the ball across the six-yard box for Bertrand to lunge at the ball and poke it into the net, but United nicked the ball away just in time for another Saints corner. Up went the noise levels yet again. The Saints fans seemed to be sucking the ball towards the Manchester United goal through every attack. Ward-Prowse sent in another perfect corner that Romeu headed on to the face of post. I don't remember, but Dan said I had leapt into the air for another goal, came down with my head in my hands, and ended up on my knees, anguished that he didn't score. We could all sense that this match was Saints' for the taking. A Saints third goal was coming.

Suddenly we could see the entire Saints half of the stadium become illuminated. Fans had turned on the torches on their smartphones, and spots of light flooded the ground from what seemed to be the majority of the 33,000 Saints fans. It was a statement of pride and satisfaction with the team. Their brave, magnificent recovery was on the verge of becoming something very, very special.

United started to respond like a boxer who has spent too much time on the ropes in realisation they are about to lose the fight, but despite their frantic efforts to get a foothold into the match, Saints still kept turning their defenders ragged and getting into great positions deep by the United by-line. In a rare United interlude, a shot was blasted over the bar, not even forcing Forster to make a save. With ten minutes to go, there were signs of tiredness in the Saints team. Tadić had already been replaced after a sterling performance. Gabbiadini left the field as a spent hero, after scoring three legitimate goals but with only two awarded. Shane Long replaced him following a well-deserved standing ovation: perhaps Long would be the one to get us this trophy in the same way he got us to the final in the first place?

United's up-and-coming young substitute Marcus Rashford shot low but Forster saved with his legs – United's first shot on target in the second half. But then, with five minutes to go, Bertrand charged into the penalty area, put in yet another great cross. The ball fizzed along the ground toward Long charging into the six-yard box. Somehow Long was unable to connect and tap the ball home and United had to scramble the ball away for a corner. From my position, it looked as though he had got there and felt sure it was going to be the winning goal – all he had to do was make any kind of connection to the ball. I could not quite process how he had not scored: it seemed that there had been an aberration in the laws of physics somehow. The resultant corner reached the young defender Jack Stephens who's shot was headed off the line by the giant Ibrahimović. Gasps of frustration were all around me, so close again.

Then Manchester United scored and won the cup. With two minutes to go, Ibrahimović wandered free and scored with a header, unchallenged, six yards out and through the flailing hands of Forster. It was another poorly defended goal, allowing one of the best forwards in the world with acres of space and all the time in the world to pick his spot.

It was like a punch in the stomach. Dan was choked with the injustice of it all. The entire Saints end was stunned into silence. Our opportunity – my opportunity – had just been snatched away when it looked as though we were going to do it. I looked at the assistant referee desperate to see his flag waving in the air for offside. There was no flag, no offside, no chance the officials could oblige by coughing up another bad decision just to level things up. It was over and the dream had suddenly died.

Now, any Saints fan will tell you that we have been on the end of last minute goals by opposing teams many, many times. We have had more practise than most in the sudden desolation that is felt when you see the pocket of away supporters go mad at such a terminal blow at the end of a match. Often you can sense it coming, either from the pressure brought to bear on the Saints goal, or merely when it seems the twisted hands of fate are working against you. The number of times that Dad used to cry out exasperatedly at the injustice of it all, "I bloody knew it!" or "You knew it was going to happen!". There often seemed to be a sense of inevitability and foreboding about the final few minutes of some matches and often the dread became reality. But today, I felt none of that. I felt better and better throughout the match. I could sense that the winning goal would come from our next attack. It didn't concern me that Saints were tiring – I felt sure that going into extra time Saints would boost their energy levels and go on to win the game. I even thought if we scored a third, we may even get a fourth – we had been that rampant at times. I was completely blinded by the performance and foolishly did not see the United goal coming.

It was now the other half the stadium going mad, with people around us jumping for joy as well. I felt sick and unprepared for this and I could scarcely believe it.

Shortly after the final whistle blew. For eighty-seven minutes I had been enthralled, the comfy seat I had paid top dollar for was criminally underused as I bounced up and down off the edge of it. But now, with the match over and the game was lost. I really didn't care anymore, and I don't much care for adding much of a description of it. I should, at this point, describe the scenes at the end of the match, with the overjoyed Manchester United fans and the devastated Saints fans. However, I don't want to. As my daughters would say when they were six, "whatever!".

Dan asked if we should leave the stadium. In 2003 Dad had said after Arsenal had beat us, that we should stay behind and watch the trophy ceremony. He said it was important to do so, it was the sporting thing to do, it would show respect for the other team, but also that you needed to see what you were missing out on – and that it will make you hungrier all the more next time. That day I watched, wallowing in the deepest envy as the Arsenal players cavorted around the pitch, trophy in the air, party music blaring over the speaker system. So I told Dan we should stay and remain for the trophy ceremony just as Dad had taught me. It was the right thing to do.

Thirty seconds later I thought, bollocks to that, and we left.

Monday

Dan had parked the car in the hotel car park so we had got back to the car at roughly the same time that Wayne Rooney (who hadn't even played in the match) lifted the trophy. We drove back to Debs to stay overnight. The trip was overly long and miserable. There were the inevitable queues in and around the stadium, and there were accidents on the motorways to additionally slow us down. It was pouring with rain and the visibility was low. It was a hard drive for Dan.

One word texts seemed to be the order of the post-match text message analysis coming into my inbox. Niall texted me. "Robbed!" he put. Debbie sent me a more emotionally fuelled summing up of the game: "Wankers!"

I could sense that Kellie and Shauna were gutted for me. I responded to the texts as best I could, making sure my replies didn't expose any suicidal tendencies so as not to worry them. As my absolute text roaming limit was close to being reached, there was one more text that I wanted to send.

I still have Dad's mobile phone number in my phone, filed as 'Dad's Mobile'. For some reason I can't bring myself to remove it. I don't believe in life after death and I don't believe that Dad has moved into some omnipresent floating heavenly state (I hope not, it would be awkward at times). But I did want to text him and I wanted him to text me back. My last proper text to him was on Christmas Day in 2011. "Happy Christmas you grumpy old bugger," I'd wrote.

"When can I see you," was his last cogent text to me.

I sent him a number of texts after this. One text I sent him was, "Sarah has asked me if 'wanker' is a swear word, so I've grounded her for a week." His reply was unintelligible. And despite further texts from me after that point, "I'm up watching the match", "Saints were crap today" and "Are you causing trouble again in the hospital?", there were no further replies. My one remaining line of communication with my Dad was gone nearly two months before he died.

I just wanted to send him one more text and get one more reply in return. I think I would tell him how it was. "We blew it, Dad. Lost 3-2. Murdered 'em but were done in the last minute by a player who looks like a girl."

I'm sure his response would be sweary but nonetheless conciliatory. He'd have told me to hurry my arse over to Mums and look after her.

I didn't send a text to him in the end.

The drive to Debs should have been about ninety minutes and took about three hours. The after-match talk radio was tedious. Typically, the radio presenters were patronising to Saints, reflecting that we were a 'small club', and that we probably enjoyed the day win or lose. Most of the talk though was about United's big striker who won the game for them.

Zlatan Ibrahimović is an odd creature. He looks like something that is better suited to Eurovision rather than the football field, with his very feminine looking face and hair, junkie-like goatee beard and protractor shaped nose. He was 35 when he arrived at Manchester United, an age when most players would be over the hill or retired. He had played for Malmö in his native Sweden, Ajax in the Netherlands, Juventus, AC Milan and Inter Milan in Italy, Barcelona in Spain and Paris Saint Germain in France. He had scored 302 goals in 484 games – a phenomenal rate of goals per game ratio in modern football – and had won a staggering thirty trophies in his career. He has an extreme arrogance, ranging from outrageous soundbites to the media, to violent incidents with team mates. He has been Sweden's best ever player and remains a global phenomenon and a football superstar.

It was a privilege to watch him play. He was by far United's biggest threat during the match. He seemed to spend much of the game ambling or drifting seemingly aimlessly up front, unconcerned and uninterested in the match going on around him. All of a sudden, he would have the ball at his feet. With lightning-fast reactions and a slight and subtle shift of the body he would receive the ball in a tight area but would fashion a yard of space in which to play in, the defender either suddenly out of the game or bouncing off him in a vain attempt to retrieve the ball.

Saints certainly had their work cut out, and at times it took two or three players to retrieve the ball off him during the match. He was on a different level to everybody else on the field.

Big clubs buy big players for days such as these, when things don't go to plan, when you are playing below your best, or your opponent keeps exploiting a weakness in your line up, you need a player like this to act as a Get Out Of Jail Free card that can keep you in the game and go on to win it. That is the role that Zlatan played in this game. United were on the ropes for much of the match but used their Get Out Of Jail Free card to great effect (for them).

Dad would have loathed him and would be public enemy number one as far as he was concerned. Irrespective of any master class or imperious performance witnessed at a match or on TV after this game, he would no longer have been Zlatan Ibrahimović, he would be simply known as 'prick'.

I have to concede that he was the difference on the day and unquestionably a class act, but no matter how much you concede to his brilliance or secretly marvel at his play, he stole my chance of winning a trophy and for that reason I can't join in with the TV pundits, TalkSport radio presenters or even neutral fans waxing lyrical about his performance. I can't bring myself to read about his heroic exploits about dragging United over the line. Right now, he's ruined everything.

I've had the privilege in watching some of the best players in the world through watching Southampton matches. These include our own players such as Kevin Keegan and Peter Shilton – who I saw at their absolute peak, and Matt Le Tissier – who I regard as the greatest player I ever saw and will ever see in my lifetime (there is no 'arguably' about it, his extreme brilliance is not open for debate – you should consider it fact). I also saw players such as Mick Channon and Alan Ball after their peak years, and Alan Shearer prior to his.

I've also had the privilege of watching opposing team players. Glenn Hoddle, Paul Gascoigne, Kenny Dalglish, Ian Rush, Bryan Robson, Jürgen Klinsmann, Ruud Gullit, David Ginola, Marco Van Basten, Steven Gerrard, Ronald Keoman, Thierry Henry, Frank Rijkaard, Robin Van Persie, Gianluca Vialli, Frank Lampard, Eric Cantona, Gianfranco Zola, Sergio Agüero, Didier Drogba and Denis Bergkamp. I admire them all and consider it a bit of an honour to watch them play, even if Saints may have lost that day (or England in the case of some of the Dutchmen in this list) or even if they were beyond their prime years. I can thereafter watch them on television with a certain personal affinity with them, as if they are part of some exclusive club and I have to admit Zlatan, Paul Pogba (who was very poor in this particular match) and David De Gea into that club as well.

Begrudgingly though, I don't have the same level of loathing that Dad had, but my admiration for the Swede is tainted. Next time I watch him on TV it will be with a blackened dislike for him based on what he did to me, my nephew and my team. That is just the way it has to be.

Me and Dan had discussed what it would take to win and, unsurprisingly, we didn't meet the requisite requirements. But we had played well. I'd had Nathan Redmond all wrong: I'd been disappointed – irritated at times – with his contribution in matches, but he had an excellent game and was involved in so much that was good about our performance going forward (shortly after he was named in the England squad). Tadić and Ward-Prowse (also now an England player) had excellent games, and Romeu and Davis were integral in ensuring that United attacks were few and far between. Cédric and Bertrand were both excellent, pushing forward at every opportunity and causing so much damage deep in United's wobbly defence. I think I saw Maya Yoshida play his best game in a Saints shirt – he was heroic at times, and I am convinced that Jack Stephens could be one for the future. Man of the match of course was Gabbiadini who scored three excellent striker goals (yes, three, not two). Liverpool fans were excited by his performance and wondered on social media whether he would be Liverpool's latest signing from Southampton. Our poorest performer on the day was perhaps our England goalkeeper, Fraser Forster, who was at fault for the first goal at least: I don't think he's had the best of seasons and appears to concede a lot of goals compared to the number of shots he faces. I think it is over-reaching to blame him for the third, winning goal, but it did seem to go through him. The blame for the third goal does go to the overall defence, stretched as they were attacking moments earlier, getting themselves into positions that were marking nobody when the killing cross came in. For the second goal, as a team we didn't defend well, standing off the United players giving them the freedom of Wembley, with Lingard given time to pick his spot to score. And Oriel Romeu must take blame for his rash challenge that gave away the free kick, although I'll never forget just how much goal Zlatan had to shoot at.

Generally, my scrutiny of blame towards the goals we conceded is unfair. It was a herculean effort overall, particularly from being two goals down, and of course we deserved to win rather than lose. As we had wanted, Saints had played as well as they possibly could. And Manchester United were accommodating. They played below their best. Paul Pogba was picked up by the media as being poor, but many of United's forward-thinking players found it hard to get into the game, whilst their defence was run ragged all afternoon.

Our other point didn't go our way, concerning the officials getting the decisions right. On Sunday night we watched Gabbiadini's disallowed goal, and saw it again on the Monday morning, and again on the Internet. It's an absolute shocker that gets worse and worse with each viewing. There were calls after the game to introduce video evidence to support goals that were disallowed. This is something I've always been against, but I'm all for it now! (I know, you can feel the raging hypocrisy leaping from the page – German scientists are wrong about the goal in the World Cup final in 1966 because the referee had absolute authority and gave the goal, whereas in 2017 the referee does not give the goal but is wrong because it goes against my team. I never said at any stage supporting a football team has any form of sane consistency or logic to it, quite the reverse in fact – you'll just have to get with the programme!)

The goal would have changed the entire structure of the match, and an underdog team can ill-afford to have a goal taking off them for incompetence. The failure to send off Lingard was also a diabolical decision in retrospect. Television analysts, including ex-referees suggested because Nathan Redmond didn't dive and collapse at the time of the challenge, then the referee did not see that as a yellow card offence – notwithstanding that Stephens had attempted to play on for the identical challenge by Lingard in the first half where he was booked. But the analysts agreed, Lingard should have gone, which would have given the Saints thirty minutes at 2-2 with an extra player. I imagine the score might have been very different.

So in some form of summary, you could argue there were question marks about our defending for the United goals, but like most Saints fans, I feel more aggrieved at the quality of 'big game' refereeing decisions which would have looked out of place in a Sunday pub league. We said we couldn't afford to get 'done' by the referee, but we did.

I went to bed after midnight and Skyped Kellie for a bit of emotional support. I felt a lot better going to sleep and eventually did.

I woke up on Monday morning to the creepy silence, punctuated by the haunting sound of crows. When opening the curtains, I expected to see the sky scored with the vapour trails of the many aircraft, criss-crossing the sky like scars. But this morning was most typically English. Grey, wet, cold and gloomy.

It was good at Debs, nice and relaxing. She was willing to spoil us and cook us breakfast. Deb was never much of a cook. When I was a kid she cooked me pancakes once that I think to this day is the very worst taste ever to go into my mouth. I shudder at the thought of it now. Dan had a busy week at work so could not afford time off ill, so we limited Debs breakfast offer to toast only, which was, thankfully, edible. I wished I had spent more time of my stay there.

Today was all about visiting Dad. It was five years to the very day that we lost him. For me he'd died tomorrow, a day later in New Zealand time, but this wasn't the time to argue semantics. We'd go and pick up Mum and Tracey and go as a family, something I was very much looking forward to.

We had lunch first at the Alma Inn in Wickham, near to the home Dad ended up in. It was a nice, typical, Hampshire country pub, serving a roast carvery selection for five pounds (yes, a full roast dinner for five pounds, about nine dollars). I soon realised why the cost of the meal was a fiver, it was not great. But the company was. Kate joined us with Dan and had a really good time. Kate was disappointed about not being able to go to Wembley as well as the result, and the boys were devastated, angry at the injustice caused by the referee and his assistant. It was a good opportunity to talk about Dad and reminisce a bit.

Afterwards, Kate went home, as did Dan. The match was a great experience and I was glad it was with Dan. It was sad to see him go. Deb drove us to Dad's place.

Dad now lives at the back of a creepy church graveyard. I get to see him every two or three years, and it was only ten months since I'd last been back. He'd been joined by a couple of 'newcomers'. Every time I see a new slab near to Dad I can't help but wonder if Dad knew them, and if he did know them, whether he liked them. If he didn't, he wouldn't be very pleased.

"Bloody hell, what are you doing here?" he would say. "Bugger off and annoy someone else." Perhaps the church should organise some form of vetting procedure, where a grieving family need to have the desired position of their lost loved one's peer reviewed. If there is an objection, then perhaps they could be black-balled and asked to be holed somewhere else?

At night, deer come into the graveyard and eat the flowers on Dad's grave. Mum and Deb think that Dad would have appreciated that. I'm not so convinced that he would be happy with a hooved animal trampling all over him and eating. I wouldn't. It made me think about where I want to be buried when I die. Would I plump for some alluvial and volcanic earth in New Zealand or some good old mud and clay in England? Perhaps I'd want my ashes scattered over the turf at St Mary's? That kind of thing is strictly prohibited – I'd imagine Saints would be playing on an ash heap in a couple of years, were that to be allowed. I wouldn't want to be responsible for a Saints shot that was goal-bound but deflected owing to an unsightly grey mound that Shauna had tipped on to the field in a hurry. Perhaps my ashes could be expertly thrown in the direction of the opposition goalkeeper's eyes just as he intends to make a super save against us? I'd be very content with that, in the knowledge that Saints scored.

It really doesn't matter to me where I get holed up, but it will matter to the people around me and so will likely be somewhere that appeals to them rather than me. Personally, I don't like the idea of being underneath the ground at all, whether it be underneath a greedy doe or a dumb possum. For people in the UK, I don't expect this to be an issue. I am sure that future technology in that day and age will mean you can Skype the dead, just like the living.

The visit today was fleeting. There is no need for anything more. A couple of small bouquets were dropped by Mum and Deb. Hayley had already been and left a red tulip and a white tulip – a really nice touch. I placed down a Saints scarf, then thought twice about leaving it. I could imagine the RSPCA standing over a deer that choked to death on a football scarf, collapsing on Dad's stone. Dad would be raging, "Get this bloody thing off me." So I thought better of it and took it back with me.

I thought a little bit about a wee eulogy given the timing of the visit. Maybe a summary of the game, maybe a wish for Dad to have been at the match. Maybe even an apology for moving away. But as with the scarf, I thought better of it. If he is hanging around in some gloopy fog of souls then he would know it all already anyhow, about the game, the decisions, the poorly defended winning goal and my own sorrow for leaving him.

Going Home

NZ1, London Heathrow to Auckland, departing 3:30 p.m. Friday, 3rd of March, arriving 7:30 a.m. Sunday, 5th of March. Flight duration 25 hours. Premium Economy to Los Angeles, Economy service class to Auckland.

Things went from bad to worse on my trip. As well as losing the cup final, I was volunteered by Mum and Debbie to take over the quiz night in Mum's Assisted Living place.

Mum soon left our home since 1981 in Colden Common for a ground floor flat in an Assisted Living complex in Eastleigh. Our house was just too big for her to upkeep. For example, our large front garden that ran out the front of the house and up the side needed regular cutting. Mum originally received kind help from a neighbour in cutting the lawn, but that went sour when the neighbour had had enough. Evidentially he was more worried about the look of the house on the overall street rather than being neighbourly in support. All of Dad's 'friends' in the street had long since regressed back into their homes, wanting nothing to do with Dad during his illness, and certainly nothing to do with Mum after he died.

That was until Mum decided to sell. All of a sudden these people crept out of their holes and made themselves known again. There was a small strip of land adjacent to the house that was owned by Mum and Dad and therefore part of the sale. The neighbours were fretful that a buyer would want to excavate that land and potentially build on it. Potential buyers would arrive to view the house and would be met by neighbours petitioning them not to buy it. They also harassed and placed pressure on Mum. Thankfully Debbie was there to put people right and to stop Mum from feeling intimidated.

It was a blessed relief to see the house sold and eventually see her move into her brand-new accommodation with a bit of company in little Dougal and with a little nest egg to live on (although it still gets taxed – honestly how does that work – you spend all your working life paying tax only to retire and pay tax? Thieves!).

It's a nice place too. She's on the ground floor with a bit of garden for her and the dog to enjoy, and it's on a bit of an annex so she can remain a bit aloof from the main Assisted Living centre.

She likes it there, although she calls it Assisted Dying rather than Assisted Living. It's also known as God's Waiting Room. She gets on well with the staff but less so with the other 'inmates' and she is always bickering to me behind their backs. It's like having an interactive experience each week on Skype with Catherine Tate's unctuous character Nan. One of Mum's complaints was that as one of the most able-bodied members of the complex, she was asked to assist with some of the more less abled in getting them into the communal restaurant for lunch, pushing wheelchairs and the like. What a liberty! Mum stopped going for lunch in case she was asked to help again. At 83 now, she seems to still be the one who is most mobile and with the most marbles, even though many of the 'inmates' are younger than her.

My visit this time was a complete surprise to Mum. When Sarah and Shauna visited Mum in December 2015, Debbie convinced me to keep the visit secret. One morning shortly after Christmas, whilst I was on Skype to Mum, Debbie simply turned up and told Mum there were some people here to see her. It was an amazing moment to watch Mum's joy as her two youngest grandchildren, now all grown up turn up to stay with her. Mum held her head in her hands in complete disbelief. "Am I dreaming this?" she asked.

It was a good idea. It meant that Mum didn't fuss or stress or spend money on stuff unnecessarily. This time we didn't tell her in case I could not get a ticket and had to cancel my air tickets. On the Saturday, whilst I was in-flight, Debbie made her read the Echo. By all accounts she fell off her chair in surprise. Mum sent me a text when she found out: "you naughty little bugger!"

For my remaining four days I intended to stay with Mum, utilising the generous Guest Room they have in the complex. I'd used it before with Kellie, but staying there alone was creepy. The Guest Room is situated as far away as it is possible to be from Mum's place yet within the confines of the complex. This means you have to run the gauntlet of two long corridors and two separate lifts to get between the two places, without crossing some addled crazy lady. When staying there alone I didn't like it. A old fogey could wander in confused at any minute. I kept the door locked at all times and the light on.

The remaining days were dull and uneventful. Each morning I would go and see Mum, ask her if she was dead that morning, make her a cup of coffee once she confirmed that she was still alive, and walk the dog. Mum would demand that I put a coat on before going out, and I would argue that I was all grown up now and could make my own decisions, thank you very much. Mum took me for a lunch at a country pub where the soup of the day was Pumpkin soup and almost all the menu had cheese on it. I wasn't surprised to learn that the chef was from New Zealand. Mum kept telling me off for being so grumpy until her main course arrived, invaded with slabs of foul bright orange pumpkin patties (like the colour of a Belisha beacon beside a zebra crossing, or the skin colour of most Caucasian women in England in 2017) and slimy yellow cheese. Mum promptly pushed the muck to the side of her plate with a tut.

Kate and Ian took me to see the boys at football training one evening. They are both very, very good and have both been at Matt Le Tissier's own football academy. Luke is currently being coached by none other than Francis Benali who by all accounts is really impressed with Luke. Perhaps in ten years we'll see either one of them playing for Saints, although hopefully Luke doesn't get regularly sent off like Benali did!

I saw Ryan first, a bit shy and grumpy, probably thinking it's that weirdo from somewhere who turns up every so often. "G'day Ryan," I said. "What did you think of the final?"

"It's not fair!" Ryan exclaimed immediately, stung by the injustice of it all. "That first goal was never offside! The goal should have been allowed! We'd have won the game if it would have counted!"

Later I caught up with Luke. "Hi Luke, how's it going? I heard you watched the final in a pub?"

"Yeah," Luke said thoughtfully. "But it wasn't right. Gabbiadini's goal should have been allowed! Bertrand was in an offside position but he didn't score the goal! We should have won."

The training session was on a 3G artificial pitch. Believe it or not this was the first time I had ever seen or set foot on one. I put it down to the fact that I live in the football equivalent of the third world. It was good to see the boys have a kickabout despite the Arctic conditions (it was nine degrees Centigrade). When I was in England in 2015, me, Ian and Dan had a kickabout with them on a field opposite Kate and Ian's home. A number of other young boys came out of their houses in their kit and boots and challenged us to a match. It was boys (about nine of them) against Adults (three of us). They rang rings round us – particularly me I think. I was like a ballerina slipping on the grass in my Adidas trainers. At one point this tiny kid slipped the ball between my legs, and I slipped up and ended up on by back to a chortling chorus of little buggers.

Eventually, like Bambi, I found my feet and got into the swing of things. Aim a pass over here, kick a kid over there – that kind of thing. Ryan charged around with good technical skills, like a fly buzzing around you. Luke was more circumspect, moving into space, waiting for a pass, collecting the ball, playing a pass. Both good players for their age. We continued playing through rain showers and darkness until the Adults went ahead 10-9. There was a bit of fear in the kids after I had scored a blistering tap in to make it 9-9, removed by top and celebrated my goal as if I had won the World Cup, beating my chest. With moobs and belly exposed and wobbling around for the world to see, the kids looked at each other with a sense of weirdness and confusion. They'd probably been taught about the likes of me in school stranger danger classes. But we won and that is always all that matters.

On the final night of my short stay we had a meal at the local Harvester. Me and Kellie used to go there when the kids were little and it was always a bit of a go-to place when we go back from New Zealand for a bit of bland cuisine nostalgia. Everyone was there, Deb and Chris, Tracey and Colin, Hayley and her Pompey boyfriend Dan. He was quite conciliatory about the match to me which was very gracious; my response in contrast was less so, "Do Portsmouth still have a team in the city at all these days?" I asked him. Hannah and Charlie were there as was Ian, Kate and the boys. And Dan and Sama came all the way from Bristol to say hello/cheerio. Sama's driving had not improved, showing me a picture of her parking her Mini flush against a concrete pillar in a multi-story car park. It was great to catch up with everyone, although it is always difficult to circulate around the family for maximum effect and to everyone's expectations.

Luke and Ryan were in top form. The Kray twins were diligently completing their colouring in sheet that the wait staff give to children to keep them occupied. In the 'Name' field, instead of writing their names in nice, neat writing, they had both written some of the foulest, rudest things I had ever seen set to paper. I am not even sure I knew what some of the things meant!

They passed them to Mum who, without being able to read the 'names' without her glasses, was suitably impressed. Everyone else got the giggles, especially when Mum, on hearing their vile child humour demanded everybody not to laugh so as not to encourage them. Kate is an amazing mother with what she has to put up with.

Everybody wanted to know how I got on at the quiz night. I told them that there are some events in your life that you look back on and shudder at the thought. This was one of those nights.

I've no problem standing in front of a bunch of people and announcing or presenting, but figured it could be a tough crowd –

some not hearing, some not seeing, some not comprehending, some of my infectious wit may be lost on them (for example, at my wedding renewal I thanked everyone for so many gifts that we had received and that we would certainly go through the names and work out who didn't get us anything). But I agreed to do it, and regretted it ever since.

I had to stand in front of about twenty elderly people organised in tables of quiz teams. I game each team a set of answers, a pen and asked someone to scribe the answers. I also suggested each team think up a team name.

"Wha'?" one lady asked.

"A team name." I said.

"A what?" an old fella asked.

"You need to think of a team name."

"A team name?" said another.

"Yes, a team name for your group, so we know which team is which."

"Ay?"

"You need a team—"

"What?"

"A team name."

"What did you say?"

"YOU ALL NEED A TEAM NAME. PUT YOUR TEAM NAME ON THE SHEET OF PAPER!" This wasn't going to go well at all. One team couldn't think of a team name, so I suggested 'Fifty Shades of Grey Matter'. Clever, I thought.

"What?" was the confused common reply.

"Doesn't matter – just put your name on the top of the answers!" I needed to get in, get it done, and get out as quickly as possible.

I'd been given a set of questions to read. Five rounds of ten questions. Bloody hell, I'm going to be here half the night. I read the first question, then again, then again. Then again. Then again. Once the first ten questions were answered, each team asked for some of the questions to be asked again. And again.

"How long will this quiz take?" asked one agitated competitor.

"At this rate we'll finish at around 4:00 a.m." I said flippantly.

"That's nice."

I persevered.

An early question caused a riot. Which company makes the most tyres in the world? When asking for the answers, I received a number of suggestions.

"Goodyear!" one man shouted.

"Dunlop!" said another.

"Bridgestone!" said a third.

I looked at the answer. "No," I said, "it's Lego. The answer is Lego!" I thought I was going to get stabbed in the side of the head with a broken chair. The tough crowd were in uproar!

"Lego? What do you mean Lego?"

"That's a bloody stupid question!"

"What did he say the answer was?"

Even though decorum was restored, the night had further incident. Another question was, in the bible what animal appears the most. The answer on the sheet was 'sheep'.

"No it isn't! It's a lamb!" cried out this elderly gentleman.

"Well," I said. "A lamb is a baby sheep, so I suppose either will be good enough for a correct answer."

"Excuse me," said the lady to the gentleman's right. "My husband used to be a vicar and he should know the answer to the question. If he says is it is a lamb, then it is a lamb. Not a sheep!"

Cue more argument. They could have put 'aardvark' as an answer and I'd have given it to them.

Another question: what is the diameter of the earth? 8,000 miles was the answer according to the sheet.

"NO IT ISN'T!" an old guy barked at me from the front suddenly jumping to his feet. "IT'S 8,500!" I've since found the Internet says it is 7,917 miles, actually. I told him that his answer was close enough.

It was as if whoever had thought up these questions had engineered the disaster in front of me. One question was, what is the biggest island? The next question was, what is the longest river?

"What is the longest island?" was one response.

"What was the biggest river?" said another.

There was plenty of arguing amongst themselves and I was perfectly happy to let them get on with it. Mum was no bloody help at all, flirting around in an otherwise all male team, part of the rabble that would leave me needing psychiatric care.

The penultimate question: list four—

I realised I was in trouble already. List four? The old buggers could hardly list one. List four cities in Britain with a working underground metro system. Cue confusing questions. How many? Is it three? What if we put two? How many? What was the question? Was I being punished for pulling all the legs off a daddy-long-legs when I was eleven? For the record the answers are London, Glasgow, Liverpool and Newcastle.

Eventually, eventually, the night was over. I got out of there as fast as I could. The carers had gone after round one leaving me on my own. Apparently, there was a medical issue to resolve with an 'inmate'. What a load of rubbish, at the first sign of dissent, they were gone, probably up the pub. It was many hours until I was able to rock myself to sleep in my locked and boarded up room, with the lights firmly on.

The following day, one of the ladies came to visit me and Mum.

"Oh yes, he did enjoy it very much," said Mum about me to her friend.

The lady turned to me and thanked me for helping out. I don't know who does their quiz normally, but they deserve a knighthood, no question. She then asked me about the match and if I enjoyed the game. I told her it was a great experience but a shame about the result.

"I know, love," she said. "I couldn't believe it at all really. We had United's defenders in a muddle, didn't we? We kept getting in good positions in the channels and delivering quality ball into the box. Their winning goal was such a bad goal to give away, wasn't it? Nobody picked up the big man, did they? He shouldn't have had a free header like that, especially with a couple of minutes to go. We suddenly lost all our discipline right at the end and gave them too much space to play!"

I was dumbstruck.

Goodbyes are always tough. Normally, with Mum and Dad, melancholy would set in a number of days before we would part. It would cast a shadow over anything you would be doing for those last days. The sadness comes not only because it will be some while before we see each other again, but because there is always the question about whether we will *ever* see each other again. And it is never a question I can answer because each time I honestly don't know. With Mum, she has her dents and issues, but generally is a fit, tough old bird so fully expect her to be around for a long time yet (I tell Sarah and Shauna – to their consternation – that it will be some time before they get Nanny's inheritance!). But, I knew that with Dad, leaving him in October 2011 was more than likely the last time I would ever see him, although I always harboured a desire for being there at the end. As it was, it was the last time I saw him, and he knew it, and I knew that he knew it. We live too far away to say with any certainly that we'll be back soon, or we'll be back next year – it's just too hard to predict and not fair to promise. We make a genuine effort to get over every two or three years, especially now that it is not feasible for Mum to come to us, but stuff happens and life sometimes can get in the way, so it can never be a promise we can keep with any certainty. Will we both be earning? Will I be able to take a month off with my employer? Have I the savings to stay off work for an entire month? Have we the savings to make the trip? So far we've been very lucky in being able to answer these questions every time. But I sincerely doubt it will be always like this. This year I'd not be able to take a month off on my project. It could be the case next year, or the following year. Other stuff might happen that could also get in the way.

It takes Mum, and it took Dad, some weeks to get over each departure. Calls on Skype are tough as the routine of long distance calls and long discussions about what the time difference is at the moment, become normal again.

Fortunately with such a brief visit, Mum was fine up until the day I departed. The fog of sadness descended as I wheeled my packed bags into Mum's flat. She would chat with the dog, explaining to him that I won't be able to walk him anymore and that I won't be able to play with him anymore. As usual, Debbie was right there to support. The taxi driver turns up and sympathetically parked out of the way of any goodbye tears. I get my bag, grab my Mum, tell her I love her, hold her there for a bit and then let her go. Her face saddens further and the tears flow, her arms held out in front of her. Here I go again, inflicting horrible, horrible pain to my family, walking away again, leaving Debbie to take the slack and pick up the pieces once more after I leave.

The flights home were uneventful with Los Angeles once again excelling with their incompetence at security and customs. I left on the Friday afternoon and with the help of jumping forward in time I arrived on the Sunday morning. Kellie picked me up at the airport and survived the local drivers on the route home and enjoyed a quiet day. As we pulled into the driveway of our home, I could hear the sound of cicadas, their distinctive chirruping song a pleasing familiarity of home. I was soon back in my routine as if I hadn't left at all, picking up my post, messing around with the dogs, catching up with news on my smartphone, losing my glasses and chatting with Shauna about her upcoming university year. I went straight back to work on the Monday. I found out that a number of people at work watched the match (at 5:30 a.m. the previous Monday, remember) even though they had no affiliation with my team or even football, merely because I went to the game. I received commiserations aplenty during my first week back in New Zealand, almost as if I had lost a loved one. The jet lag was the worst I had ever experienced, lasting a week messing me up completely. On a couple of work days I started work at 5:00 a.m. But it was good to be home.

When you see people who are quite clearly elated say that today is the best day in their life, you wonder how much thought goes into that statement, because you can immediately alienate your family and loved ones who believe they share with you what they would feel should be the best day such as a marriage or a birth. A better approach is to categorise your memories and be careful what you say.

I cannot say that the day at Wembley was the best day of my life, because there have been many other days that were either momentous, joyous, or both. My wedding day is right up there, as is my wedding renewal in 2015 (cracking day), the birth of Sarah on the day Saints lost away at West Ham United in 1996 is an obvious one, as is the birth of my youngest Shauna born in 1998 (on a Monday so as not to clash with football). These are clearly top experiences but I could never compare one with the other to define a winner of sorts. I have other magnificent memories of holidays, events in my life, and also events arguably unrelated to me, for example Portsmouth getting relegated is always a special day, but these never qualify as my top experiences, and I venture to say that all my experiences with the Saints, whilst all monumental treasures to me, are also not my top experiences.

Not yet. But a win at the cup final could have conceivably been a top experience and one of the best days of my life.

So, in the cold light of day, as it were, did I think it was all a good idea? Certainly, going into this I felt that Saints must win for it to be worthwhile. There just has been so much upset and failure in the past that this time – this time – we would get it right. To a certain extent, the trip could only have been worthwhile if we had won.

On my return, everybody from family to friends to colleagues at work said to me that it was a shame that Saints lost, but it must have been a fantastic experience. This grated with me because I wanted it all. Not only did I want the trip, the company, the ticket to be real and the experience but I also wanted the win. Nobody remembers losers of finals and semi-finals and nobody remembers our exploits in previous competitions other than Saints fans who experienced and felt it. After the match, listening to the radio phone-in in the car, despite the fact that Saints were the better side, despite the fact that Saints made the match exciting and entertaining and despite the fact that Saints were on the end of some despicable decisions from the referee, nobody wanted to phone in and talk about the Saints. People only wanted to talk about the winners, Manchester United and Zlatan Ibrahimović. And that is the way it should be – they found a way to win the game. They found a way to stop the ball creeping over their goal line for a third (well, fourth actually) and we didn't.

So I didn't agree with this queue of people telling me that the experience was everything and that the result was incidental. For me the experience was incidental, and the winning was everything. As I've said, I would have cherished the dullest 1-0 win ever with an own goal by Manchester United thank you very much and taken it to the grave with me, rather than the exciting, pulsating game that I witnessed.

Yet, two weeks after my return to New Zealand, my attitudes have softened. I spliced together all the videos and pictures that me and Dan took on the weekend, and turned it into a slideshow. It was great watching it back, and sends shivers down the spine. It's a little unbalanced, as there is nothing at the end of the match. There are pictures of us going to the match, at the stadium all potty with excitement and some homemade clips during the game when it was 2-2, but there is nothing after, as if I had run out of space or if my smartphone had been stolen from me. As it was of course, it was the match that was stolen from me. So gutted and crestfallen at the end of it all, there was no way either of us cared to take any more photos. The last photo I took was of the Saints fans all raising their smartphones as one and putting their torches on, a winning goal for us seemingly moments away.

After multiple watches of it, my opinion changed. So everyone was right after all, the experience was everything. As the football part of my brain settles down and takes a well-earned rest following all its over-exertions and constant overdrive setting over the previous month, the more rational parts of my brain start to take over and life starts returning to normal. My focus turns to how Sarah and Shauna are getting on at university, how Kellie is getting on at work, how the dogs are, how work is, etc. and with my mind in this state I can apply a level of rationality that simply doesn't exist with my football head on. Yes, it hurt to lose, and it still does, and I would go as far as to say the result is not incidental, but the experience was definitely unforgettable. Maybe there will be a next time, maybe there won't but I created a treasure for myself that I'll never forget.

The football part of my brain is allowed to pop back into focus when matches are near or are on; it hasn't been consigned to my brain's equivalent of the pit of doom, my bargain basement. Saints won their next match away at Watford, 4-3. Manchester United could only draw at home with Bournemouth, 1-1. Zlatan Ibrahimović, by all accounts, had a nightmare match and capped it off by sending an elbow into the face of a Bournemouth player that went unnoticed by the referee but not by The FA, who gave him a three-match ban. Why, oh why could Manchester United and their enigmatic striker not have performed like that the week before? Why couldn't their match against Bournemouth been right before the final so that said striker would be banned? That always seems to be the way with the Saints.

Dan raised with me an interesting dilemma since Saints had lost. What if, next year, Saints do really well again in one of the cup competitions? How would I feel if Saints reached the quarter final or semi-final of a cup competition again? Would I be eager for Saints to lose so I don't have the problem of organising another visit? If Saints got to a final next year, would I still contemplate going?

For this globetrotting football fan the answers are relatively straightforward. Should they get close to another cup final, I will be cheering them on all the way. There would be no way that I would have my fingers crossed, sneakily hoping that Saints would lose: that is something that I am just not capable of doing. The football part of my brain would simply dominate and bully any cogent and rational thoughts to the contrary.

As is normal, with each round closer to the final, I would look at the teams left, who we have drawn, what the chances are, seeing which other big teams are left in the competition and what the chances are that they get dumped out of the competition before they meet us – all the normal things that the mind of a football fan needs to devour with their team still in the cup.

If they get to another cup final next year, I'd have a look at it, assess whether I could afford it, whether the flight tickets are cheap, whether I could get a ticket for a final, whether I could get time off work and whether my home life would permit it. If I could tick all those boxes like I could this year, then off I'd go again, no problem. I'd attempt the same level of rational thinking that the football side of my brain would permit. I am sure that I would have a bit of angst with the journey and ask myself am I being a nob again, but the football head will win out.

Kellie would be the first to send me on my way. She has been incredibly shrewd through all of this nonsense. She realised that with my football head on I would be an intolerable pain in the arse for an extensive amount of time, so it would be better for me to be an intolerable pain in the arse back with the Budden Mafia than around her. But more than that, she understands what it means to me. She knows there is no comparison to be had between her, the girls and the Saints. She knows I put them first, after all my home address is exactly 18,470 kilometres (11,477 miles) away from St Mary's stadium and that I have not, as demanded by some fans on the Daily Echo web site, set up home close to the stadium.

She knows what makes me happy, and she wants me to be happy. And I am happy. But I would be even happier if we won the cup.

Would I do it all again next year? You bet I would!

In a parallel universe somewhere, Shane Long managed to get on the end of Ryan Bertrand's late cross. It was the goal that won the League Cup for Southampton and provide their first major silverware since 1976, and gave Saints a pathway into next year's Europa League. Celebrations lasted long after the game and went on long into the night.

Dan drove us back to Southampton city centre where there was a massive party in every pub and in every street. Debbie had to come and look for us on Monday morning as we failed to get back to her place. Groggy and hungover, we celebrated for days. Mum ended up being very cross with me because I was spending too much time either out or in bed in a state. I neglected Kellie and the girls too – there was too much partying going on to stop and look for gifts for them. As usual, Kellie was amazing, texting me to enjoy myself but to go steady.

But in this version of events, Dad is there too. He hasn't had is life thieved by a cowardly disease, and whilst he is older and a bit dodderier and still loses his glasses, he goes to the game alongside me and Dan. At the end of the game he is beside himself, chuckling away at the Manchester United fans who disappear at the final whistle in an instant. Here I stay for the trophy collection and grab Dad in a massive bear hug when the trophy is lifted. Back in Southampton we lose Dad for a while but turns up very drunk, with someone else's black Labrador, and complaining that he's lost his woolly hat. We spend time during the week watching the match again and again and reminisce over the weekend. "Shane bloody Long," he tells me, shaking his head. "Who'd have thought a bloody paddy would win us the cup then? Hey Russ, shall we nip up the pub?" It's much sadder when I leave for home, but I tell Mum and Dad there will always be a next time. They don't share my optimism; they are both 83 years' old and maybe for them there might not be a next time. Saying goodbye is painful, and I find myself hurting my parents yet again.

Debbie asks me if I had exorcised my demons after all. Had the experience of Saints winning the cup freed my devotion to the team? Can I now stop getting up at 4:00 a.m. to watch the matches on a Sunday morning? Can I take a step back from it all now?

Dad answers on my behalf.

"Bollocks! It won't change a bloody thing, will it, Russ?"

No, Dad it won't.

Afterword

As I am editing, fact checking and reviewing this rubbish, I realise that I have written myself to come across as a bit of a bastard. This was not my intention at all, and I actually had thought I was quite a nice guy. This self-assessment over my life has been of a particular cross-section of it, and does not represent the whole thing which, in truth, is no more interesting than the babble in these pages. But it has made me think that the absurd strain of my life that involves football has not necessarily been a positive thing. Certainly, football can bring out the worst in people, and it does with me as it did with Dad, take the example of the Portsmouth fan in Auckland minding his own business. When Harry Redknapp came on the television Dad would enter into a screeching vitriol at the TV. This was long before he came ill. Nowadays when I see Redknapp on the telly, and unfortunately he does pop up on New Zealand television from time to time, I am absolutely the same. What kind of an example is that? It's a behaviour that could quite rightly be called Neanderthal at best.

I don't ever recall helping an old lady over the road and I have never got a cat out of a tree, but a bastard I am not, although I admit the picture I have painted of myself shook me because it was truthful.

I do not want to spend time rehashing huge great swathes of pages, or rewriting already lovingly crafted chapters just to paint me in a better light. Instead permit me to use this final chapter to obtain independent advice as to whether my obsession with my team has been a continual hindrance, the elephant in the room so to speak, and whether it is possible to lodge a case for the defence to show me as someone who is not an ignoramus, someone who doesn't put the frivolousness of football ahead of family, and demonstrate that actually I am an okay bloke. I leave it to my daughters to plead my case.

This is what Sarah said about me:

I don't think my dad was very happy that his firstborn child was a female who couldn't care less about football. I didn't care for sport at all growing up. When my little sister came along he was again a little disappointed (although he wouldn't admit it honestly) because he longed for a little boy that he could take up the field and kick a ball around with. Luckily, my little sister took up that job and played football with Dad and would get up early to watch the Saints play on TV.

Being on the other side of the world, watching the Saints play meant getting up at some awfully early times due to the time difference. My Dad would crawl out of bed and hook into his headphones to ensure the game wouldn't wake his girls up, but he forgot that he screamed like a lunatic at the screen. This became the norm in my house. For a child scared of the dark there was always something so calming about hearing my Dad screaming at the game with the hall light on and occasionally cheering. It never bothered me one bit.

When my sister was old enough to get up and watch the football with Dad, in other words when Mum finally caved in to her pestering, I started to get jealous. The way to Dad's heart was through football and my little sister was stealing the spotlight. I too, got up and started watching it with him every so often, but would fall asleep because something about middle-aged men kicking a ball around a field just wasn't exciting enough for me and frankly I had no idea what the rules of the game were (I still don't).

My dad is my best friend because he taught me the most important thing in life; everything is funny. Without this philosophy, my whole world would have been a lot darker for me growing up. Having said that, this didn't apply to Dad when his team had lost.

There's a different side to my Dad when his team has lost – the whole house falls under the plague of the disappointed Saints fan at the mercy of my Dad's stupor. He stomps around the house, makes little sly comments here and there, and why? All because Saints didn't manage to defend their lead long enough to stop Manchester from scoring (or something like that).

Don't get me wrong I was a good sport. I wore the custom-made Saints shirts with my name printed on the back and I did try my very best when kicking the ball around at the field. Unfortunately, I was graced with the clumsy and uncoordinated genes in the family and spent most of my spare time drawing and writing indoors where I couldn't get myself into trouble.

I'm sure Dad didn't really mind that I wasn't too into football. I think eventually he was relieved I stopped getting up at god awful times to watch the football with him because I would constantly ask questions like 'who is playing' and then half way through the game ask 'which colours are Saints wearing?' Even when I stopped making an effort with the games, it was still apparent football was not only a sport – in this family it was a ritual.

Family is the most important thing to me in ways you simply wouldn't understand, and football has always been something so strong, especially the Saints. After moving half-way around the world, the only thing my dad had left to connect him to his family, was football and discussing the recent game with his father and his nephew. He would text his sister in the morning when he got up to stream the games, as the other side of the world was awake then too. Later on, during his life in New Zealand, football was a way for making friends, and half-way around the world, other families of Saints supporters ended up in the same town.

My grandfather on Dad's side used to play as a goalkeeper in the Southampton youth team and my grandfather on Mum's side was a referee. Dad, obviously caught the football bug and that got passed to my sister. But after trying and failing to catch the football bug I retired my efforts, and just occasionally asked Dad the score whilst we bonded with other things, like art and literature, interests and skills I actually inherited from him.

As I said, football was still a massive part of my life whether I was immersed in the games or not. Like every teenager, I was always afraid of bringing boyfriends back to the house. Not because the idea of introducing a new boyfriend to the family was particularly scary – although it was – but if my boyfriend supported a team other than Saints, Dad's blessing wasn't up for debate. This meant that before any introductions took place, briefings with the potential partner was required.

I would instruct them before meeting Dad. "The team you support is the Saints, if you get asked a question simply reply, 'Le Tissier is the greatest player of all time,' and do not under any circumstances turn up in a football shirt that is any other team, got it?"

You may think I'm overreacting but I'm really not. Actually, what Dad was doing, was helping me understand who I was going out with; the football thing was just a lead into it. I hated it at the time, but I love him for it now. I'm glad my Dad stopped me falling in love with some awful Liverpool supporter – although the same can't be said about my sister.

When my dad found out that Southampton qualified for the Premiere Cup League final (or whatever it was) I was so excited for him. The way I understand it the rule was if my parents moved us to the other side of the world, they would go back under two conditions (this doesn't include holidays): 1) Funerals; 2) If Saint's played in the Cup League Premiere final thing.

So off he went. I couldn't be more excited for him. He was going back to see his team play and his family was getting to see him too. Football is what keeps our family closer, even if we are a world apart.

This is what Shauna said about her old Dad:

At the age of five I asked my Dad what my religion was. This was a new concept to me and I wanted to understand more about this when a girl in my new class asked why our teacher wore a cross round her neck. I said "Daddy, what is our religion?".

Dad explained to me in a sentence, "Our religion is the Saints, Shauna".

I knew much about the Saints. Dad taught me how important it was to our family so I believed that this truly was our religion, and that these footballers were the people we were supposed to worship. Not only did I know that it was important to our family, I also knew that the results had a clear effect on Dad's mood. If the Saints lost then it was well understood that we mustn't go near my Dad, for on a Sunday afternoon he would usually be grumpy. If the saints won he might spend a Sunday watching a classic film in a much happier frame of mind, although I don't think he has ever watched a movie from beginning to end because he always seems to fall asleep after the opening titles and wakes up to the closing ones.

Sometimes, Dad would wake me up in the early hours of Sunday morning to watch the football with him. I was so into my football. In my teenage years though I'm too tired to do this, so have to look up the results of games on the Internet to see the result and gauge Dad's mood.

When I was about nine I played one year of netball, because in New Zealand if you were a girl and had never played netball there must have been something seriously wrong with you. I gave it a go but found it gruelling. I didn't like the moody girls, the bitchy mums and the catty opposition teams. But Mum and Dad were very supportive. They would try and alternate between my games and Sarah's, as often our netball matches would be on at the same time. Dad was mostly the only male at the courts. He was so good and supportive — that is the kind of dad he is. I don't think he ever missed anything important in our childhoods, not even because of the football. He learnt all the netball rules, but still spent 50% of each game yelling "HAND BALL" for a joke. It only took me a week of playing to know netball wasn't my thing and by the end of the year I was definitely not going back. I didn't know what sport I would try next but I knew I loved football.

Because I was a girl I didn't think I was allowed to play. I had only ever watched boys or men play. Dad always used to say he wanted a son and when we walked to the car after netball he would watch the kids playing football on the field next to us and I knew he wanted ever so much to play himself or to watch Sarah or myself play. So, the following year I took it on myself to join a football team. I loved it. Dad used to play with me in the garden all the time, although our goal did not have a net anymore because somehow our dog Buster had gotten himself tangled in it and nearly choked himself to death.

When I signed up it seemed like everyone was happy about it, even during the sign up process my primary school teacher and the principal were over the moon to see one of their sporting students finally sign up to a sport they all knew I would be good at. I was so happy because I knew I was going to be out with boys and I was glad that I knew some of them. My Dad was thrilled and he came to all the training sessions, and he even became the team's manager although he said he wouldn't do it unless he was specifically called 'Director of Football'. He can be so embarrassing sometimes.

He taught me loads of stuff at home. He bought me the nicest boots that he travelled all the way to Hamilton to get them because I wanted pink ones and it was the only place that imported boots from England. He bought me all the socks and clothing I would need for training and he even bought me pink footballs.

The first game I ever played I was put up front, the same position my Dad played, and boy did he tell me what I needed to do: "stay on the last man," he would call out or "find space". Our team was drawing 2-2 with just a minute or two to go. I remember in that first game I didn't get much time on the ball because none of the boys wanted to pass it to a girl, but when I did get the ball none of the boys on the other team wanted to try get it off me. Our team missed a chance and their 'keeper's gone to kick the ball out but miskicked it. I was standing outside the box when the ball landed at my feet. I didn't know what to do with it. I had every parent screaming at me "SHOOT!" The most important thing I heard was from my Dad inside my head when he was teaching me, and with that I slid the ball into the bottom left corner of the net to win the game.

Not a bad start for my first game. My Dad was over the moon and I wouldn't be surprised if that was his proudest moment of me. The next Sunday morning when we spoke to my grandparents I remember my Dad describing it to my Grandad and I could hear they were both so proud and impressed. I got to tell Grandad all about it, even though he had already heard the whole thing from Dad. The season went on and I played for the next three years, until I had a bad hip injury. I was the top goal scorer one year but I seemed to have a talent for setting up most of the goals for others. But I was good. As everyone still tells me, I was very good.

My dad never missed a game and when I did score a goal me and my sister were allowed a frozen coke with our Saturday McDonald's. Over the years Grandad was sent loads of pictures of me playing and I spoke to him more and more because he was so interested. I am glad that Grandad was not sick when I played, that he got to see me play and that I got to tell him all about it, and I know he was so proud.

Once I stopped playing football, I basically stopped watching it. The time difference was so difficult and I had school and I was dancing every night and I was just so tired all the time that I just couldn't get up to watch it. Not only that but we couldn't even watch it on the TV it was such a hassle because Saints weren't in the Premier League anymore. For a moment, I lost touch with who the players were and where we were in the league. Football was something that bonded me to my dad in a way Sarah didn't have. It was so important to me because Sarah was perfect, she was smart and funny and everyone got along with her. I was very different and I know that but it was something that really brought me and my dad together. I do miss watching it with my Dad.

I think about how I don't get to spend that time with him very often. I am so busy and I now live a very separate life from both my parents, but I am at the age where I need to do that. But it makes me think that he has always been there for me and as he gets older I do not want him to experience what Grandad went through and I certainly do not want to lose touch with him or for him to miss out on his football. Dad has always been a great dad to me and has taught me so much and I believe he has brought me up to be a great person. I think football makes him who he is, it is his link between all his friends, it is his go to conversation starter, it's a part of him and a part of his life and I certainly wouldn't change that about him. Football is quite definitely his religion and it may as well be mine too.

I'm not sure either one of them have got me off the hook, you'll just have to take my word for it.

Acknowledgements

Thank you to everyone, except Harry Redknapp.

Sorry about this, still not finished. Some sincere thank you's ...

Firstly, my Kellie. Imagine the scene, we've just met and we are getting to know each other. She tells me a little about herself. I tell her a little bit about me, and nonchalantly throw in the 'I'm into football – Saints fan' line. I imagine her thought response at the time to this was 'that's okay'. Little did she know about the pain and anguish that I would put her through for the next twenty-nine years. For example, moving in to our new house the day before the England versus Portugal European Championship quarter final in 2004, when we were desperately trying to get Sky installed in time, and the paddy that ensued when I couldn't. I had to listen to the match on dial-up Internet and laid on the floor in the foetal position during the penalty shootout (remember, radio makes it much more exciting when you have to paint the pictures yourself). Of course England lost (and long as the sun rises in the east, sets in the west, England will lose on penalties) which led to an expletive laden rant to no one other than to myself, in true Basil Fawlty style. It was at this point, through the open patio doors that my new neighbour had poked his head over the fence to say hello. Literally, in twenty-four hours we had moved house, and I had ruined our relationship and alienated ourselves from the neighbours.

What about Southampton versus Newcastle United in the 1995 season? Kellie came along for that game. I have brought her along to many matches, and she is always great value. She gets right into it and is properly knowledgeable about the game too. After being 1-0 down in this game with three minutes to go, Saints equalised and then poked in a second to dramatically win the game for Saints. During the celebrations I elbowed her accidentally on the top of her head. Unknown to me, she sat dazed with her hands on her head as a third Saints goal went in before the final whistle. I was jumping around like a pogo stick running wild whilst she was seeing stars. I bent over to her when I saw her crouched down, head in hands, and said "I know! I know! I can't believe it either!" thinking she was celebrating too. I don't actually think I have been forgiven for that one, either.

So Kellie, firstly thank you for all your support with going to the final, thank you for the support for this book and thank you for the cover ideas, dubious foreword and photograph. Thank you for not leaving me after any Saints loss, and I am sorry for everything: both up to now, and in the future, when Saints get beaten in the last minute, if I wake you up inadvertently in the middle of the night cheering for a goal or kicking the breakfast bar stool over, or if we sell someone else to Liverpool, or lose to Everton because of another dodgy penalty, or get to another final. I realise with my football head on I have little or no redeeming features whatsoever, I just hope my other heads are worth it.

(Incidentally, Saints drew away at Newcastle United, the Saturday before we met for the first time, 3-3, Matt Le Tissier scored twice, no need to look that up to check…)

My own Sarah Budden, who wrote a novel at the age of nineteen, called 'Credulous'. It's very good. Nineteen? That's not even twenty! Sarah, thank you for your inspiration and cajoling for me to write this drivel. You are an inspiration to me every time I see you. I know that you are not into football, and I think that's a good thing, as it can be a curse. Please make sure you acknowledge me in your next novel as the best dad ever, and put me nearer the top of the acknowledgement list thank you.

To my Shauna, who neither has written a book, nor finished third in her final year at high school. But you were Head Girl at high school, and you did get a scholarship and most importantly are pretty good at football. Even though you have a boyfriend supporting Liverpool, you are still in my top two daughters. Thanks for sharing the journey even though at times you didn't want to be on it, especially at 2:00 a.m. You are an angel and my back says so too. You are the nicest person I will ever meet. And thank you for your text to me at the cup final which helped me to immediately confirm to 85,000 others that Manolo Gabbiadini's disallowed goal in the cup final was onside and should have been given.

Big sister Debbie. Thanks for looking after me when I was over for the cup final, and for your encouragement. I am sorry that for every day that I spend in New Zealand is another day I can't help out in England. I hope you think I did Dad a service writing this muck.

To Mum, tottering around in her Assisting Living flat, causing merry hell for the carers, winning every bingo night because you are the only one left with your marbles still mainly intact, and peddling Difflam to the other inmates or to the local youths from the nearby estate. I still remember you when I was four busying yourself getting ready to go to work as the 1976 cup final was happening seemingly oblivious to the momentous importance of what was occurring right there in your living room. It is beyond me how you stayed so detached from the football as you have done, never been to a match, and that you had never ever seen me play, yet at the same time remained so attached to Dad. Thanks for everything and I am sorry I was such a loathsome child. I'll see you soon no doubt, but I'll see the top of your head on Skype sooner; we can have a nice twenty-minute chat trying to work out what time it is here, and what messages Mr. McAfee has left you on the screen.

To Dan, thanks for a memorable week end at the match. I am so sorry I was such an appalling uncle. To Sama, thanks for letting Dan come out to play to the cup final. Thanks to all of the above and also Kate, Ian, Hayley and Hayley's Dan for allowing me to publish your names in this form, as well as young Luke's and Ryan's.

Big sister Tracey, to Colin, Hannah and Charlie and to Laura. Sorry you didn't make it in to the book very much. This is because you are not into football (or into Dirty Leeds, so same thing, really) so you miss out on all this twaddle. But like Sarah, it's probably better that way. Laura, please don't grade this rubbish.

Lewis Hastings, thank you for your support and for your iffy attempt at a Foreword (not published in this book with all reasonable attempts made to bury it). To Amanda, thank you for the chilli con carne lunches (without mushrooms) and Toblerone mousse, surely the most wondrous thing of all mankind. To the both of you, thank you humbly for solving my book title crisis.

I would also like to acknowledge some wider influences on this inconsequential tome.

A major inspiration on this book was of course Nick Hornby's masterpiece, 'Fever Pitch'. I have specifically re-read his work to ensure that I do not inadvertently follow similar themes to his work.

Another book that helped me along the way was Mick Channon Junior's tremendous book 'How's Your Dad?'. It gave me confidence to press on and keep going with my attempt to write something cogent and interesting even though I am plainly rubbish at it. I'm absolutely not saying his book is rubbish – it is in fact a real gem of a read – but clearly the author went through the same pangs of indecisiveness about writing as I did. The wonderful '32 Programmes' by Dave Roberts also helped to germinate my idea. His class publication talks about programmes and matches that he went to (32 in fact, including the day

George Best played at The Dell and promptly got sent off), interwoven with his own life.

Lewis Hastings and his huge great brick of a book 'Actually, The World Is Enough' was not only an excellent deterrent from stopping the door to the garage from slamming, but also was a genuinely inspiring piece of work to me. It certainly made me think, what a load of rubbish that is, I could do so much better. Reading this tat back though, I am not sure I have succeeded.

Finally, all Southampton fans are extremely lucky because there is a group of people, known as the Hagiology Publishing Collective, who devote their time to preserving the history of the Saints in print. I do not believe there is another football club in the country with the depth of knowledge that is in print, accessible to the public. This book would not have been able to have been written without the numerous volumes of books that have been published by these outstanding gentlemen, some of which also act as official historians to the football club. I think I used no less than eight of their publications, including 'All The Saints, A Complete Players' Who's Who Of Southampton FC' to look up player details, and 'In That Number, A Post War Chronicle Of Southampton FC' to frame up the correct results for matches, goal scorers, signings and the like. I used 'Suited and Booted, A Snapshot Of Pre-War Southampton FC In Pictures' to re-learn pre-war Southampton exploits used in the Introduction, and I used 'Tie A Yellow Ribbon – How The Saints Won The Cup' to confirm how little is known about the days between Saints winning the Cup on the Saturday and Mick Channon's testimonial on the Monday. The Hagiology Collective also were major contributors to Matt Le Tissier's testimonial programme (easily the best and most informative football programme of all time) and the Southampton versus Brighton And Hove Albion match programme, which was the ceremonial last ever game at the beloved Dell. I used my own personal copies of all these books and has been a privilege also to be a published subscriber to some of them.

(For reference, according to the Internet, Hagiology means publications about the lives and legends of saints, clever isn't it?)

And finally, finally, finally, a simple thank you, a wink and a thumbs up to the best of all men, my great old Dad.

References

I used a number of resources for fact checking and for inspiration in this book. I have tried to ensure that the words on the page are first and foremost from my memory, but always sought to corroborate how I remembered things with the stone cold hard facts. Nearly all of the accounts I gave in this book are correct according to the facts, although there are exceptions: I always remembered Peter Shilton signing for Saints before Kevin Keegan left the club. However irrefutable facts from the reference list below, and from the Internet, contradict this completely and state that Keegan left Saints before Shilton joined. In this circumstance, I deliberately inferred Shilton joining first, although did not state this.

For the Introduction, the number of kits Shauna has possessed was confirmed by the excellent web site *www.historicalkits.co.uk*. How many people might have known Saints wore blue shorts up to 1951?

Details compiled for the history of the Saints were from the following sources: 'Suited and Booted, A Snapshot Of Pre-War Southampton FC In Pictures' by Duncan Holley, 'C.B. Fry: King Of Sport' by Iain Wilton, 'Full Time At The Dell' by Dave Juson and David Bull, and 'Cult Heroes', by Jeremy Wilson, published by Know The Score. Details about Southampton as a city was sourced from 'Southampton, An Illustrated History', by Adrian Rance.

For the chapter '1976' as well as the glories of the Internet and YouTube a major resource was 'Bobby Stokes, The Man From Portsmouth Who Scored Southampton's Most Famous Goal' by Mark Sanderson. For the chapter '1979' I utilised sources from the award winning 'Provided You Don't Kiss Me' by Duncan Hamilton, and 'Sir Alf' by Leo McKinstry. For the chapter '1982' I described the events of Kevin Keegan's signing from the book 'Lawrie McMenemy, a Lifetime's Obsession', by Lawrie McMenemy, the Daily Mirror

Archives book 'When Football Was Football – Southampton, A Nostalgic Look at a Century Of The Club' by David James, and a combination of the Hagiology books referenced in the end of this section. The Lawrie McMenemy quote in the chapter '1984' after the Portsmouth FA Cup tie was taken from the Hagiology book 'Match Of The Millennium' by David Bull and Bob Brunskell. In the chapter '1986' Chris Nicholl was told to 'cut his cloth' according to the Hagiology book 'In That Number, A Post War Chronicle Of Southampton FC' by Duncan Holley and Gary Chalk.

For the chapter '2001' records of caps for England were sourced from articles in the Daily Mail (don't judge me) and Wikipedia. Statistics for Matt Le Tissier were collected from 'All The Saints, A Complete Players' Who's Who Of Southampton FC' by Gary Chalk, Duncan Holley and the legendary David Bull. Details of the English mindset in a historical context was sourced from 'Don't Mention The Score, A Masochist's History Of The England Football Team' by Simon Briggs. Thoroughly entertaining book that one.

Data supporting New Zealand being in the top five countries in child abuse was sourced from the New Zealand Government Family First article 'NZ doing bugger all to fix one of worst child abuse rates in world, says doctor' (yes, that really is the document title). The 'western world' quoted is in fact the OECD. The OECD is the Organisation for Economic Co-operation and Development. New Zealand is one of thirty-five member countries that includes North America, most of Europe, Chile and Australia. Data supporting the number of tourists coming to New Zealand is available from the Tourism New Zealand web site, and I used data from 2016. Data supporting driver crashes was sourced from the New Zealand Government Overseas driver crashes report 2015, covering 2010 to 2014. The quoted value of 'less than 4%' is specifically 3.8% in this document.

Confirmation about the New Zealand Badminton team being known as the 'Black 'Cocks' was corroborated from an article by Martyn Watterson in the New Zealand Herald, September 14th, 2005.

Details about player sales between 2005 and 2009 was sourced from my own data that I collected at the time. The last date on the file was the 2nd of June 2009. All I can say there wasn't anything on the telly that night. I also used data from the web site *www.transferleague.co.uk* which helped me confirm that only one player had won the league since leaving Saints since 2005.

Details about the importance of shooting first in a penalty shoot-out is confirmed and described in great detail in the research by J. Apesteguia and I. Palacios-Huerta, in the paper 'Psychological Pressure in Competitive Environments: Evidence from a Randomized Natural Experiment', published in the American Economic Review issue 100.

Information and basic statistics supporting the Springbok tour of New Zealand in 1981 was sourced from an article 'A Country Divided' from the New Zealand History web site at the web address: *nzhistory.govt.nz/culture/1981-springbok-tour*. Barry Davies chronicles his secondment to New Zealand in his autobiography 'Interesting, Very Interesting'.

Details about the causes and effects of Vascular Dementia was included from the United States Alzheimer's Association's web site. Details about Lewy Bodies was included from research I did in a letter responding to the Southampton, Hampshire, Isle of White and Portsmouth NHS Report issued in August 2012. The association of Lewy Bodies with the actor Robin Williams was recorded based on information from the United States Lewy Body Dementia Association (LDBA). Descriptions about Dad's care (or lack of it) were based on family recollections and reports from Southampton, Hampshire, Isle of White and Portsmouth NHS, August 2012, Hampshire Hospitals, July 2012, Southern Health Community Mental Health Team, May 2012, and Stokewood Surgery, May 2012.

Bibliography:

'All The Saints, A Complete Players' Who's Who Of Southampton FC' by Gary Chalk, Duncan Holley and David Bull.

'All Whites '82' by John Matheson and Sam Malcolmson, published by Hodder Moa.

'Bobby Stokes, The Man From Portsmouth Who Scored Southampton's Most Famous Goal' by Mark Sanderson, published by Pitch Publishing.

'C.B. Fry: King Of Sport' by Iain Wilton, published by Metro Books.

'Clough, The Autobiography' by Brian Clough, published by Partridge Press.

'Constant Paine, The Biography Of Terry Paine' by David Bull, published by Hagiology Publishing.

'Cult Heroes', by Jeremy Wilson, published by Know The Score.

'Dell Diamond, Ted Bates's First 60 Years With The Saints' by David Bull, published by Hagiology Publishing.

'Don't Mention The Score, A Masochist's History Of The England Football Team' by Simon Briggs, published by Quercus.

'Fever Pitch' by Nick Hornby, published by Penguin.

'Football Nation' by Andrew Ward and John Williams, published by Bloomsbury.

'Full Time At The Dell' by Dave Juson and David Bull, published by Hagiology Publishing.

'God is Brazilian' by Josh Lacey, published by Tempus.

'Growing Up With Subbuteo, My Dad Invented The World's Greatest Football Game', by Mark Adolph, published by Sportsbooks Ltd.

'Hard Case, The Autobiography Of Jimmy Case' by Jimmy Case, published by John Blake Publishing.

'Hillsborough, The Truth', revised Updated Edition 2016, by Phil Scraton, published by Penguin.

'How To Support A Crap Football Team' by Steve Crancher and Ash published by Ian Henry Publications.

'How's Your Dad?' by Mick Channon Jnr, published by Racing Post.

'In That Number, A Post War Chronicle Of Southampton FC' by Duncan Holley and Gary Chalk, published by Hagiology Publishing.

'Interesting, Very Interesting: The Autobiography' by Barry Davies, published by Headline.

'Lawrie McMenemy, A Lifetime's Obsession', by Lawrie McMenemy, published by Sport Media.

'Le Tissier, A Tribute To A Saints Legend' by Jeremy Butler in association with The Daily Echo, published by Thomas Publications.

'Left Foot Forward' by Garry Nelson, published by 20/20 Headline Review.

'Man On The Run' by Mick Channon, published by Arthur Baker.

'Match Of The Millennium' by David Bull and Bob Brunskell, published by Hagiology Publishing.

'Match Of The New Millennium' by David Bull and Barry Webb, published by Hagiology Publishing.

Matt Le Tissier Testimonial Souvenir Match Day Programme, by David Bull and the Hagiology Publishing Collective, published by Cedar.

'On Penalties' by Andrew Anthony, published by Yellow Jersey Press.

'Playing Extra Time' by Alan Ball, published by Sidgwick And Jackson.

'Provided You Don't Kiss Me' by Duncan Hamilton, published by Harper Perennial.

'Sir Alf' by Leo McKinstry, published by Harper Sport.

'Southampton, An Illustrated History', by Adrian Rance, published by Horndean.

'Suited and Booted, A Snapshot Of Pre-War Southampton FC In Pictures' by Duncan Holley, published by Hagiology Publishing.

'Taking Le Tiss, My Autobiography' by Matt Le Tissier, the world's greatest ever player, published by Harper Sport.

'The Bald Facts, The David Armstrong Biography' by Pat Symes, published by Pitch Publishing.

'The Diary Of A Season' by Lawrie McMenemy, published in 1979 by the Readers Union Group of Book Clubs. Incidentally, on the back cover of this old book is an advertisement promoting a forthcoming book, 'Cowpasture, The Every Day Life Of An English Allotment' by Roy Lacey. Sounds like a page turner! It's still available from Amazon!

'The Final Whistle', Southampton versus Brighton And Hove Albion Match Day Programme, by John Hughes and the Hagiology Publishing Collective, published by Cedar.

'The Footballer Who Could Fly' by Duncan Hamilton, published by Century.

'The Secret Agent, Inside The World Of The Football Agent', fully revised and updated edition, by Anon, published by Arena Sport.

'32 Programmes' by Dave Roberts, published by Bantam Books.

'Tie A Yellow Ribbon – How The Saints Won The Cup' by Tim Manns with David Bull, published by Hagiology Publishing.

'When Football Was Football – Southampton, A Nostalgic Look at a Century Of The Club' by David James, published by Haynes.

'Cowpasture, The Every Day Life Of An English Allotment' by Roy Lacey, published by the Readers Union Group of Book Clubs.

'Actually The World Is Enough' by Lewis Hastings, published by Orbis 2014. This book has the word 'cock' in it 51 times. My book only has one occurrence, coincidentally in this paragraph, whilst in two other places the word shuttlecock was necessarily abbreviated.

'Credulous' by SM Budden (that's my Sarah, wahoo!!!).

YouTube videos

Here are some of the videos that I have been watching on YouTube to help with the writing of this book. I guess over time these videos might move or disappear, so sorry in advanced if some of the web site addresses are no longer valid.

A ninety minute video from the Nineties entitled 'The Official History of The Saints' is on YouTube at *https://www.youtube.com/watch?v=C_i7zDl75Jk*. Thanks to **JPR74**.

Saints in black and white! Manchester United, complete with George Best, versus Southampton early in the 1970 season, which Saints won by four goals to one, here at *https://www.youtube.com/watch?v=VHFaZeeaQOM*. Thanks to **mox888**.

For Saints versus Manchester United in the 1976 FA Cup Final, go to *https://www.youtube.com/watch?v=he4r07yqlzU* and enjoy. Thanks to **Southampton FC**. Have a look at this version too: *https://www.youtube.com/watch?v=6gVd7y5yH-0*. It is an amazing Movietone news bulletin that would be shown in the cinemas. They even miss the winning goal! Thanks to **British Movietone** all the same. Footage of the celebrations the next day is here *https://www.youtube.com/watch?v=0Kos00-ngxs*. Have a look at those crowds! Thanks to **JPR74**. On the Monday, it was Mick Channon's testimonial, footage here: *https://www.youtube.com/watch?v=ntSloSYCU48*. Thanks to **jamiecg74**. The car on the pitch was the prize for Bobby Stokes scoring the winning goal in the cup final, the giant 'L' plates there as he couldn't drive.

For completeness, Dirty Leeds beating Saints 7-0 in 1972 is here *https://www.youtube.com/watch?v=oiiZR8UdfvY*. Thanks to **TJS Sports**. Not worth watching though, that one.

Proof that my memory holds about the team we faced on my wedding day, go to *https://www.youtube.com/watch?v=DFglcs8S86c&t*. Thanks to **Chelsea Retro TV**. It appears my wedding day was 16th September 1996.

For West Ham United versus Saints on the day that Sarah was born, go to *https://www.youtube.com/watch?v=UXoy_57RNB4*. Fortunately, Sarah was born at 9:50 p.m. long after the game was finished. Once West Ham got their penalty, the radio was confiscated from me by the midwife. As you can see there was hardly any contact on the player by Jason Dodd. Thanks to **TJS Sports**.

For a sample of It's A Knockout, go to *https://www.youtube.com/watch?v=UGdKLnC6NUc*. Thanks to **jimthegallifrey**. I told you it was crap.

The 1979 League Cup final, my first match, between Saints and Nottingham Forest, go to *https://www.youtube.com/watch?v=gTq28jEnVx8&t=448s* and then to *https://www.youtube.com/watch?v=yabChh9Wbuo*. Thanks to **FLC1960**. Have a look at this version too: *https://www.youtube.com/watch?v=XtEse9PW02g*. It is another amazing Movietone news bulletin: listen to the clipped tones of the narrator: "Saints were morally in charge as well as being actually in the lead!". Thanks to **British Movietone**.

For Saints beating Nottingham Forest 4-1 in the 1980 season, go to *https://www.youtube.com/watch?v=yK6wRZdRT4I*. Thanks to **MoreGoalsTV**.

For the magic of 1982, firstly Saints versus Manchester United including the best goal of all time that wasn't given, from Kevin Keegan: *https://www.youtube.com/watch?v=S9SXa55s2OM*; thanks to **saints80to85**. A crazy 4-3 win against Stoke City, see here *https://www.youtube.com/watch?v=v6DhuDPvG2Q*; thanks to **TJS Sports**. The match against Liverpool where you will see Mick Channon's goal for Saints, labelled the 'greatest goal of all time that counted', mainly by me: *https://www.youtube.com/watch?v=fBTaRrcV0R8*; thanks to **tallowmanother4**. The disaster against Sporting Lisbon is here: *https://www.youtube.com/watch?v=fFtRuz8IMFA*; thanks to **Planeta do Futebol LFL**. The more palatable away leg is here: *https://www.youtube.com/watch?v=e_hd2Hg5b1U*; thanks to **scpcpmemoria**.

For Saints beating Liverpool 4-1 in the 1990 season, go to *https://www.youtube.com/watch?v=_vRya0_9kCg*. Thanks to **coulditb5**. Have a look at the two assists from Le Tissier and have a wee think if there has been any other player that could do that. Seriously, I saw that every week.

For Saints versus Liverpool in the first leg of the semi-final, go to *https://www.youtube.com/watch?v=TM4KZS7ZKpE*. Thanks to **Southampton FC**.

For the second leg of the semi-final, go to *https://www.youtube.com/watch?v=rtiBvgPs-Sk* and enjoy! Thanks to **Southampton FC**.

For Saints versus Sheffield Wednesday in 1983, the game on the radio where Saints lost but saved a penalty, go to *https://www.youtube.com/watch?v=WY01yyMdYJU*. Thanks to **VintageWednesdayVids**.

For Saints versus Portsmouth in the FA Cup in 1984, watch the first half on YouTube at *https://www.youtube.com/watch?v=9REAzluTKj0*, and the second half at *https://www.youtube.com/watch?v=kc-GmmO0uSc*. Thanks to **Matt Gardner** and of course, Alan Biley.

For Saints versus Everton in the FA Cup in 1984, go to *https://www.youtube.com/watch?v=45wcFvPzm44*. Thanks to **plokijuhy251**.

For a much happier match, Saints versus Liverpool in 1984 for Danny Wallace's special goal, go to *https://www.youtube.com/watch?v=18eSIWNJIIM*. Thanks to **FootballGaffesGalore**.

For Saints versus Manchester United in the 1984 season, go to *https://www.youtube.com/watch?v=uFxJyhj0hYA&list=PLC0F18CA21C6DB340*. Watch Steve Williams second goal from a free kick and catch a glimpse of the Family Centre where Dad and I stood. Thanks to **FootballGaffesGalore**.

For Saints versus Liverpool in the FA Cup in 1986, go to *https://www.youtube.com/watch?v=UP6ha4KyOTs*. Thanks to **Dave Waller**.

For masochist completists, Saints versus Liverpool in the League Cup 2015 (the one Liverpool won 6-1), go to *https://www.youtube.com/watch?v=S8r-mcdLYGc*. Thanks to **Rhys**. Six lucky goals.

Some of Saints legends from my time. For Alan Ball, Mick Channon, David Armstrong, Jimmy Case, Danny Wallace and Steve Moran search their names and add 'Southampton' in the search – there's loads of footage but no single link with highlights; Kevin Keegan – *https://www.youtube.com/watch?v=xBwwfasqD7s*, thanks to **TJS Sports**; Alan Shearer - *https://www.youtube.com/watch?v=8Nt9WCbDp70*, thanks to **All World Football**; Marian Pahars – *https://www.youtube.com/watch?v=nb6o_zsYUMQ*, thanks to **puslaiks**; Theo Walcott – *https://www.youtube.com/watch?v=ly4wCz6ijdk*, thanks to **flipjoberg**; Gareth Bale – *https://www.youtube.com/watch?v=h0SFCNQkG-Y*, thanks to **futbolpasion2013hd**; Ricky Lambert – *https://www.youtube.com/watch?v=TYP3G8F_2WE*, thanks to **Saint Rhys**; José Fonte – *https://www.youtube.com/watch?v=itZyDP0CdiY*, thanks to **Este é Craque da Bola**; Adam Lallana – *https://www.youtube.com/watch?v=o2FDGylDpmQ*, thanks to **TVSport4**; Manolo Gabbiadini – *https://www.youtube.com/watch?v=H2YaWHjR1X0*, thanks to **Fortaleza Productions**.

For the footballing connoisseur take your pick of these best of gems: Glenn Hoddle – *https://www.youtube.com/watch?v=X1kUVf8-sp0*, thanks to **1991Sadlerc**; Paul Gascoigne – *https://www.youtube.com/watch?v=-Iu5YSqN0Ok*, thanks to **The69ersFC.TV**; Kenny Dalglish – *https://www.youtube.com/watch?v=LB2nwwFgZy4m*, thanks to **dub69charger**; Ian Rush – *https://www.youtube.com/watch?v=mQpT5V6hKG8*, thanks to **AixmhroΣ**; Bryan Robson – *https://www.youtube.com/watch?v=HYmAxqG59I0*, thanks to **Green&Gold til theclub is sold**; Jürgen Klinsmann – *https://www.youtube.com/watch?v=Rhe27vw1Z3E*, thanks to **Sam Hyde**; Ruud Gullit – *https://www.youtube.com/watch?v=5JgR0DCHXuY*, thanks to **XimerMatteo**; David Ginola – *https://www.youtube.com/watch?v=3q0fPoTupd0*, thanks to **TottenhamHotspur2k11**; Marco Van Basten – *https://www.youtube.com/watch?v=RAnrVr1oggA&t=18s*, thanks to **HeilRJ Football Channel**; Steven Gerrard – *https://www.youtube.com/watch?v=IQd996AgaBI*, thanks to **HeilRJ Football Channel**; Ronald Keoman – *https://www.youtube.com/watch?v=LiCJfeO-JHw*, thanks to **FC Barcelona**; Thierry Henry – *https://www.youtube.com/watch?v=Hwux8Y5D9t0*, thanks to **HeilRJ Football Channel**; Frank Rijkaard – *https://www.youtube.com/results?search_query=frank+rijkaard*, thanks to **onlygoalburns**; Robin Van Persie – *https://www.youtube.com/watch?v=BagwKgGqrzk*, thanks to **TopFootballContent**; Gianluca Vialli – *https://www.youtube.com/watch?v=NAZ4MipejmE*, thanks to **cevaking**; Eric Cantona – *https://www.youtube.com/watch?v=gXTk0Z2oGzM*, thanks to **Jud Nist**; Gianfranco Zola – *https://www.youtube.com/watch?v=eiN_XEPIP7I*, thanks to **Тележка**; Sergio Agüero – *https://www.youtube.com/watch?v=uCXKzQ3qczQ*, thanks to **IbraAlliance**; Didier Drogba – *https://www.youtube.com/watch?v=zBs0eCBCHuM*, thanks to **gundoganed**; Denis Bergkamp – *https://www.youtube.com/watch?v=n1ah97qHjLE*, thanks to **Football & Basketball videos**.

For Matt Le Tissier, run a search on the name and enjoy. See if you can work out why he only got eight England caps. Answers on a post card. For specific links, I would recommend adding these to your Favourites – go to *https://www.youtube.com/watch?v=wPw0XRAuzu0* and *https://www.youtube.com/watch?v=dVP9IbFi5Ag*. Thanks to **chris legunner**. I rest my case.

Also, for Matt Le Tissier, have a look at *https://www.youtube.com/watch?v=MFraoBrSNgw*. This was the last England B trial match before the World Cup, described as "the best ever performance by a player in an England shirt". Unfathomably, Le Tissier still never got picked for the World Cup in 1998. Thanks to **sp1873**.

Liverpool versus Southampton 1994, go here
https://www.youtube.com/watch?v=lTuJZ0y7AX0. Thanks to **Liverpool Retro TV**.

Bolton Wanderers versus Southampton 1996, go to
https://www.youtube.com/watch?v=VQu0KVVuuBE. Thanks to **TJS Sports**.

For the run in to survival in 1994 … Norwich 4, Saints 5, in 1994
see here: *https://www.youtube.com/watch?v=zfBSrz25ig4* and here
https://www.youtube.com/watch?v=oAD0zO3vc4l. Thanks to **SuperSfc123**.
Southampton versus Blackburn Rovers in 1994:
https://www.youtube.com/watch?v=Sws79-64Xq0. Thanks to **MoreGoalsTV**.
Southampton versus Aston Villa in 1994:
https://www.youtube.com/watch?v=Mq6cB3VUHal. Thanks to **Villa Boy**.
Southampton versus West Ham United in 1994:
https://www.youtube.com/watch?v=9pK5LFV8ANw. Thanks to **MoreGoalsTV**.

Southampton versus Manchester United in 1996 – the change of kit
at half-time, go to *https://www.youtube.com/watch?v=tSoBG9c25Pg*. Thanks
to **Александр Трянин**. I didn't even notice until someone told me!

The following season, Manchester United again, this time 6-3. See
here *https://www.youtube.com/watch?v=n6J-4RlRsms*. Thanks to **Adrian
Houghton**. Look out for goal number five and the idiot in the crowd!

Wimbledon versus Southampton 1999 – Le Tissier scores from a
corner, only to have the dubious goals panel to dubiously take the goal
away from Le Tissier. Look closely: who touched the ball if Le Tissier
didn't? See here *https://www.youtube.com/watch?v=4roQ_vF9N5s*. Thanks to
TJS Sports.

Saints versus Everton on the last day of the 1999 season, which we
won 2-0: *https://www.youtube.com/watch?v=lTxYDh2eFXY&t=44s*. Thanks to
Patrick Bateman.

The final game at The Dell against Arsenal, also won 3-2:
https://www.youtube.com/watch?v=ZX9EurbX-W8. Thanks to **Patrick Bateman**.

The final, final game at The Dell against Brighton and Hove Albion:
https://www.youtube.com/watch?v=rjcJfjuofkg. Thanks to **Patrick Bateman**.

The opening match at St Mary's was against Espanyol:
https://www.youtube.com/watch?v=tRmgm5V8cp8. Thanks to **Patrick Bateman**.

The FA Cup third round match in 2003 against Tottenham
Hotspur, which I missed because I had to be Best Man at a wedding in
New Zealand, can be found here
https://www.youtube.com/watch?v=TbRs3yFNMCg. The footage includes the
league match against the same opponents which I also missed! Thanks
to **Patrick Bateman**.

Saints' quarter final match against Wolverhampton Wanderers from
2003 can be found at *https://www.youtube.com/watch?v=x9uiiM7bEYw*.
Thanks to **Patrick Bateman**. No footage of the man with the white dot
unfortunately.

The semi-final match in that competition against Watford is here *https://www.youtube.com/watch?v=YArTpDAXBME*. Thanks to **Patrick Bateman** again.

For Arsenal's annihilation of Saints 6-1, go to *https://www.youtube.com/watch?v=j8MWbh3MWuk* and watch it in-between your fingers. Thanks to **Tigo Hussain.**

The entire 2003 FA Cup Final (another tough watch) against Arsenal is here at *https://www.youtube.com/watch?v=R2lJNLytjXA*. Thanks to **pongsanj66**. A much shorter highlights reel of the final is at *https://www.youtube.com/watch?v=JiJ0doHJvww*. Thanks to **Arsenal Retro TV**.

For Saints beating Portsmouth in the League Cup during the 2004 season, go to *https://www.youtube.com/watch?v=NQMtoFJlGqU*. Thanks to **Patrick Bateman**.

For Saints beating Charlton Athletic 3-2, go to *https://www.youtube.com/watch?v=WfwhFtrgZh8*. This footage includes an impeccable minute's silence for Mr. Southampton, Ted Bates, something that was not forthcoming in Saints' previous match against Portsmouth. Thanks to **MUFC1963's channel**. Have a look at *https://www.youtube.com/watch?v=Glytv7KT8r0*. This video is a report on what a match against Portsmouth looks like, from a cup match in 2010 when Portsmouth were in the Premier League and Saints were in League One. Thanks to **MUFC1963's channel**.

For Saints versus Portsmouth in the League in 2004, go to *https://www.youtube.com/watch?v=zDVtdEEYwkE*. Saints' first goal came straight from a corner, Le Tissier style. Thanks to **Patrick Bateman**.

For Saints winning at Liverpool that same season, go to *https://www.youtube.com/watch?v=z13Vte1FKwU*. Thanks to **Liverpool Retro TV.**

I couldn't find the Saints match at home to Manchester United which saw Saints relegated. Mind you, I didn't look for it too hard.

For Saints at Watford in the 2008 season, using much more modern computer technologies such that both Southampton goals are not paused or frozen to spoil your enjoyment, go to *https://www.youtube.com/watch?v=2uy5CpzYFoA*. This is actually the Watford review of the season so you have to skip to about fourteen minutes in. Thanks to **Watford Videos**.

For Saints versus Derby County in the 2007 play-off semi-final. The first leg, including Pele (not the Pelé but *a* Pele) and his attempt for Most Obvious Penalty Ever, is here *https://www.youtube.com/watch?v=444Q1mmYSjQ*. Thanks to **Mark B**. The heart breaking second leg is here *https://www.youtube.com/watch?v=x6-_BlF0td0&t=8s*. Thanks to **Zakariya**.

The Johnstone's Paint Trophy Cup Final, Southampton versus Carlisle United, see here *https://www.youtube.com/watch?v=UEZWNoB2Yn4*. Thanks to **MrSFC1885**.

Peterborough United versus Southampton during our promotion winning 2011 season to the Championship: *https://www.youtube.com/watch?v=JhpVunm5t4g*. Thanks to **SouthCoastClub**.

A pivotal match in Saints' recent history, Saints at home to Milton Keynes Dons here: *https://www.youtube.com/watch?v=rMaf1FBPdVw*. Thanks to **SouthamptonFC**.

Another pivotal match, the brilliant match at Brighton and Hove Albion that same season here: *https://www.youtube.com/watch?v=Q0XbYZqfWBc*. Thanks to **SouthCoastClub**.

A bit of A League action with Gold Coast United (yellow) versus New Zealand's own Wellington Phoenix (white), here: *https://www.youtube.com/watch?v=fAnzQYpTCsU*. Thanks to **Glen Wilson**.

New Zealand's All Whites journey to the 1982 World Cup is chronicled here: *https://www.youtube.com/results?search_query=all+whites+1982*.

For LA Galaxy's and David Beckham's visit to Auckland against the ropey Oceania All Stars go to *https://www.youtube.com/watch?v=X8I9NqMevIA*. Thanks to **JAYFC**. Can you think of an Oceania All Star? A bit of an oxymoron, that. Appalling night, that was.

For Saints versus West Ham United in October 2011 – the year Saints were promoted to the Premier League again, go to *https://www.youtube.com/watch?v=rk5xM3ByZ-g*. Thanks to **Southampton FC**.

For Saints versus Reading four days later, go to *https://www.youtube.com/watch?v=j6vYxLylCQ4*. Thanks to **Loyal Royal**.

Saints outstanding performance against Middlesbrough was captured at *https://www.youtube.com/watch?v=FLGo5-p0J1A*. Thanks to **Southampton FC**. The third goal was fashioned out of 26 consecutive passes, a truly beautiful goal that took me back to Mick Channon's against Liverpool in 1982.

For the cup final itself, I'd advise searching for 'EFL Cup Final 2017' and taking your pick. The link I'd used was *https://www.youtube.com/watch?v=LRYQ8MRI8j8*. Thanks to **Southampton FC**. Best to skip the last few minutes.

The Alan Partridge Dan sketch is here, *https://www.youtube.com/watch?v=fOad90BvvjM*. Thanks to **BBCWorldwide**.

For the basketball player Akil Mitchell, whose eye was poked out of his socket during his game, go to *https://www.youtube.com/watch?v=7gi0XrDaR-s*. You can also search for "nz breakers player eye pops out". Thanks to **The Elliot**.

Sarah's fantastic YouTube page can be found at *https://www.youtube.com/channel/UC_2KVRZQTh7JEFfWCD_izcQ*. The French Toast three ways is to die for.

There is also this hilarious video of a puppy *https://www.youtube.com/watch?v=dgHRwscpPlA*. Thanks to **mihaifrancu**.

Pictures

This was the picture taken for the Daily Echo. Kellie took it, and if you look closely at the window you can see one of my dogs, Buddy, wondering what is going on.

Wembley, 1st of May 1976, Bobby Stokes scores the goal that's wins the FA Cup for Southampton. As you can clearly see from this Subbuteo recreation, Stokes was clearly onside.

Fair Oak Earls' Under 10's 1981 Southampton Tyro Six Aside Consolidation Cup Runner Up team. Star goal scorer top left. You'd never imagine I had a sister who was a hairdresser.

Me (on the right) circa 1982 with my Newcastle United opponent Dougal. Notice my Mum's failed attempt at the world's first ever photo bomb.

In the early 2000's it was a hobby of mine to grow giant grass. No, this is actually a bit of turf from The Dell with a Subbuteo man (Southampton, Ref 9) for scale.

Ready for the 2003 FA Cup semi-final against Watford. Shauna on the left, Sarah on the right and Baby Born, centre (toy). (The girls were threatened with being grounded if they didn't comply with this photo opportunity.)

From the pub in Birmingham before the semi-final in 2003, just after someone farted on Dad's head.

Super Saint, the Southampton team mascot, reacted poorly when I suggested at the FA Cup semi-final against Watford, that he should consider a proper job.

Dad at the FA Cup Final in 2003 against Arsenal, indoors at the Millennium Stadium. Dad has just dropped my hot dog sausage and tipped over my large Fanta, but it hasn't dampened his spirits.

Me at the FA Cup Final in 2003 against Arsenal, indoors at the Millennium Stadium. I haven't eaten since 8:00 a.m. and Dad has tossed my lunch away, but it hasn't dampened my spirits.

At Eden Park, Auckland, early in 2005, at a New Zealand versus Australia cricket one-day international. Some local wag has informed us that in New Zealand, supporters face the other way at sporting events.

The day before the League Cup Final 2017. I've been in the country for three hours. I get the typical early symptoms for the onset of jet lag: the involuntary poking of the tongue out the side of the mouth. Dan is on the left.

My ticket for the cup final was not a fake after all! This picture was taken more than two hours before kick-off. And I have had something to eat!

Pre-match entertainment, about twenty minutes prior to kick off, at the Southampton end of the ground. In retrospect, the giant Saints shirt should have been pulled tight over the goal posts to stop us conceding.

Me and Dad, early 2011.

Dementia associations

For the United Kingdom
Dementia UK; helping families face dementia
Helpline: 0800 888 6678
www.dementiauk.org
http://www.dementiauk.org/donate/

For New Zealand
Alzheimer's New Zealand
Helpline: 0800 004 001
www.alzheimers.org.nz
https://secure.flo2cash.co.nz/donations/alzheimers/donate.aspx

About the author

Russell Budden wrote this book.
He is a totally average football supporter approximately in his late thirties, who has lived with his tolerant wife and kids in New Zealand since 2004. He has been a fan of his home town football team Southampton since he was very young.

You won't notice him, unless you live near to his home in Pukekohe, near Auckland, and it is 5:00 a.m. on a Sunday morning and Saints score a goal. Then you'll probably wish that he'd go back to bed.

This is his first book and will likely be his last book too because it is a very hard thing to do. His next project is to make an authentic recreation of The Dell out of Lego®.

25026869R00169

Printed in Great Britain
by Amazon